D1496210

*Conservative Ordeal*

# CONSERVATIVE ORDEAL
## *Northern Democrats and Reconstruction, 1865–1868*

EDWARD L. GAMBILL

*The Iowa State University Press, Ames*
1981

TO EARL AND ALLEEN

*Edward L. Gambill is Professor of History, St. Cloud State University, St. Cloud, Minnesota.*



Printed by The Iowa State University Press, Ames, Iowa 50010


First edition, 1981

**Library of Congress Cataloging in Publication Data**

Gambill, Edward L. (Edward Lee), 1936–
Conservative ordeal, northern Democrats and Reconstruction, 1865–1868.

Bibliography: p.
Includes index.
1. Reconstruction. 2. United States—Politics and government—1865–1869. I. Title.
E668.G18 973.8′1 81-1560
ISBN 0-8138-1385-9 AACR2

# CONTENTS

# PREFACE

THE DEVELOPMENT of Radical reconstruction has long been a subject of intensive investigation. In attempting to explain its evolution, historians have devoted primary attention to the inner dynamics of the Republican party. Numerous scholarly works have analyzed Republican leaders, probed Republican motivations, chronicled Republican maneuvers, and assessed Republican strategies. The interpretations have been critical, laudatory, or nonpartisan, but the underlying assumption has generally been maintained: because congressional reconstruction was a Republican policy, that party, and particularly its radical contingent, should be the major focus of historical investigation.

As a result, conservatives have been largely neglected. Where earlier studies dealt with the conservative position they generally allowed Andrew Johnson to dominate center stage. He symbolized whatever strengths or weaknesses attributed to those who opposed the congressional program. For historians who proceeded from an anti-Radical bias, the president served as a convenient instrument to articulate conservative theories and strategems. For scholars who shared the Republican perspective, he provided an easy target for caustic criticism. In either case, the unfolding of the reconstruction drama essentially pitted the White House against the majority on Capitol Hill.

The Democratic party consequently received meager attention. When Democrats did enter studies of the early postwar years, they were treated as a monolithic entity whose wartime divisions vanished with the collapse of the Confederacy. Republicans initially encouraged this viewpoint because they found political advantage in identifying the opposition with the rhetoric of its extremist members. Supporters of Johnson's policy also lumped Democrats together as indicating broad support for his presidential policy. For better or worse, Northern Democrats were depicted as united in an ineffective defense of the South, the president, the Constitution, and white supremacy.

Only recently have historians suggested the possibility of a more complex picture. Eric McKitrick drew attention to the Democrats by persuasively arguing that they played an important role in the development of Radical reconstruction; John and LaWanda Cox explored the differences between conservative Republicans and the Democrats; and Michael Perman noted the division among Southern conservatives in their response to Northern initiatives. Despite the new focus on conservative forces, much of the traditional viewpoint on Northern Democrats remains intact. The Democratic party is still perceived as unified, both strategically and tactically, in its opposition to Republican reconstruction programs for the South.

There is of course some truth in this depiction. Political parties generally function on the basis of the common assumptions, perceptions, and needs of their component elements. The Democratic party in the early reconstruction period was hardly an exception. On the contrary, the party's commonality of interests was probably greater than in many other periods and was a vital ingredient in its survival. Still, the process of survival implies adaptation, and this is especially true in times of basic national transition. Faced with such change, Democrats had to weigh their devotion to traditional principles against an accommodation to new realities. That they should disagree under these circumstances is not surprising. But the very existence of disagreement underlines the varied and complex nature of the conservative response to reconstruction.

I wish to thank St. Cloud State University for a research grant and sabbatical leave that permitted the completion of this monograph. I am also grateful for the assistance provided by the library staff at the University of Minnesota, the Henry E. Huntington Library, the Library of Congress, the Pennsylvania Historical Society, the Wisconsin Historical Society, the Iowa Department of History and Archives, the New York Historical Society, St. Cloud State University, and the New York Public Library. A special debt of gratitude is reserved for David Overy, Malcolm J. Rohrbough, and members of my family for their crucial advice and support.

*Conservative Ordeal*

# 1

## *Wartime Legacy*

IN THE SPRING of 1865, George Templeton Strong, diarist and observer of the American scene, made a bleak assessment of one of the nation's prominent political institutions. The Democratic party, he noted, lay stunned and prostrate "by blows that [have] smashed its cranium."[1] Reduced by defection, torn by internal dissension, bereft of leadership, and stigmatized by the taint of treason, the party hardly occupied an enviable position. Commentators speculated whether the Democratic party could actually survive. For contemporaries who lived through a generation of intense political instability, the issue was not entirely lacking in historical precedents. If one believed the symptoms, the Democratic party could find itself consigned to the political graveyard alongside the Federalist, Anti-Masonic, Whig, and Know-Nothing organizations.

The prospect of its inpending demise was made even more dramatic by the suddenness of this development. Scarcely a generation earlier Democrats had surged into power under the leadership of Jackson and inspired a veritable revolution in American society. Drawing on and expanding concepts expressed by Jefferson, the party ushered in the "era of the common man," with its stress on the merits of individualism and the worth of social, economic, and political democracy. In its attack on special privilege, suspicion of restrictive government controls, and in its support of expansionism, the Democractic party had seized and capitalized on prevailing forces in the nineteenth century. This legacy of the Jacksonian Revolution made the Democrats the dominant political party for the next three decades. Other organizations rose and fell, but the Democratic party persevered and continued to exert a paramount influence over the nation's affairs.

Behind the external manifestations of Democratic hegemony, the forces unleashed by the Jacksonian upheaval moved in new directions that threatened the party's image and eventually fragmented its structure. By the 1850s slavery had emerged as the dominant national issue. Out of the conflict over the "peculiar institution" arose the Republican party, which developed its own version of the egalitarian theme. Democrats were suddenly thrust on the defensive and their ranks thinned as antislavery elements in their own organization defected to the opposition. Continued focus on the slavery issue divided the Northern and Southern wings of the party. In 1860 the split was completed as each put forth its own platform and presidential ticket. It was an opportunity made to order for the opposition, and control of the White House passed to Abraham Lincoln and the Republicans.

While the Southern states responded by adopting articles of secession and moved to create a separate confederacy, most Northern Democrats scurried to save the Union. From their perspective, it made no sense to assign partisan rather than patriotic reasons for their action because the two were inseparable. Since the Democrats were the single, truly national party, only action by the Democrats could ultimately resolve the crisis. They repeatedly warned the Lincoln administration against adopting a policy of coercion and persistently resisted attempts by Federal and Northern state governments to prepare for such an eventuality. Then, having discredited the use of force, they counseled conciliation. Through proposals for national peace conferences, projected constitutional amendments, and repeal of Northern state personal liberty laws, the Northern Democrats encouraged the return of their errant Southern brethren.

When these efforts failed and Confederate guns in Charleston opened fire on federal troops at Fort Sumter, the initial reaction among Northern Democrats was a massive outpouring of support for the federal government. To be sure, a small minority disagreed with Lincoln's final call to arms and either aided the Confederacy, held their peace, or had their criticisms stifled by torrents of patriotic rhetoric. But for the mass of party members it was enough that the flag had been fired upon by the Confederates. Public declarations by Stephen A. Douglas, the Northern Democratic standard-bearer and titular party leader, set an example for Northern Democrats to make known their commitment to the Union in no uncertain terms. Party chieftains participated in mass rallies, organized and equipped volunteer regiments, and, in a number of instances, joined the army themselves. Democratic legislators on both the national and state levels renounced their earlier resistance and joined the movement to prepare the nation for war.

The onset of war created a perplexing new problem for the party. Military efforts to crush the rebellion would require a vast mobilization of Northern resources and greater efficiency in governmental operations. Continued factionalism among the people would hurt the war effort; political partisanship was suspect. This situation created special problems for the Democrats because of their unaccustomed position as a minority. A Republican president now exercised supreme command over the army as well as civil administration, and Republican governors occupied most Northern statehouses. Republicans would profit in the long run from any temporary disavowal of partisan activity. The question Democrats faced was whether they should give up partisanship or attempt the difficult role of a wartime loyal opposition.

A number of party leaders concluded that partisan activities should cease and that the administration should be supported for the duration of the conflict. The stance adopted by the White House helped reinforce this decision. Lincoln initially adopted a thoroughgoing conservative position on war objectives by asserting he had no intention of destroying Southern institutions. Though the president eventually departed from his pledge, he still refused to identify himself with the radical wing of his party. Democrats predisposed to support the administration found evidence of Lincoln's good intentions in his appointment of a prominent Democrat, Edwin Stanton, to a key government position and the selection of Democrats George B. McClellan, Ulysses S. Grant, Henry Halleck, and William Rosecrans for high military command.

Republicans also made similar overtures to Democrats on a state level. With the exception of some localities where the Radicals dominated, they attracted Democrats with military commissions and political appointments to support the war. In addition, they invited Democrats to share political power through the creation of fusion tickets. These bipartisan organizations, usually adopting the name Unionist, served as halfway houses that provided cooperation without the complete surrender of party identification. Democrats who collaborated were called War Democrats and maintained the distinction between themselves and Republicans. This, in turn, provided a degree of flexibility should they choose to return to party regularity at the close of the war or if they became dissatisfied with Republican policy.

The Union movement drew a number of influential Democrats away from their normal partisan alignments. In New York, Daniel Dickinson and John Dix, previously national as well as state leaders in the Democratic party, led the procession into the Union ranks and were joined by other prominent Democrats, such as James Gordon Bennett of the *New York Herald,* Edwards Pierrepont, John Cochrane, and Lyman Tremaine. To the south, the Unionists gained the support of John Forney, editor of the *Philadelphia Press* and battle-scarred veteran of backstairs Pennsylvania politics. Meanwhile Massachusetts enlisted Benjamin Butler; Illinois, John Logan and John McClernand; Indiana, Joseph Wright and Lew Wallace; and Wisconsin, Matthew Hale Carpenter. Alongside these leaders came a number of others—newspaper editors, former public officials, and party functionaries.

While there were internal disputes within the coalition over patronage and policy, and some Democrats departed before the end of the war, the Union movement functioned with surprising efficiency. War Democrats generally lent their support to measures adopted by the Lincoln administration to crush the rebellion, or when they disagreed they maintained a discreet silence. But they demanded and received a reward for their allegiance. Democrats elected on Union tickets in Wisconsin and Ohio served as governors for a major part of the war. Other Democrats occupied a variety of elected offices in Northern state governments. Nor was their recruitment confined to the state level; War Democrats Carpenter, Wright, and William Sprague of Rhode Island took seats in the United States Senate and had their Capitol Hill ranks augmented by men of similar political convictions in the House of Representatives. As the final capstone to the coalition movement, the Republican National Convention in 1864 chose Andrew Johnson, War Democrat from Tennessee, as Lincoln's running mate on the Union ticket.[2]

The exodus of War Democrats, following earlier defections, left the ranks of the regular Democratic organization depleted but not broken. The Republicans virtually dominated New England, the upper Midwest, and Iowa. Even here, major pockets of Democratic strength survived. There was a strong vein of conservatism in Connecticut, and Democrats sharply contested Republicans for control during the war. Farther west, Detroit and the neighboring countryside in southeastern Michigan remained strongly Democratic, as did the Wisconsin lakeshore counties stretching from Green Bay to Milwaukee. But these areas were of secondary importance when compared to the heartland of the Northern Democracy, the Ohio River valley and mid-Atlantic states. Throughout the war Democrats controlled southern Illinois and Indiana, and much of the western, central, and southeastern portions of Ohio. In the East they relied on the Appalachian counties of Pennsylvania and the region extending from east-central portions of Pennsylvania through northern New Jersey, continuing into the lower Hudson River valley and metropolitan New York. When supplemented by strong support from Delaware, the border states, and the Pacific Coast, the Northern Democrats were a force to be reckoned with.[3]

Democrats could be found in all socioeconomic levels of Northern society, but there were ethnic groups they dominated. Nowhere was this more evident than with the Irish. Forced out of the old country by English oppression and economic calamity, Irish immigrants streamed into the United States in search of opportunities, only to find the new land held its own hardships. Because they lacked capital and craft skills, they congregated in urban centers as ill-paid factory workers and day laborers, hired out in the mining areas of western Pennsylvania, or fanned out across the countryside as construction hands on canals and railroads. Everywhere they encountered hostility from native-born Americans who distrusted their religion and disliked their social customs. The nativist reaction had blossomed forth in the 1850s as the Know-Nothing movement, marked by feverish attacks on the Catholic Church, parochial schools, and demands for revision of registry laws and rigid sabbatarianism. The Irish regarded Republicanism as an offshoot of Know-Nothingism, so their attachment to the Democratic party was deep and abiding.

To a lesser extent the party received reinforcement from other recent arrivals. German Forty-Eighters, free-thinkers, and political progressive generally gravitated to the ranks of the opposition; but most German Catholics, and frequently German Lutherans, went with the Democrats. German-American farmers augmented Democratic strength in the rural Wisconsin lakeshore counties, and factory workers, craftsmen, and businessmen increased the Democrats' political base in Milwaukee, Cincinnati, Chicago, New York, and other cities. And Democrats counted on the support of the less numerous Poles, Italians, and other elements of the "new immigration."

Southern migrants and their descendants constituted still another segment in the party mosaic. Offspring of the first wave of settlers in the Midwest, these people of Southern lineage constituted over half of the region's total population in 1860 and were particularly evident in portions of southeastern and central Ohio, southern Indiana and Illinois, and the lower tier of counties in Iowa. Frequently illiterate and oftentimes located on poor hard-scrabble farms, they bore the name of Butternuts because of the dye used to color their homespun clothing. Many had left the South with no love lost for its plantation and slave economy, but they brought with them a cultural perspective that was equally intolerant of Republicanism.[4]

The Butternut democrats with their large immigrant contingent left Democrats open to the charge of being the party of ignorant and debased rabble. These claims of partisan and class characterization were misleading. Not only did the Republicans have their own contingents of recent immigrants and laborers, but Democratic leadership included many people of substantial means. August Belmont of New York, chairman of the party's national committee, had accumulated a sizable fortune as an American representative of the Rothschild interests, and Alexander Mitchell of Milwaukee headed a financial empire that made him one of the wealthiest men west of the Appalachians. Mitchell and Belmont were only two of many Democrats prominent in banking circles, but their counterparts could be found in other walks of life. Asa Packer of Pennsylvania, Erastus Corning and Augustus Schell of New York, and John Stockton of New Jersey, among others, were Democratic entrepreneurs in transportation. And in manufacturing, traditionally the stronghold of the Republican party, there were such eminent Democrat manufacturers as James English of Connecticut and Cyrus Hall McCormick of Chicago.

Whatever their socioeconomic backgrounds, many Democrats had Southern economic ties that may have contributed to their partisan outlook. Farmers in the Ohio River valley were particularly dependent on the Mississippi River trade for their surplus wheat, corn, flour, pork, and distilled spirits. Midwestern Democratic businessmen had similar vested interests; Alexander Mitchell held large amounts of Southern state bonds at the outset of the war, Cyrus McCormick looked to the Southern market as an outlet for his agricultural machinery, and Washington McLean, editor of the *Cincinnati Enquirer,* feared the impact of the closing of the Mississippi trade on his boiler plate factory. Nor were such ties confined to the Midwest; New York City served as a Northern emporium for Southern trade and commerce, and neighboring communities such as Newark and New Haven, which functioned in the New York orbit, had provided the South with shoes, clothing, carriages, saddlery, and other goods.

Democratic attitudes about the political economy reflected a combination of such vested interests and party legacy. As heirs of the Jeffersonian and Jacksonian tradition, Democrats perceived the corporate state as a violation of natural law that benefited the few at the expense of the many. Consequently many midwestern farmers, businessmen heavily dependent on agrarian markets, and immigrants who had fled from repressive governments in Europe were suspicious of federal economic intervention. This did not mean that they were always consistent. Democratic railroad promoters were susceptible to the lure of federal land grants, some Democratic bankers looked favorably on the idea of reinstituting a national banking system, and Democratic politicians from states such as Pennsylvania found it expedient to endorse protective tariffs. Nevertheless, the Democrats showed a decided disposition toward laissez faire when compared to the opposition.

This tendency was more apparent with social issues. Generally, Democrats affiliated with ritualistic churches such as the Catholic and Episcopalian that embodied a passive deference to formal doctrine and clearly defined hierarchical authority. Acknowledging the existence of sin as an integral part of man's worldly condition, their religious framework counselled moderation rather than abstinence from worldly pleasures. Individuals committed transgressions periodically and absolution provided a means for forgiveness. In this area the church and its clergy exercised authority. Thus reason dictated that government, born of man, should exercise restraint in questions of personal morality. The status of one's soul should not be determined by a Caesar.

Democrats, steeped in the ritualistic perspective, found the antithesis of their religious outlook in pietistic and evangelical Protestantism. Congregationalists, Methodists, and other related sectarians de-emphasized doctrine and institutional authority and stressed the direct relationship between an individual and a transcendent God. Consumed by the notion of a change of heart through personal conversion, they were intolerant of moral relapses in themselves or in others. The world had to be purged of evil and the Kingdom of Heaven achieved on earth. If this could be done with moral suasion and personal example, so much the better; if not, they endorsed coercive legislation. Little wonder then that Democrats, discerning Yankee Puritanism as a major force within the Republican party, viewed the opposition as provocative and potentially dangerous.[5]

Democrats fell back upon the Constitution as protection against such threats. Their viewpoint was conservative and ritualistic. They believed that the Founding Fathers had created a government based on law rather than personal whim, and they held that the strength of the document lay in its elaborate system of checks and balances. By artfully distributing power between the executive, legislative, and judicial branches and balancing the relationship between state and federal authority, the Constitution posed a middle course between anarchy and despotism. Modifications in government were of course occasionally necessary, but extreme care should be exercised or they might damage its basic structure. Serious tampering with the system could only disturb its fundamental harmony and lead to instability and disorder.

Democrats generally viewed the fragmentation of the nation in civil war as a direct consequence of such political meddling. By dismissing the Constitution and resorting to their higher law doctrine, the abolitionists created a division within the body politic. Southern fire-eaters also contributed to this devisiveness by refusing compromise and ultimately resorting to secession. Restoration of the Union required a rejection of both forms of extremism.

Thus most Democrats willingly supported the administration so long as its prosecution of the war did not threaten the Constitution or serve as a cloak for partisan legislation. Perhaps Lincoln, aligned with the moderate wing of his own party, would resist pressures in this direction. But unlike the War Democrats, regular party members harbored serious reservations, maintained their vigil, and stood ready to sound the alarm.

Many soon found evidence to justify their fears in the economic policies adopted by the federal government. In February 1861, with Southern legislators largely absent from Congress, Republican leaders on Capitol Hill secured the enactment of the Morrill Tariff, which raised duties generally on manufactured goods. Additional legislation gave further protection to manufacturers while imposing import levies on such basic commodities as sugar, tea, and coffee. Increases in excise taxes on distilled and malt liquors supplemented the new external taxes. And if tax legislation was not enough to rankle Democrats, a new system of national banks and a flood of irredeemable paper currency issued by the Treasury Department added to their concern.

A large segment of the Democratic party viewed such political tinkering as a violation of sound economic principles and as blatant discrimination. Irish and German laborers suffered when wage increases lagged behind rising prices, and farmers in the Ohio valley faced severe hardship when the interdiction on river trade produced surpluses in agricultural goods and the new excise taxes restricted local markets for their corn and barley. But while farmers and laborers faced poverty, others prospered. Northeastern railroad promoters, taking advantage of the decline in river trade, raised railroad rates. Manufacturers reaped large profits behind the shield of protective tariffs, bankers and contractors thrived on the government's need for money and military supplies, and speculators capitalized on the country's general economic instability. As many Democrats saw the lion's share of opportunities going to Republican businessmen, they called the opposition's demand for nonpartisan patriotism a cruel hoax.[6]

If Republican economic policies angered Democrats, they were even more disturbed by other wartime measures. Lincoln at the very outset of hostilities took actions that raised troublesome constitutional questions. By unilaterally imposing a blockade on the South and spending federal funds without congressional authorization, the president served notice that he was not bound by conventional restrictions on executive authority. Democrats, placed on their guard, carefully scrutinized his actions for any flagrant abuse of the president's emergency powers. They soon found evidence in the wave of arrests that followed Lincoln's suspension of the writ of habeas corpus. Some individuals who were seized and incarcerated had obviously aided the Confederacy, but others appeared merely to have criticized the administration's conduct of the war. Concern aroused by such prosecutions mounted when the government sanctioned trial by military commissions in noncombat areas. Because Democrats were subjected to such procedures, many party members concluded that the Republicans intended to stamp out all forms of opposition, whether loyal or disloyal.

Violations of free speech were all the more troublesome when accompanied by what appeared to be a fundamental change in wartime objectives. In July 1861, Congress endorsed the Crittenden Resolution that denied any intention of prosecuting a war of subjugation or emancipation. Yet the ink was scarcely dry on the pronouncement when events indicated another direction for government policy. A newly enacted confiscation act provided for the seizure of property used in the rebellion, and several military commanders proceeded on their own initiative to free slaves in their jurisdictions. The following year Congress passed legislation emancipating blacks in the District of Columbia and the territories and enacted a supplementary confiscation bill that broadened the scope of seizures and specifically included slaves in its provisions.

Lincoln also shifted his position. Democrats found little fault with the president's initial pronouncements on war aims, and they applauded his forceful action against generals who moved beyond the boundaries of administration policy. But within a year there was mounting evidence Lincoln had succumbed to pressures from the radical wing of his party. The first troublesome sign came with the extension of diplomatic recognition to the black republics of Haiti and Liberia. The president followed these steps by proposing voluntary compensated emancipation in the border states. Finally, in September 1862, Lincoln took a bold step that shocked the country. The president threatened through his preliminary Emancipation Proclamation to make slavery a casualty of the rebellion and by doing so expanded political dissension in the North.

Almost to a man Democrats attacked the president's decision. The proclamation, they charged, was a flagrant act of executive usurpation. If Lincoln could unilaterally destroy existing property rights sanctioned by the Constitution, then limitations on his exercise of dictatorial powers were nonexistent. The proclamation fundamentally altered the nature of the war. Rather than merely a change in tactics dictated by military or diplomatic considerations, it entailed a major reversal in policy, negating earlier pledges by president and Congress that the sole objective of the government was to preserve the Union. In so doing, the declaration could only harden Southern attitudes and prolong the conflict.

Objections on constitutional and strategic grounds were only part of the Democratic objections. Of equal concern was the long-range impact of emancipation on society. A mass freeing of slaves, coupled with efforts already under way to utilize blacks in the Union army, would lead to pressure for black civil, political, and economic equality. The inevitable result would be a continuation of national turmoil and strife. Democrats at once exhibited and sought to capitalize on the racial aversion of most American whites toward blacks, an aversion apparent among Radicals as well as conservatives. Democrats claimed the Radicals could be hypocritically charitable because Southern whites and Northern workers would be the ones to compete with cheap black competition and bear the major burden of upheaval caused by emancipation.[7]

Democrats charged that the adverse public reaction to administration policies was responsible for a decline in volunteers and led to the government's sanction of conscription. Resorting to the draft only compounded the problem. Conscription not only marked a departure from American tradition, but it also fell heaviest on those who were least inclined to identify with the war's objectives. Well-to-do businessmen could escape compulsory military service through a three-hundred dollar exemption payment. Marginal farmers and immigrant laborers found it exceedingly difficult to raise this sum. Thus national conscription revealed the discrimination inherent in Republican policy. The conflict, Democrats complained, had become "a rich man's war, and a poor man's fight." Party spokesmen, voicing their criticism of the war, had tangible evidence that a large segment of Northern voters shared their concerns. The 1862 fall elections were the first major test of public opinion, and the results were gratifying. Democrats posted gains in every midwestern state except Iowa, secured control of the legislatures in Indiana and Illinois, elected a number of state officials, and increased their representation in the House of Representatives. Along the eastern seaboard, the Democrats swept into power in New Jersey and New York and the following spring came close to unseating Republicans in Connecticut. Reaction to conscription underscored the intensity of public disaffection. Draft riots in Boston and New York and in Wisconsin's lakeshore counties as well as isolated attacks on enrollment officers indicated a sizable segment of the population vehemently opposed being drafted to fight a war for the abolition of slavery.

An absence of easily recognized and credible national leadership was a major impediment to further Democratic efforts to exploit this unrest. The death of Stephen Douglas in the summer of 1861 removed the one man of sufficient stature who might have provided the Democrats with some semblance of unified direction. Of Douglas's Northern colleagues who remained in the Senate, only Henry Rice of Minnesota, James A. Bayard of Delaware, and Jesse D. Bright of Indiana were veterans of the Democratic power structure on Capitol Hill. But Bright faced expulsion because of alleged pro-Confederate sympathies, Bayard resigned in protest over government policies, and Rice found his political powers curtailed as a Democrat in a heavily Republican state. Other Democrats of national prominence who occupied Senate seats during the war were border state Congressmen James Pearce and Reverdy Johnson of Maryland who, for a variety of reasons, exercised only limited influence in Northern party circles.

Nor could the Democrats draw on an abundance of experienced executives. The sole role remaining for Franklin Pierce was that of elder statesman, and James Buchanan, battered and bruised by political infighting during the fifties, had retreated to his Pennsylvania estate where he busied himself writing a defense of his presidential administration. Only two Northern Democrats became governors during the course of the war; of the two, Joel Parker had virtually no exposure outside of New Jersey, but Horatio Seymour possessed more imposing credentials. Noted as a conciliator within New York party circles, Seymour had been nominated five times for the governorship, elected twice, served as keynote speaker at one national convention, and mentioned as a possible presidential candidate at another. Yet many perceived the governor as acting irresolutely during the New York draft riots, and his political reputation suffered accordingly. Consequently his future political prospects were in doubt.

The void in national leadership came at an unfortunate moment. Mounting disillusionment with administration and congressional activities provided the Democrats with a choice opportunity. If the party marshalled its forces, developed a coherent policy, and broadened its base, it might regain control of the White House and Capitol Hill. But such an approach necessitated a degree of internal unity on the validity and conduct of war, and on this issue the Democrats were divided. Lacking central direction, the Democrats were once again beset by internal dissension and factionalism.

Occupying one wing of the intraparty spectrum was a loosely knit coalition of peace advocates known as Copperheads. The most volatile group within this coalition consisted of a small number of Southern sympathizers and ideological purists who either proclaimed the right of secession or insisted that the government had no authority to coerce the South. These extremists, easily identified by their violent rhetoric, condemned the Republicans for precipitating the national crisis and urged noncompliance in the conduct of the war. On occasion they even called for the recognition of the Confederacy. A much larger segment of the Peace Democrats adopted a more cautious approach. While attributing major blame for the disruption of the Union to the Republicans, they conceded a limited culpability to Southern fire-eaters and most were reluctant to withhold support for federal armies in the field. But their concern over the devastation brought by war and the tactics and objectives adopted by the administration forced them to conclude that the Union could not be restored by existing policies. They demanded an armistice to be followed by a national peace convention that would offer concessions to the South.[8]

Republicans generally charged that Peace Democrats were traitors and disunionists. Such claims were misleading, for although they applied to Copperhead ideologues, those who favored an armistice and negotiations were not as easy to categorize. Some, it is true, claimed they favored peaceful separation in the event the Confederacy spurned their overtures. Others pledged their commitment to a restored Union and to a resumption of war should negotiations fail. But most, either because they desired flexibility or believed their proposals would ultimately succeed, left the question unanswered. Thus Republicans accused them of treason before they had actually been disloyal.

The aspersions made against Democrats by the opposition were not limited solely to the peace wing. They were directed against the broad mass of moderate party regulars who reacted with vigorous and heated denials. While the Democratic moderates stoutly proclaimed their support of the government, they rejected Republican efforts to confuse their position by claiming they backed the administration. For some, criticism of Lincoln's policies remained restricted and differed only slightly from the position held by War Democrats. A larger number found increasing grounds for complaint, from infractions of civil liberties to changing the objectives of the war. On this level the moderates occupied common ground with their peace colleagues.

Where moderates differed from the Copperheads was on the prosecution of the war. Firmly committed to a restoration of the Union, the moderates hesitated to counsel any action that might indicate support of the Confederacy. They took a dim view of the Peace Democrats' tendency to welcome Union defeats as a necessary prelude to Northern concessions and to suggestions of noncompliance with federal law. They generally believed that Southern leaders were firmly committed to independence, and they held that reunion depended upon Northern strength. Negotiations predicated upon an armistice were out of the question. This did not mean that Northerners should disregard peace deliberations based on mutual compromise, but if and when the opportunity came, such efforts should be coupled with sustained pressure by the military.[9]

The division within Democratic ranks precipitated an intense struggle on the state level for control of the party machinery. In Ohio, the moderates led by Hugh Jewett, Austin Ranney, and editor George Mannypenny of the Columbus *Ohio Statesman* managed to exert a dominant influence during the first two years of the war. In so doing, they encountered increasing opposition from a formidable assortment of Copperhead malcontents. Samuel Medary, an old wheelhorse in Democratic circles, used the editorial columns of the *Columbus Crisis* to pronounce reunion impossible and to call for a peaceful separation of the states. Meanwhile Alexander Long and William Cory of Cincinnati pressed their own inflexible notions of state sovereignty and denied the federal government had any authority to coerce the South.[10]

More important than the ideological purists was the peace faction headed by Clement Vallandigham of Dayton, Ohio. As a three-term congressman, former secretary of the National Democratic Committee, and Douglas's choice to manage the party campaign in 1860, Vallandigham carried considerable weight beyond his own local bailiwick. But his increasingly dovish tendencies as the war progressed eroded the support of his congressional constituency and cost him his reelection in 1862. The defeat made him more strident. He returned to Washington as a lame-duck congressman and angered Capitol Hill by pronouncing the war a failure and calling for an armistice. Four months later he provoked the military commander in Ohio to order his arrest. The trial and subsequent banishment from the North made him a celebrity and the state convention reacted by nominating him for governor in absentia. While Ohio voters rejected Vallandigham in the fall elections, the campaign served to link other influential Ohio Democrats—George Pendleton, George Pugh, and Washington McLean—with the peace faction of the party.[11]

The contest between the peace and moderate elements in Iowa was more evenly divided. There the Copperhead contingent was inspirated by the leadership of Henry Clay Dean, LeGrand Byington, and editor Dennis Mahoney of the *Dubuque Herald*. The peace advocates achieved a limited platform victory at the July state convention when the assembly expressed its discontent with a war pursued for emancipation but avoided the armistice issue. The balloting on the gubernatorial nomination ended in a virtual deadlock between Byington and Gen. James Tuttle. Byington withdrew his candidacy, and a majority of the delegates swung behind Maturin L. Fisher, a compromise selection. The solution was temporary; Fisher refused to accept the convention's endorsement. The party finally fielded a ticket after the state executive committee met and chose Tuttle by a split vote.[12]

The struggle in Wisconsin closely paralleled that of Iowa. Wisconsin's dissatisfaction with the war surfaced in the fall of 1862 when Edward G. Ryan seized the occasion at a special Democratic meeting called to condemn the Lincoln administration and its policies. When the regularly scheduled state convention met the following summer, the peace faction—Ryan, Frederic Horn, and editor Marcus "Brick" Pomeroy of the *LaCrosse Democrat*—managed to secure approval of the criticisms Ryan had made in his earlier address. The platform adopted by the delegates called for negotiations to end the conflict only if there was widespread evidence of Southern willingness to return to the Union. The gubernatorial nomination finally went to Henry Palmer, a member of Milwaukee's "Jenny Lind Club," who viewed Ryan as a political adversary. Despite the moderate nature of the platform and the gubernatorial nominee, the convention created enough dissension to cause a number of influential Democrats to defect to the Union ticket.[13]

In the midwestern states of Illinois and Indiana, where there were no statewide elections in 1863, the intraparty division took other forms. The Copperhead faction at Springfield, taking advantage of the new Democratic majority in the legislature, introduced resolutions denouncing federal policies, urging an armistice, and calling for a national peace convention in Louisville. Although the resolutions passed the assembly, moderates joined the War Democrats in defeating peace advocates in the Senate. Moderate leadership in Indiana, headed by Thomas Hendricks and David Turpie, and supported by the *Indianapolis Sentinel*, kept a tight rein on the Hoosier party organization and successfully curbed Copperhead activities there. A number of resolutions were introduced in the legislature for an armistice, but they languished in committee and never came to the floor for debate.[14]

The success of moderate Democrats in handling similar peace proposals in New Jersey was largely Joel Parker's doing. Parker, recently elected governor, faced an imposing array of Copperhead spokesmen, including *Newark Journal* proprietor William Wright, ex-Governor Rodman Pierce, and a contingent of state legislators from Bergen County headed by Thomas Dunn English and Daniel Holsman. The strong peace sentiment in the state capitol was evident when the Democrats chose Wright to fill a vacant Senate seat in Washington. But Parker mounted a vigorous counterattack when the Copperheads sought to have a party caucus adopt resolutions favoring a six-months truce. The Governor succeeded in toning down the report so that it called for negotiations without an armistice and fought off attempts by English and Holsman to modify it during general legislative debate.[15]

In Connecticut, the Copperhead movement was stimulated by certain well-defined attitudes. Not only was peace sentiment widespread and long held, but two of the state's most prominent Democratic leaders, Issac Toucey and Thomas Hart Seymour, were active supporters. In 1863 the antiwar faction capitalized on the backlash from administration policies and military reverses and launched a concerted effort to gain control of the state government. Copperheads at the Democratic convention dominated the resolutions committee and drafted an uncompromising peace plank. Adoption of the platform signified defeat for moderate spokesmen Congressmen George Woodward and James English, but the high point of the meeting was reached with the nomination of Seymour, who promised to campaign against the enforcement of conscription.[16]

Copperheadism was less apparent in Pennsylvania than in New Jersey or Connecticut. Nevertheless, peace sentiment did exist and in Philadelphia drew much of its inspiration from individuals of prominent old-line families. Moved to action by the Emancipation Proclamation and recent Democratic victories, Charles Ingersoll, George Wharton, William Reed, and Charles Biddle launched the Central Democratic Club, used it as a peace forum, and published its proceedings through the newly organized *Philadelphia Age.* Neither the Philadelphia group nor its out of state allies were able to sway the statewide moderate leadership that included William Wallace, Charles Buckalew, and William Bigler. In April the Democratic-controlled legislature adopted resolutions asserting its unalterable opposition to any division of the Union, and the party state convention two months later passed a moderate platform.[17]

New York moderates made up a broad spectrum of the local Democratic leadership. Upstate, the most powerful faction was the Albany Regency, which was closely affiliated with the New York Central Railroad. Dean Richmond of Buffalo, vice-president of the line, shunned public office and appearances but was a master of offstage political maneuvers. Erastus Corning, on the other hand, was finishing his second term in the House of Representatives while serving as president of the railroad. Other members of the Regency inner circle included John Pruyn, attorney for the New York Central and member of the House of Representatives, William Cassidy of the *Albany Argus,* and Cassidy's brother-in-law, Peter Cagger.

The Regency maintained close ties with a conservative business-oriented group in New York City that included August Belmont, Samuel Tilden, Samuel Barlow, and the young editor of the *New York World,* Manton Marble. This generally well-to-do faction was a lucrative source of funds for Democratic operations, but Tammany Hall was the major organizational structure at the grass-roots level. During the war years Tammany experienced internal difficulties, as leadership underwent a transition from older figures such as Elijah Purdy, to a newer generation of politicos led by Peter Sweeney and William Tweed. Yet its commitment to the Union was unwavering, and it could count on the support of the neighboring Brooklyn machine led by Henry Murphy.[18]

Copperhead opposition to the war in New York was centered primarily in Mozart Hall and its leaders the Wood brothers. Fernando Wood had created the organization in the late fifties, following his defection from Tammany, and used it to win a third term as mayor. During the secession crisis the mayor showed his antiadministration bias by his proposal that New York become a free and independent port city. The outbreak of war temporarily checked his dovish tendencies, but he soon joined his brother Benjamin, editor of the *Daily News,* in demanding peace. By 1863 the two operated in tandem with local Copperheads James McMasters of the Catholic *Freeman's Journal,* James Brooks of the *New York Express,* and C. Chauncey Burr of the *Old Guard,* and they carried their message to Washington as newly elected Congressmen.

Horatio Seymour tried to steer a conciliatory course between the two political camps. As governor, the Utica Democrat tried first to reinstate civil law in New York by bringing to trial metropolitan police commissioners for permitting arbitrary arrests and imprisonment without benefit of the writ of habeas corpus. But the governor quietly yielded when the commissioners refused to appear before the court in Albany. Later, Seymour's protests against federal conscription, followed by his conciliatory attitude during the New York draft riots, caused some observers to conclude that he actively encouraged resistance to national policy. He discounted these charges and used his official powers to modify conscription in New York rather than defy it. Seymour set the tone for the party platform at the September state convention by rejecting disunion, calling for conciliation, and judiciously avoiding the issue of an armistice.[19]

Northern intraparty struggles in 1863 centered primarily on contests for state office but also served as a rehearsal for the approaching national elections, and political observers of all persuasions scrutinized the returns for some indication of the public's attitude. The results marked a general reversal of Democratic advances from the previous year. Moderates concluded the setback could be blamed on Copperhead activities associated in the public mind with treason, and they warned that further temporizing on the peace issue would end in disaster. The antiwar faction refused to concede the argument. From their perspective, the Democrats, with few exceptions, failed to take a forthright stand on principles. They had alienated many of the party faithful, who sat out the elections, and the voters were left with no meaningful alternative to the opposition. Hope for the future lay in an unequivocal denunciation of a war that was clearly doomed to failure.

During the continuing debate over policy, both factions rallied behind potential presidential candidates. The moderates' favorite was George B. McClellan, the former commander of the Army of the Potomac. New York

Democratic leaders began courting him immediately after his dismissal by Lincoln and by the fall of 1863 secured a public confirmation of his identification with the party. When the general indicated his willingness to run, Tammany Hall leaders started ward clubs in his behalf, and similar organizational efforts quickly developed throughout the North. The response indicated the obvious merits of McClellan's candidacy. There could be little question of the general's commitment to the Union, and his military record could be utilized to emphasize differences over the administration's wartime strategies rather than the war itself. Moderates looked to McClellan to draw support from soldiers, with whom he was popular, as well as War Democrats and conservative Republicans.

Copperheads were strongly opposed to his candidacy. To endorse McClellan was tantamount to sanctioning a war they had vehemently rejected. Moreover, the general's transgressions were not limited to a misguided effort to coerce the South; as a military commander, he had disregarded certain civil liberties in areas under his control. His nomination would rob the Democrats of one of its most effective criticisms of the administration. Appalled by his candidacy, Peace Democrats were prepared to fight. They considered a number of leaders who might be strong enough to stand up to McClellan, but the man most frequently mentioned was Thomas Seymour, the recognized leader of New England Copperheadism.

Both factions of the Democratic party began an intense struggle for advantage in the preconvention maneuverings. The moderates benefited by the decision to hold the national meeting in Chicago rather than Cincinnati. In addition, they prevented the Wood brothers from becoming delegates, blocked an attempt to have Vallandigham named delegate-at-large from Ohio, and secured a dominant position among the contingents chosen from such populous states as New Jersey and Pennsylvania. Time and the war aided the Copperheads. By the summer of 1864, Union military forces appear stymied, victory was nowhere in sight, and peace sentiment was increasing. The Copperheads took advantage of the situation and sponsored a series of mass meetings throughout the North. At the largest meeting, held in Syracuse, peace advocates were addressed by Fernando Wood and Vallandigham, chose another delegation to represent New York at Chicago, and refused to support any nominee who favored "further prosecution of this useless, bloody, and ruinous war."[20]

An obvious danger in such infighting was that it might fragment the party, but leaders of both factions were sensitive to the problem and anxious to avoid a repetition of the Charleston fiasco of 1860. Whatever their differences, they shared a common belief that reelection of a Republican administration would be a national calamity. To save the country they must first save the party, and this required forbearance and compromise. A concerted effort was made to keep the lines of communication open, to seek a basis for agreement, and to provide guarantees that neither faction would be excluded by the platform or nominees.[21]

This overriding concern for unity was evident when the convention delegates assembled in late August. A number of party leaders, including Vallandigham, arrived in Chicago pledged to support the outcome of the proceedings, and their choice of Horatio Seymour as permanent chairman reflected their conciliatory outlook. The report of the Committee on Resolutions provided something for nearly everybody. Moderates took satisfaction in those portions of the platform that pledged "unswerving fidelity" to the Union and praised soldiers for their patriotism. Copperheads won major concessions in a statement that condemned the war as a failure and pledged to seek an immediate armistice as a precedent for peace negotiations. The convention acclaimed General McClellan, the presidential nominee, who was expected to stand by the party platform and chose George Pendleton as his runningmate.

Democrats left Chicago satisfied that a ruinous split had been avoided. The real test of their deliberations lay ahead, and events soon indicated trouble for the party. Almost immediately following the convention, Northerners received the electrifying news that Sherman had captured Atlanta. The impact of the event seriously damaged claims that the war was a failure and left McClellan in an unenviable position. Discontented with the peace plank in the first place, the general faced intense pressure to disavow it. He consulted with advisors, weighed the risks, and finally spoke out. In a carefully constructed public statement, the Democratic presidential nominee asserted that the end of hostilities should come only after successful peace negotiations.[22]

The Copperhead reaction was predictable. Vallandigham was furious; he claimed he had been deceived and threatened to cancel his scheduled campaign appearances. Washington McLean managed to soothe Vallandigham's feelings and secured his reluctant agreement to support the ticket. Other Peace Democrats were more stubborn. Benjamin Wood and James McMasters called a meeting in New York City that condemned McClellan and discussed the possibility of an independent presidential nomination. William Cory, Alexander Long, James Singleton of Illinois, and other midwestern Democrats sponsored a similar gathering in Cincinnati. Efforts to organize a third-party movement were stillborn, but many Copperhead purists nursed their grievances and decided to sit out the election.[23]

Lack of support from some of their most vehement activists was not the only misfortune that hindered the Democrats during the campaign. In September military authorities arrested a handful of men, members of a secret organization known as the Sons of Liberty, and charged them with plotting insurrection. Because several of the individuals—most notably Lambdin Milligan of Indiana—were well known Democrats, party spokesmen regarded the conspiracy to be a politically inspired fabrication of the opposition. But evidence presented before a military commission largely substantiated these charges and revealed that Vallandigham was the national commander of the Sons of Liberty. The trial was a godsend to Republicans. Ignoring the absence of evidence implicating Vallandigham in the plot, Republican orators charged the Democrats and Vallandigham with treason.[24]

Internally divided and on the defensive, the party suffered a devastating setback at the polls. In the national election McClellan polled 45 percent of the total vote and carried merely three states—New Jersey, Kentucky, and Delaware. The final count gave the Union ticket of Lincoln and Johnson 212 of 233 electoral votes. Nor were Democrats defeated only in the presidential contest, for the congressional returns stripped them of nearly half their seats in the House of Representatives. Seymour failed in his bid for reelection as governor, and Republican control of nearly all the Northern state legislatures insured further Democratic reductions in the United States Senate.

The party faithful were understandably despondent, and the trend of events following the election was less than reassuring. McClellan, dispirited by his venture into national politics, announced his departure in January for an indefinite stay in Europe. This decision, as had Douglas's death in 1861, once again deprived Democrats of their titular leader at a crucial moment. Virtually every day brought news of new Union victories, and it was soon apparent that the end of the war was in sight. The Republicans were entrenched in power on all levels of government, and Democratic regulars had little on which to base their claim to a share of the glory. They had staked their future on a policy of opposition to the administration's handling of the war, a highly risky stance at best, and lost. The legacy of that opposition was a stigma that would not be easily removed or forgotten.

# 2

## *New Horizons*

ALTHOUGH the power and prestige of the Democratic party had reached a record low, there was still time to recoup its losses. The mass of party regulars had little reason to doubt the wisdom of their political identification and provided a central core on which to rebuild. The success of Union armies negated Democratic claims about the futility of the war but also offered the possibility of a change in party fortunes. As the war drew to a close, the way was once again open for major political readjustment. The Republican opposition, as Democrats repeatedly noted, derived from and continued to exist on a narrow sectional base. In contrast, the Democratic party had functioned throughout its history as a national party with strong support on both sides of the Mason Dixon line. With the defeat of the Confederacy, the Southern states could return to a Union dominated by Democrats, with the Republicans again in the minority.

Of course, the Democrats realized such a scenario depended on several crucial variables. First, a return of Southern states to the nation's political councils implied a willingness by Congress and the White House to permit the resumption of normal relations within the federal system. Second, normalization would have to be accompanied by minimal changes in the Southern power structure. In either case the federal government would have to adopt a policy that conflicted with the interests of the currently dominant Republican party. Yet this development was not beyond the range of possibility. After all, Republican dominance during the war years had been achieved in large measure through the Union coalition, an organization created for temporary and limited objectives. With the war drawing to a close, War Democrats might return en masse to party orthodoxy. New concerns created by peacetime might attract additional recruits. In such an eventuality, the Democrats could force a reentry of Southern states on conservative terms and guarantee their own political future.

Political realignment in the North, as a prerequisite for the conservative restoration of the South in the Union, depended on the solution of older issues that had worked to the party's disadvantage. Chief among these was the vexatious problem of black slavery. In an egalitarian age, their stand on chattle slavery had converted the Democrats' image from champions of the common man to defenders of aristocratic privilege. Black slavery was the emotionally charged problem that divided the party and fomented secession and civil war. Democratic efforts to punish the Republicans for converting the war into an abolitionist crusade had met with fleeting success; in 1864 the opposition won a landslide victory on a platform committed to the abolition of slavery by constitutional amendment. Obviously, there was little political capital to be gained in supporting the "peculiar" institution, even if by indirection. As far as the Democrats were concerned, it was an issue to avoid.

Democratic attitudes toward slavery took on added significance in early 1865 when the House of Representatives began consideration of the proposed emancipation amendment. Proponents of the resolution needed minority votes to secure its passage, and campaigned for the moderate Democrats' support. Lincoln invited Representative Samuel Cox of Ohio to the White House and found him amenable, particularly when the president promised to reciprocate by initiating peace negotiations with the South. The selection of Cox was not mere happenstance. Not only did the four-term congressman have considerable influence among Democrats on Capitol Hill, but he had developed close ties with the New York party leadership during McClellan's presidential campaign.[1]

The stance of the New York leadership was of strategic importance because of its moderate position and weight in national Democratic councils. If it could be converted, passage of the resolution was assured. With this in mind, Cox conferred with Tilden, Barlow, and Marble and was assisted in his lobbying efforts by several influential War Democrats and conservative Republicans. Democratic opposition to the amendment, they noted, would be futile. Reports from the South indicated the Confederates were actually considering freeing their slaves in order to raise additional manpower and as a concession to secure last-minute European recognition. Republican dominance in the next Congress and control of Northern state legislatures meant that the amendment would be adopted in a matter of time. Montgomery Blair, conservative Republican spokesman, queried Barlow on this point: "What then can the northern Democracy gain by holding on to slavery?"[2]

The New York moderates had their reservations. Part of their difficulty stemmed from the administration's linkage of the constitutional amendment with the peace negotiations. Lincoln had initiated discussion with Confederate representatives with the understanding that Democrats would provide the support for passage of the emancipation resolution. But the Democrats realized that by making peace dependent upon emancipation they might paradoxically fortify Southern resistance, undermine the negotiations, and prolong the war. In addition, they were concerned over the precedent embodied in the resolution; if Congress could interfere with private property rights sanctioned by the Constitution, then authority for even more drastic changes by Republicans might be assumed. Given these considerations, the New York leaders finally settled on a noncommittal position, neither endorsing nor opposing the Amendment.[3]

An ambivalent outlook also characterized the party's congressional representation. While there was a solid core of Democrats committed to defeating the resolution, others had difficulty making a final decision; predictions of the eventual tally varied from day to day, stimulated by rumors of bribery, political arm twisting, and conflicting information on the status of peace negotiations. A party caucus held to discuss the issue indicated that a number of House minority members favored adoption. However, late reports on peace efforts at Fortress Monroe caused many Congressmen, including Cox, to change their minds. The final vote recorded a large majority of the Democrats opposed, thirteen supportive, and eight abstaining. Nevertheless the Democratic yeas and abstentions were crucial because they provided the narrow margin to carry the resolution.[4]

For a number of conservative spokesmen, passage of the Thirteenth Amendment promised a revitalization of the Democratic party by allowing concentration on issues that had previously worked to its advantage. George Bancroft, a New York War Democrat, counseled Cox that the death of slavery would remove the barriers separating conservatives and force a major political reorganization. "We Democrats are right on the coming financial question and the country knows it," Bancroft asserted; "do away with slavery and the Democrats will be borne into power on their sound principles of finance." Manton Marble of the *World* agreed. Future political battles would revolve around economic problems inherited from the war. Northerners had reason to be concerned about the tariff, national banking structure, and the federal debt. And in the South, the primary task for the administration was to provide an atmosphere for growth and development. Nor were these sentiments confined to New York circles. George Paul, editor of the *Milwaukee News* and Wisconsin's representative on the party's national committee, surmised there were twenty to thirty thousand voters in his state who supported the Republicans solely because of the slavery issue. With this problem out of the way, there should be no question about future political trends because the remaining national issues would be those "which originally divided the democratic and federalist parties."[5]

Many Democrats were not convinced of the primacy of economic concerns in the future. Samuel Medary's editorial successor on the *Columbus Crisis* dismissed claims that emancipation would terminate the black issue as "an absurdity"; passage of the constitutional amendment would dramatize the problems relating to black social and political equality. The editor of the *Harrisburg Patriot and Union* concurred. Emancipation, he asserted, would lead inevitably to a demand for black suffrage. Once this was conferred, there would be pressure for social and economic legislation for the freedmen. The scramble for black votes would make race a central theme in American politics for years to come. From the viewpoint of these critics it seemed obvious that the Republicans would not allow the issue of black rights to die with slavery. Whether the Democrats would make widespread gains with the end of slavery was still open to question.[6]

Democrats who proclaimed the future political significance of race had ample evidence to support their predictions. Congress, debating the Thirteenth Amendment during the early months of 1865, considered several proposals that dealt with the reorganization of Southern state governments and the conditions for their readmission to the Union. Although all were eventually rejected, the issue of voting rights for freedmen figured prominently in their discussion. Moreover, the political status of Northern blacks was a subject of contention. In Minnesota, Michigan, Wisconsin, and Connecticut, Republican-dominated legislatures drafted resolutions to include black suffrage in their state constitutions, and Ohio Republicans tried to repeal the "visible admixture" law that defined racial qualifications for the state's electorate.[7]

The attempt to extend voting rights to blacks had ominous implications for Democrats. It was generally assumed that wherever blacks were granted the franchise they would align themselves with their emancipators, the Republicans. The limited numbers of blacks in the North did not constitute an immediate threat; but black immigrants had been increasing in recent years, and there were fears that an end to the war and emancipation might expand the movement. A more pressing concern was the possibility of political rights for the mass of Southern freedmen. Blacks in Mississippi and South Carolina constituted a majority of the population and could conceivably dominate local governments. Black enfranchisement elsewhere, when joined with restrictions against ex-Confederates, might provide the margin to alter the balance of power. Whatever the process, the possibility of a Republican organization in the South with massive black support was less than reassuring to the Democrats.

On the other hand, Negro suffrage might prove to be a double-edged sword that could be wielded to the Democrats' advantage. Republicans would have to overcome widespread Northern resistance against black enfranchisement. By 1865 all New England states, except Connecticut, allowed blacks equal voting rights. In New York, nonwhites voted only if they could meet the $250 property qualification, and other mid-Atlantic and midwestern state constitutions expressly limited the franchise to whites. Should Republicans encounter a setback in their efforts to remove these disqualifications at home, they would find it difficult to impose black suffrage on the South. In the meantime they ran the risk of seriously eroding their existing constituencies and creating mass defections to the Democratic party.

Congressional consideration of reconstruction proposals early in 1865 illustrated the potentially disruptive impact of the suffrage issue for Republicans. Some Radical Republicans pressed for unrestricted black enfranchisement and tended to oppose plans that excluded it. Many conservative and moderate Republicans either favored a white electorate or voting rights for those blacks who met restrictive qualifications. This conflict enabled Democrats to prevent legislation by alternately aligning themselves with one faction against the other. Senator Thomas Hendricks of Indiana viewed the scene as precursor of what was to come. "The discordant elements of the Republican

Party are exhibiting themselves here," he noted, "and I venture to prophesy that a like exhibition will be witnessed over the country within a few years." Hendricks concluded that "the Democracy will eventually have some gains from gentlemen who will not go the extreme doctrine."[8]

By summer, as the Republican dilemma became increasingly apparent, Democratic prospects for a resurgence based upon the suffrage question were strengthened. Noting evidence of general Northern opposition, Charles Walker of the *Detroit Free Press* commented "that from present appearances the Republican Party will be shipwrecked on the question of granting to blacks of the South the right of Negro suffrage." Washington McLean, Hamilton County boss and editor of the *Cincinnati Enquirer,* agreed. "The split in the Republican Party promises to be complete," he declared. "The question of Negro suffrage is the wedge." There was no obvious or easy solution for the Republicans. Having adopted a policy of emancipation, they would be unable to guarantee blacks political status and influence. McLean concluded: "The party in power will stand responsible for having undertaken what they were unable to complete with all the consequent sufferings and disadvantages."[9]

Among other factors, recognition that agitation over the political rights of freedmen might work to the advantage of the Democrats defused resistance to the Thirteenth Amendment. In February delegates to the Connecticut party convention summarized the prevailing mood by declaring the proposed amendment "a covert attempt to overthrow and destroy the great Democratic idea of 'States Rights.'" When the resolution came before Northern state legislatures for ratification, Democrats generally voted against it. Nevertheless there was a growing tendency to view this rejection as a formality that should not be given much attention in the party press. By summer many state party conventions ignored emancipation altogether and a few actually endorsed it. Indicative of the partisan reorientation, Minnesota Democrats greeted the end of slavery with "unfeigned satisfaction" and attacked the opposition on Negro suffrage and related issues.[10]

Constitutional scruples prevented most Democrats from giving any but tacit endorsement of the amendment. In so doing they were able to put themselves in a position on suffrage that was consistent with conservative principles and conducive to partisan objectives. If states had no authority to secede, as the administration and Congress had asserted, then they had never been legally separated from the Union. Control in the South had temporarily passed into the hands of rebels, who could be legally cited and punished if they persisted in treason. In accord with this view of secession, termination of the rebellion implied that Southern state governments would resume normal relations with the federal government with all their rights and privileges intact. It would be the states, rather than the president or Congress, that ultimately determined the qualifications for participation in the federal political system.

Thus Democrats rejected Republican theories of state suicide or reversion to territorial status embodying an extension of federal authority over Southern affairs. Nor were they willing to accede to Northern intervention under the constitutional guise of guaranteeing republican forms of government to the South. This debate between Republicans over whether the executive or legislative branch should determine the reconstruction process was largely irrelevant in that both positions derived from illogical assumptions. Lincoln, in his 10 percent plan, and congressional Republicans presumed that the status of the Southern states within the federal structure had been altered and that prior relationships had to be reconstructed. Neither had the right to do more than insist that loyalty to the Union be reaffirmed.

Ironically, Lincoln himself came close to adopting the Democratic position in the closing weeks of the war. He originally launched his 10 percent plan as an expedient for restoring civil government in limited areas of the South under Union control, but the president shifted his policy with the rapid deterioration of Confederate armed resistance. An order to military authorities in Virginia called for reassembling the existing legislature. General Sherman, acting in concurrence with the directive, recognized the legitimacy of established state governments when he negotiated peace terms with Gen. Joseph Johnston. Although Lincoln changed his mind and countermanded the order, Democrats perceived the president's emerging policy as conservative in outlook. Consequently, the reaction of the vast majority of Democratic party members to Lincoln's assassination was one of revulsion against the crime and fear about the consequences for the nation.[11]

Much of the apprehension stemmed from concern about Lincoln's successor in the White House. As a War Democrat, senator from Tennessee, member of the Joint Committee on the Conduct of the War, and military governor of his state, Andrew Johnson was clearly neither an orthodox conservative nor strict constructionist of the Constitution. On several occasions he publicly tolerated charges that associated Northern Democratic regulars with treason and repeatedly demanded punishment for those who started the rebellion. Johnson's background did not inspire much Democratic enthusiasm when he assumed the vice-presidency. His apparent intoxication at the March inauguration seemed to provide further confirmation of his incapacity for high political office. Democratic critics charged, quite unfairly, that the Tennessee tailor-turned-politician was an "ignorant, insolent, drunken sot" and a potential despot of the caliber of a Nero or Caligula.[12]

There were few such barbed attacks when Johnson became president. Democrats privately expressed their apprehensions but publicly greeted their new president with deference and respect. The circumstances surrounding the transfer of office and traditional political protocol only partially accounted for the reaction. With Congress adjourned and the war virtually ended, Johnson would have great influence on the development of reconstruction policies. Besides he was still a Southerner who refused to identify himself fully with the Republican party. It made little sense for regular Democrats to oppose the president until his policies on postwar national affairs were fully known. On the contrary, their most expedient course would be to offer nonpartisan support in the hope that they might win his endorsement of their conservative policies.[13]

Democratic support of the president during his first month and a half in office was not without its difficulties. His actions on more than one occasion gave cause for alarm. Johnson's persistent verbal attacks on Confederate leaders and threatened confiscation of large landed estates raised fears for the survival of the South's traditional economic power structure. His failure to declare peace officially, when the war had clearly ended, aroused speculation about continued violations of civil law. In early May the administration confirmed these fears by announcing that the trial of those charged with Lincoln's assassination would be conducted by a military commission. Democrats who found the decision reprehensible were even more appalled when the defendants appeared before the court in chains and the presiding officer announced there would be no public release of testimony. Because rumors spread implying that the government sought to link Jefferson Davis with the conspiracy, apprehension was expressed that the trial would not end the assault on Anglo-Saxon legal custom.[14]

Washington insider, Montgomery Blair, was acutely aware of Democratic fears and sought to prevent a breach between the party and the White House. Having ingratiated himself with Johnson by inviting him to the family's Silver Springs household following the unfortunate episode at the vice-presidential inaugural, Blair was known to have the Tennessean's personal confidence. He used this advantage in a persistent effort to maintain support for the administration by the New York moderate Democratic leadership. Democrats, warned the Maryland conservative Republican, should not make the mistake of criticizing Johnson for minor sins of omission or commission. Rather, since the president was seemingly conservative in his outlook, the Democrats should extend their support and prevent his preemption by the Radicals. In so doing, they would further their own interests and render the "highest service to the country."[15]

Despite their obvious reservations, most Democrats were not ready to forego a possible rapprochement with Johnson. Much of the president's vehement rhetoric against Confederate leaders, they reasoned, stemmed from passions generated by the war and Lincoln's assassination. It was hoped that time would temper the intensity of those feelings. Other instances in which the administration appeared to overreach its authority could be traced to Johnson's sudden elevation to the presidency and the temporary pressure to grant cabinet members discretionary authority. Yet department heads were subject to criticism, and Secretary Stanton bore the brunt of the attack. Led by the *New York World,* the Democratic press launched a full-scale attack designed to generate friction between the secretary of war and the president and force Stanton's removal. They charged he had needlessly humiliated Gen. William T. Sherman by rebuking him publicly for his handling of peace negotiations with Gen. Joseph E. Johnston and was directly responsible for the shameful mishandling of the Lincoln assassination conspirators. For the good of the president and the nation, Stanton should be replaced by someone who more adequately reflected administration policy.[16]

The assumption that Johnson might gravitate toward the conservatives was not based on wishful thinking. During April and May the president showed an inclination to disavow the Radicals. Johnson told an Indiana delegation a week after the assassination that he rejected the notion that when the Southern states seceded they had either committed suicide or reverted to territorial status. Democrats applauded the president's declaration as a projection of states' rights convictions but awaited the translation of this theory into practice. Their hesitance stemmed from the president's failure, as yet, to state where he drew the line between state and federal authority. Through public statement and private interview, Clement Vallandigham and William Bigler let the president know that party regulars would not make an issue of his support of the Thirteenth Amendment, but that further federal intervention into Southern domestic affairs, and in particular suffrage, would be unwarranted. Late in May Johnson largely quieted such fears by counseling a group of blacks against looking to Washington for support and by informing Francis Preston Blair, the family patriarch, of his intent to leave the question of black suffrage to the states.[17]

Johnson took another step towards clarifying his position at the end of the month by issuing two proclamations that had direct bearing on the reconstruction process. In the first of these the president granted amnesty to all Southerners who took part in the rebellion with the exception of individuals in fourteen categories. Those who qualified would have to take an oath of future loyalty and accept earlier presidential proclamations concerning slavery. The second proclamation, issued on the same day, outlined the procedures for reinstituting civil government in North Carolina. Johnson appointed a provisional governor empowered to call for the selection of delegates to a state constitutional convention and designated requirements for the electorate. Whites included under the amnesty, or who subsequently received a pardon, were generally permitted to participate in the election. Individuals not entitled to vote at the outbreak of the rebellion were expressly denied a role in politics.[18]

Democrats for the most part viewed the president's program as falling short of their expectations but regarded it as the best that reasonably could be expected. Obviously Johnson rejected the notion that Confederate state governments constituted lawful authority in the South and that repeal of the articles of secession was all that was necessary for normalization. Furthermore, the president's fourteen categories of individuals exempted from amnesty was even more proscriptive of ex-Confederates than Lincoln's terms had been. Party regulars took particular note of the restrictions against former rebels who held property in excess of twenty thousand dollars and complained this constituted a form of class warfare that denied the South much of its leadership talent. Nor were they pleased, as a matter of precedent, with the amnesty requirement calling for acceptance of presidential proclamations on slavery.[19]

The exclusion of blacks from the initial stages of the reconstruction process more than compensated for the program's apparent shortcomings. By prohibiting black participation in the election of the North Carolina convention, Johnson had taken a major step towards embracing the conservative position. In so doing he had publicly rebuked the Radicals and furthered division within the ranks of the Union political organization. The obvious discomfort of Radical spokesmen, and reports of disagreement between the president and Stanton over black suffrage, provided additional support for this conclusion. Wilbur Storey of the *Chicago Times* asserted "there is nothing more certain in the immediate future than that the radicals and President Johnson will pursue different paths." William Cassidy agreed and sounded the death knell for the Republican party: "Its day to live has passed," he gloated; "its time to die has come."[20]

Despite such jubilation, many Democrats looked for additional confirmation of Johnson's conservative orientation. After all, the reconstruction process prescribed for North Carolina might not be applicable to other Southern states. Furthermore, some party regulars nursed suspicions about the president's position on black suffrage as stated in the North Carolina Proclamation. Johnson had denied blacks participation in the election of convention delegates, but he had expressed no opinion on how the constitutional convention or future state governments should handle the suffrage issue. Conceivably he had left the way open for an endorsement of black suffrage at a later date. Noting this possibility, the editor of the *Columbus Crisis* theorized that the president could compel North Carolinians to enfranchise blacks "by means of military force or bogus elections." Accordingly, the editor concluded that the composition of the Southern electorate was "still in doubt."[21]

A public condemnation of black political rights would have created other problems for Johnson. Most Democrats, particularly those from the Ohio valley and lower mid-Atlantic states, subscribed to the notion of the biological inferiority of blacks and held that they had no place in a "white man's government." But this sentiment within the party was not universal. In New York and New England, where blacks already had the franchise, and in the upper Great Lakes states, where blacks were relatively few in number, there was evidence of a more moderate attitude. William Cassidy, Manton Marble, Charles Walker, and Editor William Galloweigh of the *Boston Post* all allowed for the eventual enfranchisement of freedmen if they were given adequate education and time to overcome the limitations of their slave heritage. The president, by claiming that political rights were ultimately a matter for state determination, reasserted a traditional constitutional principle and took the only position broad enough to encompass the diversity of Democratic opinion.[22]

Other matters contributed to Democratic uncertainty. Party regulars had been willing to grant Johnson time to formulate his own policy and in the interim exempt him from responsibility for actions by his department heads. But there was no firm evidence following the North Carolina Proclamation that the president intended to reorganize the cabinet. Nor did he fulfill Democratic expectations in the matter of civil law. Johnson postponed the execution of Lambdin Milligan and others convicted in the 1864 Midwest conspiracy trial and ordered the release of some testimony on Lincoln's assassination. The Washington military commission continued its deliberations, and rumors spread that Jefferson Davis and Robert E. Lee were to be charged with treason. In mid-June Gen. John A. Dix, the military commander in New York, ordered the arrest of John Mitchell, Irish nationalist, Confederate sympathizer, and newly hired member of the editorial staff of the *New York News*. Because of his reputation for inflammatory rhetoric, Mitchell's imprisonment appeared to be a continuation of wartime infringements on the freedom of the press.[23]

The arrest came at an inopportune moment. The National Democratic Committee was scheduled to meet in New York the following day, and Johnson's supporters hoped to secure a resolution of endorsement. In preparation for the meeting, Congressman John Chanler lobbied for a commitment to Johnson by the New York City Democratic party. Both efforts for Johnson failed. Samuel Barlow, writing to Montgomery Blair, expressed the sentiments of the New York party hierarchy by asking: "Are we never to be freed from the meddling interference of Provost Marshalls . . . ? Are we never again to have trials by jury?" The New Yorkers let Johnson know they expected the termination of the Washington military tribunal after the Lincoln conspiracy trial and its findings turned over to the courts for final review.[24]

Although the president and the Democrats remained at odds over the application of martial law, during the last half of June they drew closer together on reconstruction issues. Johnson issued pardons without prior consideration by the courts and indicated he favored a rapid bestowal of political privileges on ex-Confederates who had been exempted from amnesty. He soon demonstrated that his plan for North Carolina was not unique by issuing in quick succession similar proclamations for five other Southern states. Late in the month in an interview with a South Carolina delegation, Johnson provided additional insight on his views on black suffrage. The president revealed that he subscribed to the widely held assumption that freedmen were docile and easily manipulated and should be granted the ballot because they would be influenced to vote as their former masters dictated. In so doing he sought to make his policy more palatable to a wide range of political interests. Actually, most Democrats were willing to overlook this veiled attack on traditional Southern leadership and noted that Johnson had suggested a general disposition against Southern black suffrage.[25]

The president's reconstruction position was enough to convince at least one prominent Democrat that the time was ripe for an official partisan endorsement. In the latter part of June Charles Mason visited Johnson in the company of several other Democrats and found the discussion "highly satisfactory." Mason left the meeting convinced of the president's commitment to "a white man's government" and the principle of states' rights. Johnson had won an important ally. A West Point graduate, former resident of New York, one-time Chief Justice of the Iowa Supreme Court, and practicing attorney in the District of Columbia, Mason had wide and varied political contacts. In

1863 he had served as secretary to the Society for the Diffusion of Political Knowledge, a short-lived national organization for the dissemination of party propaganda, and in the following year became chairman of the Washington Resident Committee which served a somewhat similar function. It was as chairman of the Resident Committee that Mason wrote an open letter early in June calling for the Democratic endorsement of Johnson. "All the acts of the president," he asserted, "have tended in the right direction." And although Johnson was somewhat laggard in restoring of civil law, Mason concluded "no great harm seems to have resulted from the delay. Mason reasoned that since Johnson was fully in accord with the Democratic party on reconstruction, the president deserved the enthusiastic support of "his political brethren."[26]

Mason's timing could not have been worse. In early June the military commission in Washington concluded its deliberations, found the defendants guilty, and sentenced them to be hanged. Democrats conceded that the testimony warranted a guilty verdict except for Mary Surratt, but they expected the president to send the proceedings to the courts for final review. Yet Johnson approved the sentences and denied last-minute appeals for a writ of habeas corpus for Mrs. Surratt. The Democrats were incredulous and indignant. Angered by the hangings and new reports of a plan to try Jefferson Davis, Robert E. Lee, and others for treason, many party spokesmen concluded the president had lost his mind. Samuel Barlow noted that at a meeting of "the most prominent leaders" of the Democracy "not a man present was willing to lend his support to the administration." Under these circumstances the reaction to Mason's appeal was rejection.[27]

In time the outrage of moderate party leaders began to subside. Charles Mason, understandably chagrined by the episode, was inclined to close the door to further communication; discussion with Montgomery Blair subsequently convinced him this would be unwise. Blair, urgently seeking to patch up the rift, explained that the president had recently been ill and under the temporary but pernicious influence of Stanton and Secretary of State William Seward. Now Johnson's health had improved, and Blair gave assurances that the imposition of martial law had ended. Shortly afterwards Mason and other prominent Democrats interviewed the president at the White House and left "much gratified" with Johnson's identification with the Democrats. A transformation of Democratic sentiment ensued. Samuel Barlow informed Blair that he, Samuel Tilden, and Dean Richmond wanted to visit the president and inform him that as far as the New York leadership was concerned, "the whole party is today a Johnson party."[28]

The New Yorkers did not speak for the Copperheads. Many of the former peace advocates had demonstrated a pragmatic bent since the end of the war and were willing to accept moderate leadership and grant concessions in the effort to win over Johnson. The most notable exception was the small contingent of party ideologues led by Alexander Long and William Cory, who continued to nurse grievances over McClellan's nomination in 1864 and viewed both Johnson and the Democratic hierarchy as disloyal. But the Cincinnati clique's sharp attacks on the administration and rejection of accommodation gained little support until after the execution of the Lincoln conspirators. Other Copperhead spokesmen joined in the assault and persisted in their criticism even when party moderates moved toward a rapprochement. C. Chauncey Burr of the *Old Guard* asserted it was illogical to assume that Johnson could ever return to the Democratic faith and charged that individuals who sought his favor were "thieves, speculators, and spoils-hunters of their respective parties."[29]

By early August other events lent credence to the critics' claims. When municipal elections in Richmond, Virginia, resulted in the selection of a number of former secessionists, the military commander in charge annulled the returns and left all but two city offices vacant. Statewide elections in Kentucky shortly thereafter also brought military intervention. General John Palmer, a fervent emancipationist, ordered that Confederate veterans and those who gave aid or comfort to the rebellion be excluded from the polls. The deployment of black troops to police the election added insult to injury. Conservatives were able to carry the contest by slim majorities, despite military supervision, but Johnson's refusal to intercede raised troublesome questions about the president's attitude. Nor did Johnson help matters by his widely publicized interview with Congressman Robert Schenck, a prominent Ohio Republican. The president reportedly acknowledged his responsibility for the Richmond intervention, claimed he would do so again in similar instances, and explained that the plan set forth in the North Carolina Proclamation was merely experimental.[30]

Military intervention in the Virginia and Kentucky elections once again confused the public about the direction of national politics. Johnson's use of the military lent substance to Radical charges that Southerners were unrepentant and that he would prevent secessionists from reassuming power. If the administration would use force to prevent such a possibility in the fully organized states of Kentucky and Virginia, then the door would be open for federal interference in the reconstruction process in the deep South. From the Democratic perspective, the president had undermined his own reconstruction guidelines. Amnesty, pardon, or a willingness to swear their future loyalty were apparently not enough to guarantee ex-Confederates full political rights. The editor of the *Dubuque Herald* spoke for those Copperheads who had already written off Johnson by asserting that the Virginia and Kentucky incidents proved the folly of Democrats believing the president "would ultimately come out squarely for liberty and popular rights." Meanwhile, New York moderates made known their displeasure by scrapping plans to visit the White House.[31]

Johnson's apparent concessions to the opposition, restricting the political activity of former Confederates, raised the possibility of similar changes in his policy on black suffrage. Moderate party spokesmen Manton Marble and Charles Walker, seeking to forestall this prospect, suddenly altered their own positions and called on Democrats to view black political equality as a national rather than local issue to be opposed "root and branch." The president, under conflicting pressures, used the Mississippi constitutional convention in mid-August to treat the issue of black suffrage on other than constitutional grounds. In a telegram to the state's provisional governor, he urged the assembly to formally terminate slavery and prohibit its reintroduction by legislative enactment. The president further advised an extension of the vote to blacks who met restrictive literacy and property qualifications. Should Mississippi make these concessions, he concluded, it would "completely foil" Radical plans to deny Southern representation in the next Congress.[32]

Johnson's intervention, while not disclosed to the public, indicated the extent of the president's flexiblity that Democrats feared. Perhaps the president's sole motive was to defuse the Radical attack so that he might secure the admission of Southern representatives. Democrats could hardly have been convinced that this concession, even if it were granted by the South, would produce the desired objectives. In the meantime it created a dangerous precedent. By advising Southern acceptance of qualified black suffrage, the president not only conceded legitimacy to the proponents of universal black enfranchisement but also inferred voting rights were a matter of federal concern. Advice could conceivably turn into demand and transform suggestion into precondition. At this point constitutional objections to the Radical program would be obliterated. By his support for qualified black suffrage, Johnson was again at odds with the Democratic party and rumors of the administration's backsliding clouded the atmosphere at the August Democratic state conventions.

The reaction of Pennsylvania Democrats was compounded by problems of a personal nature. During the summer Montgomery Blair sought Pennsylvania's support for the administration through the Buchanan faction of the party led by the former Senate spokesman William Bigler, former cabinet member Jeremiah Black, and Congressman Adam Glossbrenner, who had once served as secretary to the ex-president. Blair turned to the Buchananites primarily because of their influence in state party circles. The Pennsylvanians, for their part, were willing to use Blair to gain access to the White House. Yet the relationship, born of immediate political necessity, was an uneasy one because of mutual distrust dating back to Buchanan's removal of Blair from public office. While the Pennsylvania Democrats were willing to support Johnson when his position served national party interests, they had reservations about the Blair family's obvious designs to control the president, or a possible accord between Blair and the Pennsylvania Unionist clique led by John Forney. These doubts heightened their response to White House lapses from conservative doctrine.[33]

When the Pennsylvania Democrats assembled in convention on August 24, there was strong sentiment against a blanket endorsement of the administration. This did not mean that the delegates had determined to resurrect old issues, or that they rejected the possibility of partisan realignment. On the contrary, the selection of Union veterans to head the ticket and the rejection of slavery indicated a disposition to overcome the legacy inherited from the war and broaden the Democrats' appeal. But the platform made clear their determination that any conservative realignment would have to be on Democratic terms, defined by the regular party organization. The resolutions offered tentative approval of the president with the qualifications that he refrain from future use of military tribunals and prevent military intervention in state elections. On the question of black suffrage, the convention not only denounced federal control of voting qualifications as a "high crime against the Constitution" but also as a "deliberate and wicked attempt . . . to degrade the white race morally, and socially, as well as politically." Irate over the platform, Blair complained to Black that the Democrats had raised "too many qualifications," and the relationship between the Maryland conservative and his erstwhile Pennsylvania allies soon degenerated into an exchange of insults.[34]

Democrats adopted a similar position in Ohio. McLean, Pendleton, Pugh, Thurman, and other party leaders sought to revitalize the party's image by affirming their desire to discard "dead issues of the past" and raising the threat of black suffrage. The Columbus convention went outside the traditional party hierarchy to select George W. Morgan of Mount Vernon to head the ticket. A general in both the Mexican and Civil Wars and an early advocate of McClellan's presidential nomination, Morgan could hardly be denounced as hostile to the military or an abettor of secession. His wartime opposition to black troops had already established him as an opponent of black equality. Thus the choice of the gubernatorial candidate coincided with the convention's decision to affirm state control over suffrage and demand exclusion of blacks from the polls. The platform pledged the party's support to Johnson "in all Constitutional efforts" to restore the Union. But it also made it clear that federal tampering with voting qualifications, infringements upon the freedom of the press, trial by jury, or free and open elections would constitute a violation of constitutional principles.[35]

Although the Ohio convention and New Jersey's a week later did not meet the expectations of Johnson's advocates, Iowa proved more satisfactory. Democratic regulars favorable to the president, led by ex-Senator George W. Jones, allowed a coalition of War Democrats and conservative Republicans to take the initiative. On August 23 delegates to a "Soldiers' Convention" in Des Moines constructed a "Soldiers' Ticket" headed by Thomas Hart Benton Jr., a nominal Republican and nephew of the former senator from Missouri. The regularly scheduled Democratic convention met the following day and, after some internal feuding, ratified results of the Des Moines meeting. In his letter of acceptance, Benton set the tone for the campaign by ignoring the administration's infractions of civil liberties and focusing on Radical efforts to extend the franchise to blacks in Iowa and the South.[36]

The midwestern conservative movement for political reorganization was not without its difficulties. The Iowa Copperhead contingent led by Dennis

Mahoney and Le Grand Byington condemned the Des Moines convention and denounced Benton as a "renegade." The Copperheads refused to be bound by the subsequent Democratic endorsement of the ticket and they scheduled their own convention and nominated candidates for state office on a platform that stressed civil liberties. Nor was factionalism spawned only by efforts to create new pro-Johnson political organizations. Alexander Long and William Cory stoutly resisted efforts by the Ohio Democratic hierarchy to modify party principles in order to broaden its appeal. Failing in this, they launched an independent State Sovereignty party that endorsed the principle of state nullification and nominated Long for the governorship.[37]

While Democrats in Ohio, Pennsylvania, Iowa and New Jersey launched their campaigns in late August, party regulars elsewhere awaited clarification of the administration's position. The deliberations of New Yorkers, scheduled to hold their convention on September 6, drew special attention and were expected to influence the Northern Democrats' general approach to the fall elections. Relations between the New York party leadership and the White House showed signs of improvement. Late in August Johnson gave private reassurances of his conservative stance on reconstruction. Southerners such as Russell Houston of Kentucky, Thomas Pratt of Maryland, and Richard Taylor, a former general in the Confederate Army and son-in-law of Jefferson Davis, visited the president and reported their favorable impressions of their meetings to Barlow. They noted that Johnson had reasserted his resolve to leave the suffrage issue to state determination, promised that pardoned ex-Confederates would not be treated as second-class citizens, and guaranteed that martial law would end once a state became fully organized. Given these assurances, they urged Democratic support of the administration.[38]

The president had left similar impressions on previous occasions, but the direction charted by Johnson during late August indicated that his promises were not mere rhetoric. Mississippi concluded its constitutional convention without Washington intervention and without endorsing black suffrage. Rather than displeasure, Johnson wired his approval and congratulations. And he kept his promise to restrict martial law when he countermanded the residing federal commander's order prohibiting local militial units and confirmed the right of Mississippians to provide for their own public safety. Moreover, the president countered Radical demands for further controls over the South by removing existing restrictions against trade and commerce and allowing pardoned ex-Confederates to leave the country freely. Conservatives also welcomed reports of Johnson's alleged intervention in the military trial of the Andersonville prison commander and his quashing of complicity charges against Jefferson Davis and Robert E. Lee.[39]

Although the president allayed fears over future administration reconstruction policy, New York Democrats had a continuing concern about political organization on the state level that involved William Seward, secretary of state. Earlier rumors and predictions notwithstanding, Seward remained in the cabinet and provided a link between the White House and the New York

Republican faction that included Thurlow Weed and Henry Raymond of the *Times*. The Seward presence was a major factor in the deliberations of New York Democrats' future relations with Washington. They distrusted Seward's professed conservativism, for they remembered only too well his earlier radical rhetoric. But most importantly, they feared his influence on legions of federal officeholders who could have a decisive impact on any political campaign. If there was to be political realignment, Democratic regulars were determined that they should control the patronage that was the basis of partisan power.

The New York Democratic leaders believed it was imperative that Seward be replaced and during the summer had repeatedly pressed their views on the president through editorials as well as personal diplomacy. By late August their objective appeared within reach. Thomas Pratt visited the White House on the seventeenth for an interview with Johnson in which he voiced Democratic reservations about the secretary of state and their desire for his removal from office. Johnson recognized the concession was the price for the party's support; he relented and agreed to an eventual reorganization of the cabinet. Barlow, elated over this news, wrote Pratt of his satisfaction with Johnson's position. Asserting his belief the president would secure the backing of the Democrats, he added a postscript disavowing any intention of dictating appointments: "The most that anyone could think of doing," he concluded, "would be to suggest those who *should not* be appointed."[40]

Johnson's commitment to changes in the cabinet, as well as his assurances on reconstruction, provided the incentive for New York endorsement of the president. Samuel Tilden went to Washington before the convention for a final confirmation of the president's policy and when he returned he met Barlow and Marble to arrange a draft of the platform. They traveled to Albany to test the Regency's reaction and, after minor modifications, secured the approval of William Cassidy and Dean Richmond. The resolutions adopted by the convention delegates were basically moderate in their outlook. The platform condemned any federal interference with state suffrage requirements but was phrased to exclude any blatant racist rhetoric. Although the New Yorkers did not ignore the issues of martial law and civil liberties, their language avoided the appearance of any direct criticism of the administration. Cassidy noted that "the endorsement of President Johnson . . . was strong without servility, and all the more forceful for its reserve.[41]

The regular party leadership, firmly in control, constructed the ticket to convey the appearance of a major party reorganization effort. John Van Buren, a War Democrat bearing one of the most prominent names in state party history, received the nomination for attorney general. The delegates endorsed the incumbent comptroller, Lucius Robinson, a Republican since the fifties and a former critic of Lincoln's conservative policies. The Democrats' new profile was strengthened by the nomination of Gen. Henry Slocum for secretary of state. His choice constituted an apparent contradiction of the reconstruction plank; Slocum's order disbanding the state militia in Mississippi had been countermanded by the president. But as Manton Marble asserted in the *World,* the ticket demonstrated the extent to which the convention was willing to prove "that the Democratic party is not a hidebound, illiberal set of impracticables [sic], fighting over the bodies of dead horses slain in former battles. . . ."[42]

Other Democratic conventions held in September followed the New York precedent. Minnesota regulars met the day after the New York convention and selected Henry Rice, who had bolted the party in 1864 to support Lincoln's reelection, as their gubernatorial candidate. Democrats in neighboring Wisconsin similarly condemned black suffrage, strongly praised the president, and chose Gen. Harrison Hobart, a War Democrat, to head the list of nominees. The Massachusetts chairman of the state central committee and author of the party platform, notified Johnson that the endorsement of the Massachusetts Democrats was both "unanimous" and "unqualified." Special meetings were also set up in states where there were no off-year elections to voice support for the administration. Thus the Northern Democrats generally, except for third-party movements in Ohio and Iowa and Copperhead dissidents such as Benjamin Wood of the *New York News,* went into the fall campaign committed to party reorganization and support of the president's reconstruction program.[43]

Democrats had difficulty drawing a sharp distinction between their position and that of the opposition. In New York, for example, they assumed that Radicals would control the Republican platform and nominations and force moderates and conservatives to identify with the Democrats. The assumption was ill-founded. When the opposition met in Syracuse, the Seward-Weed-Raymond faction dominated. The Committee on Resolutions, chaired by the *Times* editor, praised Johnson as "a statesman of ability, experience, and high-toned patriotism" and approved the administration's relaxation of military authority in the South. To placate the Radicals, the platform made full restoration of civil government dependent upon the preservation of order, exclusion of slavery, and guarantees of republican forms of government. But it omitted direct reference to black suffrage and inserted instead a general statement that affirmed the need for Southern states to perpetuate "the full rights of citizenship of all their people. . . ." The Union Convention also nominated Henry Slocum for secretary of state and selected several former Democrats to round out the ticket.[44]

In other states the Democrats ran into similar problems. Iowa Republicans held their convention early in the summer and were formally committed to black suffrage by their platform. By fall the conservative campaign mounted by Thomas Benton forced the Union gubernatorial candidate to deny the significance of the suffrage issue in the election. Wisconsin conservatives and moderate Republicans, led by James Doolittle, drafted resolutions supporting Johnson, shelved a Radical proposal demanding enfranchisement of freedmen, and proposed a constitutional amendment basing congressional representation on eligible voters. Ohio Democrats confronted an even more perplexing dilemma: the Republican gubernatorial candidate not only refused to disassociate himself from the president but also sought to outflank his opponent on racial matters by proposing the colonization and segregation of freedmen in a separate black state. Most Union and Republican organizations vied with the Democrats in their endorsement of Johnson and were reluctant to adopt a forthright position on voting rights for either Southern or Northern blacks.[45]

Under these circumstances, the Democrats were forced to do battle with an elusive foe. Their response was to accuse the opposition of deceit and to publicize Radical statements in behalf of black suffrage as indicative of the objectives of the party at large. Once they characterized their adversaries as proponents of black enfranchisement, they forecast the worst if the enemy were elected. Party spokesmen in the Ohio valley argued that changes in their state constitutions would attract numerous black migrants who would compete with returning soldiers for jobs. Democrats further north called for the defeat of black suffrage referendums as a mandate against granting the vote to Southern freedmen. They claimed that universal suffrage would lead to political chaos, as it had in Haiti and Jamaica, and eventually to a debilitated, mongrel society. Nor were they willing to countenance qualified suffrage based upon literacy or military service. They reasoned that whites owed nothing to black veterans because blacks had fought for their own objectives and had been rewarded by emancipation. If literacy was enough to merit the ballot, then women should be accorded the right to vote. Moreover, to immediately bestow suffrage in any form on the freedmen would be an affront to European immigrants who were obliged to wait a lengthy period before naturalization.[46]

By making black suffrage the central issue of the campaign the Democrats were able to link their position to that of the administration. Johnson's advice to Southerners to adopt qualified black suffrage was either ignored, denied, dismissed as facetious, or deemed irrelevant because of his broader commitment to state control over voting rights. Nor were Democrats forced to accept claims of the president's disposition to moderate his stance and seek a compromise with the opposition. On the contrary, official actions of the administration during September gave evidence of Johnson's conservative orientation. The president had ordered the restriction of land confiscation in the South and a withdrawal of black military units. In a discussion with a Southern delegation he commended Southerners for their general attitude, denied that the administration wished to treat them harshly, and condemned efforts to concentrate further power in the federal government. Criticism of Johnson by Radical spokesmen Thaddeus Stevens and Charles Sumner revealed the fundamental differences between Republicans and the president and made it clear that the Democrats were the only party favorable to the administration.[47]

Returns from the October elections indicated the Democratic strategy was only partially successful. In Connecticut a black suffrage amendment to the state constitution was defeated by 6,000 votes out of 60,000 cast. Connecticut demonstrated strong public sentiment against black enfranchisement, but the results from other contests did not transform that sentiment into a Democratic victory. The party in Pennsylvania lost the two statewide offices in the election, and Republicans carried the Iowa and Ohio gubernatorial races. The Democratic percentage of the total vote in all three states was larger than the previous year, although this was not much consolation in view of the extent of McClellan's defeat. If the voters did support the administration, they did not necessarily perceive their support as a partisan action.[48]

These attitudes were in accord with Johnson's aims and objectives. Troubled by persistent claims in the Democratic press that he had returned to party orthodoxy, the president in an interview with Boston Republican George L. Stearns disavowed charges that he had been captured by the Democrats. Johnson asserted that although he believed control of suffrage should be left to the states, he personally favored a gradual extension of voting rights to blacks based upon property, literacy, and military service qualifications. In addition, he subscribed to a widely held principle in Republican circles that state congressional representation should be based upon the number of qualified voters, which would sharply reduce Southerners' power in Washington if they failed to give freedmen the vote. The Democrats were offended and put on the defensive by this widely circulated interview and sought not too successfully to explain away the apparent discrepancy between their position and that articulated by the president.[49]

There were other troublesome matters that concerned the party. The November elections assumed added significance after the setbacks in Pennsylvania, Ohio, and Iowa, and the Democrats feared that new reverses would prevent future party realignment. Samuel Barlow, noting Johnson's erratic course, concluded that the president was temporarily "trying to ride two horses" and would eventually cast his lot with the party that emerged the victor. Barlow feared that a Republican victory in New York would leave the Democrats with the unpleasant choice of political isolation or as an appendage to the Seward-Weed-Raymond organization. To forestall this possibility, party regulars demanded that the opposition be denied the support of Republican officeholders. They hoped that Johnson's appointment of a former Democrat to head the Customs House and a refusal by the secretary of the navy to restrict Democrats in the Brooklyn Navy Yard were encouraging signs. But actions by Republican appointees against the Democratic ticket soon forced Barlow to demand that "Johnson call off his dogs and do it effectively and publicly. . . ."[50]

The November elections confirmed Democratic apprehensions. Party gains of a month earlier suddenly vanished when the opposition won large majorities in Minnesota, Wisconsin, and Massachusetts, increased its control over New York, and won the governorship and legislative dominance in New Jersey. The defeat of the black suffrage referendums in Minnesota and Wisconsin were the only redeeming features for Democrats in these elections. Democrats correctly assumed Northern resistance to black enfranchisement, but, as the elections demonstrated, they had been unable to turn this to their advantage.

Thus their earlier expectations of a major party reorganization during 1865 remained largely unrealized. The evolution of the president's reconstruction program clouded rather than clarified the picture. Although Johnson's Southern policy appeared to favor conservatives, it was often inconsistent and occasionally contradictory. Politicians of both parties, solicitous of White House prestige and patronage, had tailored their actions accordingly. Moderate Democrats mollified their opposition to presidential inconsistencies in policies, hoping that Johnson's eventual affiliation with them would undermine the Republican organization. Neither Johnson nor the Republicans conformed to their scenario. Instead, the Democrats renewed and intensified their own internal conflict between the apostles of principle and the advocates of expediency.

# 3

## *The Breach*

WHILE AVOIDING the black suffrage issue in the 1865 elections, Republicans capitalized on the claims that the North stood to lose the fruits of military victory. The South, they charged, was unrepentant. They elaborated on this accusation by asserting that former secessionists, encouraged by their Northern Democratic allies, sought to gain control of the new state governments at the expense of Unionists. It was feared that once they were in power, these advocates of rebellion would sanctify their treason by payment of the Confederate debt and repudiation of federal financial obligations. Republican orators argued that Southerners demonstrated a decided reluctance to accept the eradication of slavery as a consequence of war. They warned Northern Unionists not to be deceived by acknowledgements of emancipation from ex-Confederates, for these assurances merely masked their intention to create a de facto servitude by new legislation. Congress must spurn the normalization of sectional relations and extract concessions to protect Union policies.

Democrats sought to counter Republican demands for additional guarantees by rejecting the assumptions on which they were grounded. In response to charges that the South was falling back under the control of "rebels" and "traitors", Democratic spokesman noted that treason had ceased with the termination of military activities and the collapse of the Confederacy. They presented evidence from Southern newspapers, travel accounts, and other sources to support their conclusion that the overwhelming majority of Southerners accepted the results of the war and were anxious to resume their responsibilities as full-fledged citizens of the republic. As for the blacks, Southern whites knew their needs best and should be allowed to provide for the transition to freedom with a minimum of outside interference. Whatever racial turbulence existed in the South should be attributed to Republican agitators, whose objectives were personal and partisan gain.[1]

Although Democrats generally subscribed to the South's acquiescence in defeat and rejected the need for further federal demands, they disagreed over whether such Southern passivity should be maintained indefinitely. For some, and especially those of an ideological bent, the logic of the conservative position dictated that the South make no additional concessions to Northern opinion. Washington McLean declared that Southerners needed recognition of their basic rights as citizens, and he claimed they would "not gain these by voluntarily conceding them away, nor by selling them for a consideration." Benjamin Wood defiantly charged that prominent Confederates need not refrain from political activity to quiet Republican suspicions; treason had died with the Confederacy and the North should not expect Southerners to act like traitors.[2]

Other Democrats disagreed with such reasoning. Like their hard-line colleagues, they believed that Republicans were diverting attention from black suffrage and attempting to devise a rationale on other issues to exclude Southern representatives from Congress. They claimed that the best strategy for Southerners would be to undermine Republican attacks by quieting Northern fears and suspicions. Manton Marble criticized Wood for being "more pro-southern than the South itself" and warned Southerners against adopting the "suicidal course" proposed by the *New York News*. These pragmatic party spokesmen stressed that the South must avoid selecting prominent ex-Confederates for public office, take positive steps to acknowledge the end of slavery, and guarantee freedmen legal protection in the courts.[3]

When Southern state conventions assembled in the fall, their increasingly truculent attitude troubled the president and moderate party regulars. The South Carolina assembly convened on September 13, acknowledged emancipation, repealed rather than nullified the articles of secession, and refused to repudiate the Confederate debt. These actions were protested by Northern Unionists and forced Johnson to pressure for moderation by subsequent conventions in North Carolina and Virginia. Although the president's intervention prevented a repetition of the South Carolina experience, other difficulties arose. The Mississippi election of public officials under the new constitution resulted in the selection of an unpardoned ex-Confederate as governor and the installation of a legislature that enacted the notorious, restrictive black codes. The Mississippi pattern, repeated in other states, once again forced the president's hand. He responded by requesting provisional governors of North and South Carolina to remain temporarily in office, urging Southerners to endorse the Thirteenth Amendment, and refusing to countermand orders from Union officers disallowing black codes in several states.[4]

Johnson's actions added to the mood of uncertainty among Democratic regulars. The president appeared to be mandating new conditions beyond those called for in the North Carolina proclamation. He may have been trying to outflank the opposition by depriving it of issues effectively utilized in the fall elections, but he may have been making overtures to the Republicans to avoid future confrontations with Congress. Democratic leaders were especially troubled by reports of interviews between Johnson and influential Republican politicians and claims that the administration's Southern policy was largely experimental. If so, the administration might make more concessions and eventually give in to Republican demands for black suffrage. Most party spokesmen believed the results of the Northern state referendums on black enfranchisement rendered this possibility unlikely. They resolved to continue their support for the president and looked to action by Congress in early December to clarify national attitudes.[5]

Democrats were in an unenviable position when representatives of the legislative branch converged on Washington. The election of 1864 had severely weakened the Democrats and reduced their bloc in the House to less than twenty-five percent of the total membership. Gone were such prominent wartime figures as William Holman, Alexander Long, Samuel Cox, William J. Allen, Fernando Wood, George Pendleton, and James English. With their departure went vital legislative experience. Republican ranks may have been augmented by a sizable number of freshmen congressmen, but a significantly higher percentage of the Republicans had served one or more terms in the House of Representatives. So Democrats faced a definite disadvantage in the number of Congressmen knowledgeable in Capitol Hill affairs.[6]

Nevertheless there were those who were qualified to lead. For Speaker of the House, Democrats nominated James Brooks, a former Whig congressman and publisher of the *New York Express*. Brooks' role in the Thirty-ninth Congress was limited by his eventual removal in a contested election, as was Daniel Voorhees, a prominent member of the Indiana delegation. With the loss of Brooks and Voorhees, moderate party regulars led by Samuel J. Randall of Philadelphia played a larger role, and New Jersey's Andrew Jackson Rogers emerged as principal spokesman for party hard-liners. In addition, Charles Eldridge of Wisconsin, Sydenham Ancona, Benjamin Boyer and Adam Glossbrenner of Pennsylvania, Michael Kerr and William Niblack of Indiana, Samuel Marshall of Illinois, William Finck and Francis LeBlond of Ohio, and Henry Grider of Kentucky would achieve some distinction among the House minority.

In contrast to the House, Senate Democrats were distinguished by their extensive and varied experience. Reverdy Johnson, the dimunitive, aged, and nearly blind senator from Maryland, was one of the most respected figures on Capitol Hill and was a national authority on constitutional law. Although Johnson's role as prosecuting attorney in the Dred Scott case once earned him the emnity of Republicans, he had transformed his image by his support of Lincoln's wartime policies and early endorsement of the Thirteenth Amendment. Similarly, James Guthrie, Kentucky's foremost businessman and onetime secretary of the treasury in the Pierce administration, was one whose devotion to the Union could not be questioned. Nor could the opposition find fault with the wartime records of California's James McDougall, Oregon's James Nesmith, or Indiana's Thomas Hendricks, the latter already demonstrating the talents that destined him to national party leadership. Their relatively moderate attitudes, reinforced by the modest and quiet decorum of Pennsylvania's Charles Buckalew, gave the Senate minority a temperate quality that was marred only by the occasional vehement rhetoric and intransigence of Delaware's Willard Saulsbury and Kentucky's Garrett Davis.[7]

The limited number of the congressional Democrats posed a problem for the party strategists. They were in no position to dictate the course of reconstruction, but their posture could certainly have a definite influence on the formulation of Republican policy. Congressional Democrats were aware of this and used their influence to exacerbate divisions within the Union coalition. This strategy consisted of support and encouragement for the president in conservative policy decisions, muted criticism when he strayed from desirable doctrine, and provided tactical procedures to subvert legislation that created a consensus among the opposition. At the same time they had to be on guard against creating a conservative and moderate Unionist backlash that might jeopardize their ultimate objective. The nature of this strategy required a delicate balancing act that was often threatened by the indiscretions of party militants. Most party regulars sought to offset adverse reactions by denying any intention of exploiting disagreements between Unionists, refraining from identifying Johnson too closely with the Democratic party, and, when it was to their advantage, allowing Republicans to take the initiative against the Radicals.[8]

The weaknesses in this strategy were evident on the opening day of the session. The clerk of the House, backed by the Republican majority, omitted the names of Southern members-elect from the role call. Democrats were forewarned of the move and were prepared. When the clerk ignored the pleas of a Tennessee Unionist, James Brooks took the floor and exploited a possible division between the White House and the Republican congressional contingent. The New York Democrat noted that the Republicans were denying representation from Johnson's own state and inquired whether their policy implied that a Tennessee resident could not legally hold the office of president. Brooks protested a subsequent motion to create a joint committee on reconstruction on the grounds that the House should first receive the president's annual message. The protest failed, and the resolution passed over Democratic opposition, but not without angering conservative Republicans. The *New York Times* showed little interest in criticizing Congress for this decision, asserted that Democrats had no right to speak for the administration, and warned against similar action in the future.[9]

If the Democratic diversion was prompted by fear of an accommodation between the White House and the Republicans, Johnson did little to alleviate these suspicions. To the dismay of Democrats, the president, on December 1, issued a proclamation on civil law that restored habeas corpus guarantees in the North alone. The move foreshadowed Johnson's general position on reconstruction that he presented to Congress on the second day of the session. Democrats had hoped for a firm conservative commitment, but the message fell short. On the other hand, Johnson reaffirmed his belief that the South had never been legally out of the Union, acknowledged that the South had met the requirements outlined in his initial program of restoration, and voiced his conviction that control over suffrage was a prerogative of the states. Yet he conceded that Southerners must ratify the Thirteenth Amendment, protect the freedmen's lives and property, and agree that Congress had the authority to determine its own membership. Many Democrats regretted that the message gave no clear indication of the administration's future policies.[10] To more pessimistic party spokesmen, it was obvious that Johnson would "fizzle out completely and go down on his belly before the fierce fanatics of Congress. . . ."[11]

Johnson's address provided a new dimension on the House resolution for the creation of a joint reconstruction committee. Many moderate and conservative Republicans perceived the message as an indication of Johnson's flexibility and his desire to avoid confrontation. Thus there was the possibility that the generally more conservative Senate might vote down the House proposal. Fresh from a discussion with the president, Montgomery Blair confided to Barlow he expected the resolution to be defeated in the upper house but believed that if passed, Johnson would veto it. Barlow relayed Blair's prediction to another confidant, along with his own conviction that Johnson would soon proclaim the South fully restored. His expectations of a breach between the White House and Congress were ill founded. When the issue came up for debate, Republicans ignored Reverdy Johnson's objection that the Senate should have more members on the committee and adopted the House version virtually intact. The one important modification was to change it from a joint to a concurrent resolution, thereby obviating the necessity of Johnson's signature. The president chose not to protest, and Manton Marble warned Johnson that he "must not wait many days without sounding the keynote of war on the Republican majority."[12]

Republican initiatives on black suffrage contributed to the Democratic sense of unease. Hoping for some form of detente with Johnson and mindful of public attitudes reflected in the recent elections, moderate and conservative Republicans members resisted proposals for congressional imposition of black voting rights in the South and rallied behind the idea of a constitutional amendment that would reduce Southern representation if blacks were denied the ballot. Democratic party spokesmen believed that the proposal would fail, despite its obvious benefits for Republicans. Democrats may have disagreed with Johnson's pressure for Southern ratification of the Thirteenth Amendment, but they recognized the South's inclusion in the process had established an important, and not altogether detrimental, precedent. If by chance Congress mustered enough votes to recommend further revision of the Constitution, Southern conservatives could prevent final ratification.[13]

The unknown variable was the administration's eventual reaction. It was conceivable that Johnson might endorse the amendment and reaffirm his identity with the Union coalition. Despite their concern over the president's annual message and his failure to attack publicly the formation of the joint committee, Democrats proceeded on the assumption he would not. Consequently, they moved to clear away possible sources of friction between themselves and the administration. To counter Republican charges that the party was at odds with the White House on the issue of war debts, House Democrats sponsored a resolution proclaiming the federal debt to be "sacred and inviolable" and by a two-to-one majority supported another resolution against payment of Confederate financial obligations. To focus attention on what they considered to be the paramount question before the country, they proclaimed suffrage qualifications a state prerogative and challenged Republicans to acknowledge that admission of Southern representatives was not dependent upon the South's adoption to black suffrage.[14]

Democrats received little criticism from potential Republican allies when they confided their statements of policy to these issues but ran into difficulties when they openly linked their position with the administration's. A speech by Thaddeus Stevens on December 18, attacking the president, was such an occasion. Several days later Henry Raymond, spokesman for conservative Republicans in the House, came prepared to respond, only to find that Daniel Voorhees and William Fink had seized the opportunity to identify themselves with the president. Frustrated, Raymond turned on the Democrats and emphasized the differences between Unionists and the regular Democrats. An impassioned Senate speech by Willard Saulsbury provoked a similar reaction. Members of the Union coalition, disturbed by the scene, wrote Johnson that such Copperhead endorsements would jeopardize the president's political base and should be rebuked.[15]

In reply, Democratic spokesmen reasserted that their support of the president was tentative and dependent upon Johnson's adherence to conservative doctrine. Manton Marble declared:

> We reprobate . . . any declaration of Democrats claiming the President as a convert . . . of assuring him of any other support than that which is implied in a straight-forward adherence to our well-known principles. It will not aid the President or strengthen the party to hold up, either as an expectation or a proposal, the idea of an approaching coalition between him and us.

Representative Michael Kerr of Indiana proclaimed that "if anything that shall fall from my lips shall seem a defense of him, it must be taken as tending in that direction simply and solely because in my judgement it is right, and not because he is my President in any partisan sense or I his champion."[16]

With both Democrats and a major segment of the Republican party professing support of the administration, attention shifted to a bill to regulate suffrage in the District of Columbia. The proposal, introduced early in the session, called for direct bestowal of voting rights on blacks in the nation's capitol. Radicals strongly favored the measure because it reinforced their claims of congressional control over suffrage qualifications. Since Congress clearly had the authority to govern the District, sponsors of the bill recognized that the constitutional concerns of conservative and moderate Republicans made them reluctant to defy the administration on the states' rights issue. The proposal provided a convenient means for the party to maintain some semblance of internal unity, promote its interests, and at the same force a clarification of Johnson's position on black suffrage. Thus the bill was rushed through committee and scheduled for debate in early January.

In the interim the Washington City Council scheduled a referendum on the issue; of the 7,000 votes cast only 36 were favorable. The results supported the position of congressional Democrats, who conceded that Congress had the constitutional authority to enfranchise blacks in the District but claimed the referendum imposed a moral obligation not to do so. They linked the sentiment of white Washington residents to that recently shown by Northerners in the fall elections. They pointed out that during the campaign the opposition had generally denied any intention of promoting black political rights, but their present action revealed that their real objectives were in defiance of the election mandate.[17] "This contest," declared Sen. Garrett Davis of Kentucky, "is but an experiment, a skirmish, an entering wedge to prepare the way for a similar movement in Congress to confer the right of suffrage on all of the Negroes of the United States."[18] House Democrats, led by Benjamin Boyer and Andrew Jackson Rogers, agreed and predicted the worst for the republic should the Republicans be successful.[19]

In the tactical maneuvering over the proposed legislation, Democrats took advantage of a division that was evident quite early among the opposition. Radicals who had drafted the original House bill favored the extension of the ballot to all blacks residing in the District. The more conservative Republicans tried to tone down the proposal to accord with the president's preference for qualified suffrage and moved that the bill be returned to the committee with instructions to include literacy and military service requirements. In keeping with an earlier agreement with Thaddeus Stevens, Democrats joined the Radicals to defeat the motion. The bill passed the House in its unamended form, with a handful of Republicans joining the minority in opposition.[20]

If the Democrats sought to split the Union ranks, they were only partially successful. A large number of conservative and moderate Republicans clearly favored a compromise solution; when forced to choose between the Democratic or Radical position, most reacted against the Democratic party's meddling and aligned themselves with the Radicals. This show of Republican unity raised questions about the administration's possible response. Democrats conceded that the president might now endorse the enfranchisement of male black voters in the District in its unamended form but gambled he would not and called for the Senate to follow the House precedent. Their expectations were not realized. Apprehensive about a confrontation with the White House, Republican senators clouded the issue with a proposal for governmental reorganization of the District and sent the pending legislation back to committee, where it was buried for the remainder of the session.[21]

A widely disseminated interview on January 28 between Johnson and Sen. James Dixon of Connecticut prompted the Senate decision. In the discussion Johnson charged that the District suffrage bill was "ill-timed, uncalled for, and calculated to do great harm." He reiterated Democratic claims that the proposal set the stage for Radical efforts for black enfranchisement and predicted it would result in a war of racial extermination. Johnson took a dim view of additional amendments to the Constitution but left the door open for a possible compromise. If they wished to change the Constitution, he declared, he favored representation on the number of legal voters, leaving suffrage qualifications to the states.[22]

The president's position was at odds with the shifting perspective of the Republicans. After closer scrutiny, Republicans began to have reservations about basing representation on the number of legal voters. When they calculated the impact, they found that the Northeast would lose representation because of its population distribution. The Joint Committee on Reconstruction modified the proposal to avoid this disruptive impact on the North and prevent a divisive sectional controversy within the Union coalition. The constitutional amendment reported to the House in late January based congressional representation on the population of the respective states, excluding Indians not taxed, but provided that any abridgement of the vote by race or color would entail the exclusion of the entire disfranchised group from the basis of representation.[23]

While discussion of the issue revealed differences of opinion among Republicans, Democrats themselves were not in total accord. Representative Henry Grider of Kentucky, one of the three minority members of the joint committee, favored the existing ratio provided by the census of 1860, thereby including three-fifths of the freedmen in the Southern population base. Andrew Jackson Rogers saw in emancipation the chance to enhance Democratic power and called for representation based upon population without penalty for racial discrimination. Reverdy Johnson was the sole Democrat on the committee who favored basing representation on the number of legal voters, and he had little support among his fellow Democratic congressmen. When an attempt was made in the House to substitute representation based on voters to accord with the President's views, only three Democrats from Illinois and one from Maryland joined twenty-five Republicans in voting for the proposal. The House adopted the joint committee's recommendation by the necessary two-thirds majority, with only a handful of conservative Republicans joining the Democrats in opposition.[24]

Democratic regulars seemed disinclined to follow the president's advice. Although they welcomed the problems the Dixon interview created for the opposition, they were troubled by the White House tendency towards compromise. Once again Johnson appeared to be withdrawing from direct confrontation with Republicans by allowing for the possibility of further changes in the South. From the Democratic perspective, this continued ambivalence had dangerous implications. Already both political parties were preparing for the spring elections, and Democrats were urging Johnson to act quickly to maintain his prestige and power by breaking with the Republicans and by firing federal officeholders who might be disloyal.[25]

It was just such an event that many Republicans wished to avoid, and they looked to another matter under consideration to strengthen the ties between themselves and the White House. This was the Freedmen's Bureau bill that called for an extension of the federal organization created during the final days of Lincoln's administration to provide relief for refugees dispossessed by the war. It also provided for protection of blacks against violation of their civil rights as defined in a separate and companion proposal. The president's earlier declaration of their need for protection was sufficient ground for the Republicans' belief that Johnson would not oppose them. There was no apparent basis to assume that Johnson disagreed with the use of military courts to enforce these rights, since he had not hesitated to use military justice and had excluded the South from his proclamation restoring civil law. The bill was supported by such conservative adherents of the president as Congressman Henry Raymond and Senators James Doolittle, James Dixon, and Edgar Cowan.

Democrats were unanimously opposed. Senator Thomas Hendricks declared he had no objection to public lands being set aside for freedmen by the government, but was firmly against land confiscation. More aid, he claimed, would make Washington a national poorhouse, threaten the checks and balances system, and constitute an enormous drain on the Treasury. But if the relief features of the bill were bad, the civil rights section was worse. Hendricks claimed that Northern fears for the former slaves were largely unwarranted and Southern whites were already taking steps to guarantee their protection. The Indiana senator pointed out that the term civil rights was vague and subject to conflicting interpretations. Democrats capitalized on this by voicing their suspicions that the Republicans intended to expand its definition to include suffrage and racial intermarriage. They viewed the plan as a threat to Northern as well as Southern society; the result would be the reintroduction of martial law in areas where the president had already restored civil authority and the use of force to achieve social, political, and civil equality.[26]

The passage of the bill by the House on February 6, following Senate adoption two weeks earlier, forced the administration to reveal its policy. Republicans appeared confident of the president's endorsement, but Democrats expected a veto. The day after the House vote, Johnson granted an interview to a black delegation, reiterated his previous pronouncements against black suffrage, and suggested that the only solution to the nation's racial dilemma was black emigration. This raised questions about the president's commitment to the federal protection of the freedmen, and Democratic spokesmen stressed these statements as evidence of Johnson's conservatism. Moreover, there were indications the president was irritated by the Radicals' persistent verbal assaults and was ready to counterattack. One Washington insider confided to Manton Marble that Johnson's attitude toward the Radicals was "strong enough to induce him to *veto any* bill that comes from that quarter." By the middle of the month there were reports that the president had already voiced dissatisfaction with several provisions of the Freedmen's Bureau proposal.[27]

The suspense continued until Johnson's veto message on February 19. Its impact was all the more dramatic since it repeated the same criticisms raised by the Democrats. Johnson questioned the bill's constitutionality because of the vast expansion of military power in peacetime and the threat it posed to the judiciary. He asserted that the Founding Fathers never intended the federal government to provide relief to the indigent and certainly not by any process of land confiscation. Such a program would keep the freedmen in a dependent and indolent status, interfere with the natural law of supply and demand, greatly expand the federal bureaucracy, and compound the problems of the nation that needed fiscal retrenchment. The president concluded that it was improper for Washington to adopt the legislation with Southern representatives excluded from Congress.[28]

The veto message brought a sharp reaction from the Republican leadership. Angered by the message, majority members of the Joint Committee on Reconstruction turned from the consideration of Tennessee representation and unanimously endorsed a concurrent resolution that no Southern congressman or senator be admitted until Congress approved. Democrats regarded this as an affront to Johnson and identified themselves with the president. Henry Grider asked to present a minority report when the resolution came before the House, but Thaddeus Stevens objected and imposed the gag rule. The Democrats resorted to obstructionist tactics and called for a series of diversionary roll calls to prevent the resolution from coming to a vote. The legislative impasse finally broke after six hours of parliamentary maneuvering, and the resolution passed over the Democrat's opposition.[29]

The senate response was more temperate. Unlike the House, where only a small handful of Republicans led by Henry Raymond joined the Democrats in support of the administration, Democratic senators were aligned with a sizable and significant segment of the opposition. In a vote to pass the Freedmen's Bureau bill over the veto, eight Republicans who had previously supported the measure reversed their position and voted to sustain the president. The defections were enough to prevent a two-thirds majority and killed the bill. Democrats, elated over the outcome, were more than willing to allow conservative Republicans the initiative. When Senate members of the Joint Committee on Reconstruction introduced the resolution against admitting Southern congressmen, minority party militants Garrett Davis and Willard Saulsbury merely listened while Dixon, Cowan, Doolittle, and others carried the burden of debate. The House acted quickly on the proposal, but the Senate postponed consideration of the resolution until after the holiday commemorating Washington's birthday.[30]

The Washington Resident Committee met earlier in the month and planned a mass meeting for February 22. Ostensibly billed as a nonpartisan affair, the gathering featured a number of prominent conservative Unionists as well as Democratic congressmen. The crowd listened to speeches extolling Lincoln and Johnson and proceeded to the White House to serenade the president. Johnson's response reflected anger against the Radicals. The country, he declared, had suffered great agony because of the treason of Southern conspirators. Yet after four years of civil war, treason was not dead but had reappeared among Northerners who sought to keep the Union divided. When a member of the group shouted to Johnson to name these Northern traitors, the president cited Thaddeus Stevens, Charles Sumner, and Wendell Phillips. He intimated that the Radicals were somehow responsible for the death of Lincoln and were probably plotting his own assassination. Proclaiming himself to be the true defender of the Constitution, Johnson called upon the nation to rally behind him and his program of Southern restoration.[31]

Democrats regarded this speech as the final confirmation of an irreparable division in the Union coalition. Elated over the outcome, the Democratic party press showered the President with praise, prominent party leaders offered to visit Johnson in Washington, and well-to-do conservatives in New York City offered him membership in the recently established and exclusive Manhatten Club. Despite their elation, the need for caution was recognized, for if many conservative Unionists supported the president they made it clear they did not disavow their party identification. Samuel Barlow concluded the Democrats should avoid antagonizing potential recruits by refraining from extensive claims to patronage. In keeping with this strategy, Manton Marble and Washington McLean advised their readers that the conflict was primarily among Unionists and the proper role for Democrats was that of interested spectators.[32]

Their immediate concern was the impact of the president's veto and speech on the proposed constitutional amendment. There had been sporadic Senate debate on the joint committee resolution during February but no concerted effort to resolve the issue until March 8, when the Radicals produced a substitute proposal that flatly prohibited black disfranchisement. This was soundly defeated. Garrett Davis sought to have his colleagues prevent state legislatures from acting on any constitutional provision until after the fall elections. Only two conservative Republicans joined the Democrats in supporting Davis's motion. Republicans once again divided on the resolution, and the proposal fell short of the two-thirds necessary for adoption. Doolittle offered an alternative resolution basing representation on voters, but the Senate's response was to postpone further consideration.[33]

This schism in Unionist ranks allowed the Democrats to hope for partisan dividends in the spring elections. New Hampshire Democrats endorsed John Sinclair for the governorship on a platform that supported the administration and charged the opposition ticket with being Radical. Republican candidates for state office rejected this indentification, stressed their common Unionist ties with Johnson, and professed allegiance to the president. Their campaign gained momentum when the postmaster general replied to an inquiry from a New Hampshire Republican congressman that the administration planned no proscription of federal officeholders in the state and denied any partisan ties with the Democrats. Republicans publicized the letter and claimed it constituted an endorsement of their ticket. Adding further credence to such claims, the commissioner of Internal Revenue made a number of speeches for the Republican gubernatorial candidate, and New Hampshire clerks in Washington were granted leave to vote in the election.[34]

Democrats were apprehensive. Edmund Burke, Concord editor and former political lieutenant of Franklin Pierce, wrote Johnson that the postmaster general's letter could cost the Democrats 3,000 votes and the election. Burke asserted that New Hampshire public opinion favored the president, but he feared that the Radicals would claim a Republican victory to be a vindication of congressional policy. Democratic pressure did produce a statement from the secretary of the navy that workers in the Portsmouth Navy Yard would not be punished for voting the Democratic ticket, but the party needed more than an indirect confirmation of White House neutrality to offset the activities of federal officeholders and Republicans. Sinclair lost the election by 5,000 votes, a smaller margin of defeat than in the previous gubernatorial contest, but one that contrasted sharply with early Democratic expectations.[35]

The New Hampshire setback gave added significance to the scheduled spring election in Connecticut. The prospects for a Democratic victory were much brighter here. Conservative sentiment was stronger than in other areas of New England, and the referendum the previous year clearly indicated strong resentment against Radical suffrage demands. The state Democratic party, already acknowledged to be one of the best organized in the country, appeared all the more formidable for its willingness to cast aside wartime internal divisions. Sensing the possibility of success, Origen Seymour, a prominent peace advocate seeking the governorship, agreed to withdraw from the race prior to the state convention and allowed James English to receive the nomination by acclamation. The Democrats' selection of English, a moderate party regular with a record of support for Lincoln's policies, had an obvious potential appeal to conservative Unionists. All that was needed to swing the state into the Democratic column was a public statement of White House support that would enlist the aid of the Connecticut conservative contingent led by Sen. James Dixon and Secretary of the Navy Gideon Welles.[36]

Early in the campaign the Democrats had reason to believe administration intervention would be forthcoming when John Coyle of the Washington *National Intelligencer* and recognized spokesman for the White House, wrote an editorial extolling English and the Connecticut platform. But Johnson's apparent neutrality caused concern, and Democrats intensified their pressure on the administration. Manton Marble and Samuel Barlow, co-owners of the *New York World,* departed from their policy of detachment and publicly called for the president to use his patronage powers, or they would hold him personally responsible for a Democratic defeat. Alfred Burr used his longstanding relationship with Gideon Welles to warn the administration that failure to curb the activities of federal bureaucrats would be construed as partiality towards the Republican ticket, and this would have disastrous implications for the president's political prospects.[37]

In mid-March English traveled to Washington and called at the White House. After a short meeting with Johnson, the Democratic gubernatorial candidate returned to Connecticut convinced he had the President's promise to draw a tight rein on local officeholders. Democratic efforts to publicize the meeting as an endorsement of English were soon offset by a Republican countermove. In Connecticut as well as in New Hampshire, Union candidates had no intention of jeopardizing their election by launching an attack on the president. Joseph Hawley, the Union standard-bearer, arrived at the executive mansion shortly after English and sought some symbol of Johnson's support. Although Johnson had personal misgivings about Hawley, he confirmed his allegiance to the Union Party. This was all the Republican politicians needed, and upon his return to Connecticut he claimed the President's identification with the Union coalition was tantamount to an endorsement of the state Union ticket.[38]

Democrats were again put on the defensive. They protested that Johnson's ties with the Union Party were past history and had no direct bearing on the current contest. They made the charge that in reality the coalition was defunct in Connecticut; there were no War Democrats on the state ticket and much of the Republican press supporting Hawley was critical of the president's Southern policy. Such claims did little to offset the opposition's argument that Johnson's obvious distrust of the Democrats indicated a negative attitude toward all Democratic candidates. Concerned over the drift of the campaign, Alfred Burr traveled to Washington to confer with the president. He presented a letter from the Hartford postmaster, who announced his intention of voting for English and offered his resignation should Johnson deem it necessary. The president's rejection of the offer confirmed the administration's neutrality, but did not slow down the Republican bandwagon. Consequently Democrats saw their earlier expectations of victory dashed by defeat.[39]

Johnson's role in New Hampshire and Connecticut once again confused the politicians in the nation's capital, and Democrats had difficulty understanding its future implications. The president had asserted in his Freedmen's Bureau veto that Southern representatives should be admitted before the adoption of further reconstruction legislation. Republican rejection of this premise indicated little common ground between the White House and the Republicans. Yet Johnson hesitated to declare war on those who opposed his position. Did this mean, as some suggested, that he contemplated some new party organization and was content for the moment to keep his distance from both existing parties? Or was he having second thoughts about severing ties with the current Union coalition? Certainly Johnson had not yet withdrawn his support for an additional constitutional amendment that had the backing of Unionists of all ideological persuasions. But he could be merely keeping his options open while he waited for the outcome of the spring elections.[40]

Deliberations on the Civil Rights Bill heightened Democratic fears about the administration's position. This measure, introduced early in the session along with the Freedmen's Bureau proposal, passed the House on the day of the New Hampshire election and was confirmed by the Senate two days later. It conferred citizenship on persons born in the United States, excluding Indians not taxed. Citizens were explicitly guaranteed the right to make contracts, to sue and give evidence, and to hold and transfer property. Beyond this the Republican sponsors refused to go, and they cautiously avoided mentioning the right to jury service, suffrage, or officeholding. The proposal, by specifying only those rights already granted by most Northern states, was framed to enlist the support of a broad Unionist consensus. Republican moderates assumed that Johnson agreed with the bill's intent because of his public statements about the need to protect the freedmen. Since it was to be enforced through the federal courts, it avoided his objections found in the Freedmen's Bureau proposal to the use of military tribunals.[41]

These were not the grounds on which Democrats would have chosen to do battle. The pressure of time, the rejection of Southern representation in Congress, and the unresolved relationship between Johnson and the political parties determined that it was not a moment for retreat. In attacking the specifics of the proposed legislation, the Democrats were limited to questioning the omission of such groups as unnaturalized immigrants or to expressions of concern over the provisions for federal prosecution. Party regulars focused on what they perceived to be an unfolding Radical plot and charged that the Civil Rights Bill was but a single thread in the web of this larger conspiracy. Even though there was no direct mention of political rights or social equality in the proposed legislation, they claimed it provided the means to secure these rights, and they cited Republican opposition to amendments explicitly excluding political rights from the bill as justification for their apprehensions.[42]

Democratic regulars used the press to encourage a presidential veto, leaving direct personal diplomacy to conservatives Francis P. Blair, George Morgan, and Edgar Cowan. On March 27 Johnson revealed his position in a veto message that branded the bill unconstitutional and damaging to local controls over suffrage qualifications and social segregation. The veto was all the more significant because the president issued it several days prior to the Connecticut election rather than waiting for the outcome of the contest. On the day Connecticut voters went to the polls, Johnson took another step advocated by Democrats and proclaimed the rebellion officially ended.[43] For all intents and purposes the link that had so tentatively bound the President to the Republican majority had been severed. One enthusiastic New York Democrat wrote Montgomery Blair that the line was drawn between the president and his enemies, and Republicans could "no longer deceive him by professions of friendship while secretly working to circumvent his policy and effect his destruction."[44]

At issue was whether Johnson had the congressional support to sustain his position. Conservative strength in the House clearly fell short of the votes required to uphold a veto. The situation in the Senate was more tenuous, and even a slight change in its composition might tilt the balance either way. A Colorado statehood bill, introduced early in the session, threatened such a change. The sponsors faced a number of difficulties. Democratic critics questioned whether the territory's population was adequate to merit the transition and pointed out that a recent referendum indicated many residents were strongly opposed. Discussion of the bill involved the sensitive issue of black suffrage. Radical Republicans, seeking to establish a precedent for the South, introduced an amendment to give blacks the ballot. Failing in this, they joined with Senate Democrats in defeating the unamended bill.[45]

Although the Colorado statehood question surfaced again later in the session, a contested election involving Sen. John Stockton of New Jersey had more immediate significance for the Civil Rights Bill. The case had its origins the previous year when the New Jersey legislature began deliberations over a replacement for Republican John C. Ten Eyck. The Democrats, who had just won a majority in the state senate and an even division in the lower house, were in a position to dominate any joint legislative session and control the senatorial selection. But New Jersey Democrats were divided between peace and moderate factions and controversy over the railroad and canal clique identified with Stockton. Daniel Holsman attempted to enforce party unity by introducing and securing passage, with substantial Republican support, of a resolution requiring a majority vote for election. When it became evident that some Democratic dissidents could not be whipped into line, party leaders changed their strategy and rescinded the Holsman proposal. Thereupon Stockton received a plurality and the Senate seat, amid Republican protests over the changes in the rules.[46]

When Congress convened, it provisionally seated Stockton and placed his contested election with the Senate Judiciary Committee for review. The committee reported at the end of January in favor of the New Jersey Democrat, but the Senate failed to act on its recommendations for seven weeks. On March 22, one week after passage of the Civil Rights Bill and five days before Johnson's veto, the issue came to the floor for debate. On the first roll call the following day the Senate cast twenty-one votes for Stockton and twenty against. At this point a Maine Republican Lot M. Morrill requested that he be recorded against, producing a twenty-one to twenty-one tie. Charges and countercharges were made by both sides over a previously agreed upon pair between Morrill and William Wright, Stockton's ill and absent Democratic colleague from New Jersey. Angered by the turn of events, Stockton cast his vote in his own behalf and, in the furor that followed, offered to withdraw it if the issue was referred to the Judiciary Committee. Republican floor leaders were in no mood for delay, and on the day of the president's veto message they ousted Stockton from his Senate seat.[47]

Four days later Connecticut voters went to the polls and dealt the Democrats another setback. While party totals indicated a gain over the previous state election, English lost his bid for the governorship by 5,000 votes. Democratic spokesmen blamed the president for his lack of support and the Republican press for deliberately distorting the administration's position, but this hardly compensated for the loss of a crucial contest that both sides expected to influence the wavering or uncommitted. When the Senate voted shortly thereafter on Johnson's veto, only five Republicans broke party ranks to support the president. The combined conservative tally fell one vote short of the margin necessary to sustain the veto. Concurrence by the House in the Senate decision on April 9 merely provided a final reminder of the deterioration of conservative influence at the congressional level.[48]

Democrats had some reason for optimism despite the adoption of the Civil Rights Bill. The party, recuperating from losses in New Hampshire and Connecticut, showed signs of renewed strength, reinforced by victories in St. Louis and several other cities in April municipal elections. Democrats believed the conservative trend would have been even more dramatic had the conflict between the president and the congressional Republicans surfaced earlier. Now that the breach between the White House and Congress seemed complete, Democrats expected that a coalition with conservative Republicans and the administration's patronage powers would enhance their position. Representative John Hogan of Missouri sounded an optimistic note when he advised his House colleagues that "it is the terrible thunder of the Democratic Party that gentlemen are now hearing, which is to roll up like clouds in the summer sky when storms are brewing."[49]

Hogan's metaphor carried a promise for the future, but it admitted that previous forecasts of a Democratic deluge had been premature. In retrospect, the first session of the Thirty-Ninth Congress did not result in any resounding party victory. Democratic courtship of the president and opposition to compromise, particularly evident in the House, had angered the Republicans and bound them together. Congressional Republicans skillfully skirted the suffrage issue, where Democrats hoped to make major gains, and focused the nation's attention on the freedmen's civil rights and physical security. These concerns posed no direct threat to most Northern constituents and implied a broad humanitarian appeal. When the breach came between Johnson and the congressional majority, the number of Republicans supporting the president fell far short of conservatives' estimates or hopes. Congressional Democrats found they had too few Republican allies to sustain the president's vetoes and prevent the evolution of congressional policy.

# 4

## *National Unionism*

ALTHOUGH Johnson's veto of the Civil Rights Bill was a great advantage to Democratic strategists, a problem remained: how to translate the president's breach with congressional Republicans into party advantage and power. A coalition between the Democratic and Union party dissidents, abetted by White House patronage, could conceivably produce conservative victories in the fall elections and force the admission of Southern representatives on conservative terms. But such a scenario depended upon several crucial variables. The extent of disaffection among Unionists would not be fully determined until Congress concluded its deliberations over the proposed Fourteenth Amendment and spelled out its final requirements for national reunification. There was also the problem of organizing any bipartisan coalition of conservatives into an effective political force. Sporadic state efforts at political reorganization the previous year had not always been successful and indicated wartime animosities and partisan prejudices might remain an obstacle to the nationwide movement for political reorganization.

Initiation of a formal coalition in support of the president came immediately after Johnson's veto of the Civil Rights Bill. On March 29 a group of War Democrats, Democratic regulars, and conservative Republicans met in Washington and organized the National Johnson Constitutional Union Club. The assemblage chose Montgomery Blair and Charles Mason as president and corresponding secretary, respectively, and named a vice-president from each of the states, including the South. After discussion of strategy and tactics, the group agreed to establish local clubs throughout the country and solicit funds for printing and distributing political propaganda. On April 11 Blair and Mason announced the organization's existence, forswore any intention of creating a new party, and called upon conservatives of all persuasions to rally behind them in support of Johnson.[1]

The movement drew a mixed response. Clubs were organized in some communities, and toward the end of the month the local Brooklyn organization sponsored a successful rally, highlighted by speeches from John Van Buren, Representative Lowell Rousseau of Missouri, and a letter from John Dix. Many Democratic regulars were suspicious. Despite assurances to the contrary, some feared the organization threatened the party's titular identity and advised their colleagues against involvement. Others expressed concern about a further erosion of basic Democratic principles. And the movement rekindled long-standing personal animosities. James Buchanan asserted he was unwilling "to fall into line under Montgomery Blair as a leader of the Democratic Party," and Manton Marble declared against any affiliation with Republicans Seward, Weed, or Raymond, whose "hands are . . . red with blood and their pockets . . . plethoric with public plunder."[2]

Certain conservatives were reluctant to affiliate with the Democrats. James Gordon Bennett, editor of the *New York Herald* and political maverick, publicly condemned both Democratic Copperheads and Radical Republicans and extolled the president's policy. When conservative Unionists staged a rally in Hartford, Connecticut, Bennett praised the participants for "avoiding any entangling affiliations" with the Democrats and proclaimed the Democratic party "must go the way of the old Federal party." A small group of individuals, who shared similar views, met in Washington in late April and organized a National Union Club. They elected Alexander Randall, former governor of Wisconsin and assistant postmaster general, as their president. The resolutions adopted by the organization were conservative in outlook. They called for Southern representation, state control over suffrage, and support for Johnson. But in their demand that treason be punished and federal offices be denied Southerners who violated previous oaths by joining the Confederacy, the National Union Club clearly set itself apart from the mass of Democratic regulars.[3]

Friction between the various conservative factions showed itself in other forms. For some time advocates of the president's policy had called upon Johnson to use his patronage powers against the Radicals and staff the federal bureaucracy with administration loyalists. He persistently rejected these appeals. Johnson's reluctance stemmed in large part from his ambivalent relationship with congressional Republicans and his inability to determine which officeholders were his opponents. Until these problems were resolved, the president saw no advantage to a patronage war that might force many federal bureaucrats to alter their professions of support or their attempts to remain neutral. Openings occurring through death or resignation revealed another dimension to the president's patronage dilemma; War Democrats, Democratic regulars, and conservative Republicans vied with one another over the spoils.

The death of the collector of the port of New York in the fall of 1865 was one such occasion. Initially, Democratic state leaders hoped for the appointment of a party regular who would give them influence over the powerful Customs House bureaucracy. But War Democrats, led by Edwards Pierrepont and John Cochrane, the moderate Republican faction headed by Edwin Morgan, and the Seward-Raymond-Weed contingent vigorously rejected any such choice. Johnson, fearful of identification with the "Democracy" and apprehensive that Congress might reject his nominee, claimed the selection of a Democrat would be unwise. New York party chieftains, anticipating that a breach between the White House and Congress might affect the administration's patronage policy, used delaying tactics and hoped the President would change his mind. The veto of the Civil Rights Bill finally resolved the issue by eliminating the Morgan faction, which defected to the opposition, forcing the other groups to compromise. The appointment went to Henry Smythe, a conservative banker not aligned with any of the rival cliques. Although Smythe's nomination forestalled immediate criticism, his lack of political experience raised questions about his future effectiveness in the administration's cause.[4]

The president faced intensive pressure to carry the war to the Radicals by exercising his power of removal. Suddenly in late April Johnson responded by removing several Pennsylvania officeholders who were proteges of John Forney and Thaddeus Stevens. The president hoped to avoid a moderate Republican backlash because Pennsylvania Republicans had nominated a moderate to head their ticket at the March state convention and endorsed a platform that lauded Johnson for his fidelity to the Union. But this occurred prior to the Civil Rights Bill veto, and most Republican moderates, faced with the choice of supporting the White House or Congress, began to rally behind congressional policy. Since Pennsylvania Democratic leaders refused to collaborate with Republican conservatives and selected a straight party slate of candidates, Johnson had no party organization in the state with which he could identify. Nevertheless, Radicals used his removals to claim he opposed the Unionists and supported the Pennsylvania Democrats.[5]

Senate Republicans responded to the president's initiative by attempting to curtail further use of executive patronage through the amendment of a pending Post Office appropriations bill. The proposal would withhold salaries for offices requiring Senate confirmation if appointments came after Congress adjourned and were occasioned by forcible removal of present incumbents. Republican advocates of the amendment charged Heister Clymer, the Pennsylvania Democratic gubernatorial nominee, with wartime dovish tendencies, cited accounts alleging Johnson's intention of awarding federal offices to former peace advocates, and claimed Johnson's policy would revitalize the Copperhead faction. Democratic spokesmen discounted extremism within their ranks and noted the president's appointees in Pennsylvania, as elsewhere, were Unionists. Though Democrats were willing to support the president on principle, they claimed they had evidence that Johnson intended to maintain his ties with the Union coalition.[6]

Democratic expectations and Republican fears of a widescale removal of officeholders not loyal to Johnson failed to materialize. In mid-May it became evident that Johnson was reluctant to use his patronage weapon, and the Senate voted down the Post Office Bill amendment. Democrats were disturbed by what they perceived to be other signs of White House timidity. Two weeks after the April proclamation on civil law in the South, the assistant adjutant general issued a communiqué permitting the continuance of military tribunals in cases involving the Freedmen's Bureau. Johnson, despite persistent pressure, also refused to issue a general amnesty. Party spokesmen attributed such deviations from conservative objectives to the treacherous influence and double-dealing of Johnson's heads of war, interior, post office, state, and justice departments and urged that he replace them with loyal supporters.[7]

The administration's handling of the Fenian crisis in early June reinforced these convictions. Reports of the invasion of Canada by bands of pro-Irish nationalists from the United States posed a dilemma for the White House. Should the government fail to act, it risked charges of violating its own neutrality laws. However, government intervention to curb the Fenians might mean alienation of the sizable and influential Irish-American constituency. The initial Washington response reflected the crosscurrents of conflicting pressures; United States authorities arrested and then immediately paroled a number of Fenian leaders. Finally, five days after the initial conflict, the attorney general directed federal marshals and district attorneys to take forceful action and Johnson belatedly issued a proclamation enforcing the laws of neutrality. Democrats declared that the president was legally bound to act and those who found fault with the government's policy should first turn to Congress. Privately, many believed that the administration had bungled the affair under pressure from cabinet officers who sought to involve the President in new difficulties.[8]

Johnson was reluctant to press for political reorganization because of the uncertain nature and fate of proposals for a Fourteenth Amendment. Following the Senate's failure in early March to endorse the joint committee's recommendation on representation, there was public discussion of alternative plans offered by individual Republicans. The ongoing debate illustrated the diversity of opinion in Unionist ranks and again raised the question of whether the Republicans could achieve a consensus on the prerequisites for Southern admission. Failure to do so would benefit the Democrats who had charged that the Republicans were seeking to prevent normalization of sectional relationships. Well aware of this, majority leaders reconvened the joint committee on April 21, determined to devise an acceptable plan. A week later the committee recommended a revision of its earlier proposal on representation and added new sections on legal equality, disfranchisement of ex-Confederates, and prohibitions against payment of Confederate debts or compensation awards for former slaveholders.[9]

The committee included the financial claims primarily because of the position adopted by a small contingent of congressional Democrats. Andrew Jackson Rogers, spokesman for the group, had on more than one occasion voiced his opposition to Washington's interference with state contractual obligations as destructive of the federal system. Because of Roger's membership on the reconstruction committee, Radicals identified him as a party leader and insisted his views were a projection of conservative objectives. Democratic moderates disavowed Roger's alleged leadership and dismissed charges that they intended to sanctify the rebellion by payment of its debts. They noted there was no movement among bankrupt Southern governments to assume these obligations, and Congressman Benjamin Boyer declared there was little reason to assume "any man outside of a lunatic asylum ever dreamed it would be paid by anyone else." Nor was there strong sentiment in the party, apart from the border states, to claim compensation for slaveholders. Democrats generally ignored the section on financial claims and focused their criticism on other parts of the resolution.[10]

They regarded the provision for legal equality to be a tacit Republican admission of the unconstitutionality of the Civil Rights Act. Their critique included the charge made against earlier legislation that Republicans sought authority to enfranchise all blacks by federal decree. This objective was even more transparent when the constitutional amendment's general statement on legal rights was compared with the enumerated civil rights included in the bill passed over Johnson's veto. In an attempt to force the Republican's hand, William Niblack of Indiana announced that he would offer a revision prohibiting Congress from using the amendment to regulate state suffrage requirements. But he did not have a chance to move his proposal and could not substantiate his claims about Republicans' ultimate objectives.[11]

While Democrats perceived the legal equality section as a means of securing black suffrage, they viewed the statement on representation as an interim measure designed to punish the South. It made little difference that the joint committee moderated its earlier position by omitting any mention of race or by excluding only disfranchised adult males from the basis of representation. The result was the same; Southern states with sizable Negro populations would have their congressional power sharply reduced, while Northern states that disfranchised blacks faced no such penalty. Democratic spokesmen drew a sharp distinction between representation and suffrage; women, children, and unnaturalized citizens would be technically represented in Congress under the resolution, while tax-paying blacks denied the ballot would not. They charged that the scheme was a covert attempt to enhance the power of New England and pointed out that representation based upon the actual number of voters would be more equitable to other sectional interests.[12]

Although Democrats disliked the representation provision, they reserved their strongest criticism for the section curtailing Southern white voting rights. The joint committee proposal prohibited all who had aided the rebellion from participating in congressional or presidential elections until 1870. Minority party critics insisted that Southerners could not be expected to agree. This exclusion was designed to guarantee rejection of the amendment and ensure Republican control of the federal government after the next presidential contest. Republicans might brand former secessionists and Copperheads as disunionists, but Democrats characterized such rhetoric as hypocritical. In reality, the extremism of the partisan Republican majority prevented reconstruction and divided the nation.[13]

A number of Unionists considered the amendment as too extreme and believed modifications were needed to avoid a backlash by the electorate. Thaddeus Stevens, in reporting the resolution, sought to prevent its revision by moving that it be recommitted. The Pennsylvania Radical later called for the previous question and attempted to force a final vote on the unamended proposal. At this point Democrats divided. Nineteen moderate party regulars aligned themselves with sixty Unionists who favored some basic changes in the sections on representation and Confederate disfranchisement. But twelve Democratic representatives, led by Rogers and Eldridge, sided with the Radicals and provided the margin to prevent consideration. In so doing they may have been trying to split the Republican ranks and defeat the committee's report. If this was their strategy, they miscalculated. The opposition coalesced on the final vote and secured the two-thirds majority necessary for adoption.[14]

After Democrats prevented revision by the House, Senate Republicans caucused and developed a compromise proposal. The financial section was expanded to guarantee payment of federal debts incurred during the war, and citizenship was expressly defined to exclude unnaturalized immigrants. Renewed discussion of basing representation on voters was finally rejected by the majority in favor of the joint committee's recommendation. The major change came over Confederate disabilities, as the caucus replaced extensive disfranchisement with a milder prohibition against holding state or federal offices. Democrats welcomed this modification as an improvement but were powerless to effect additional revisions. Determined to maintain a united front, Senate Republicans brushed aside Democratic efforts to amend and on June 8 adopted the caucus proposal by a vote of thirty-three to eleven. Party discipline was apparent a week later when the House adopted the Senate plan after limited debate.[15]

Congressional approval of the constitutional amendment was a decided setback for Democratic strategists. At best they had hoped that debate would exacerbate divisions within the Republican party, prevent a final settlement of the issue, and provide conservatives with a platform for the fall elections. Instead the Democrats appeared more isolated. Many conservative Unionists were offended by the opposition of House Democrats and accepted the final compromise. It was also possible that the president might endorse, or at least not attack, the amendment. Certainly there was little in the proposal, apart from the section basing representation on population, that conflicted with Johnson's public pronouncements on reconstruction. And insofar as the framers pointedly avoided stating that ratification by Southern states was necessary for their admission, the congressional plan met the president's declarations against preconditions for normalization.[16]

After some deliberation, Johnson finally responded in a message to Congress on June 22. The president declared the administration's transmittal of the resolution to the states was merely ministerial and not indicative of White House endorsement. But he refrained from a direct attack on the substance of the amendment and instead criticized its construction while Southern representatives remained excluded from Congress. In so doing he stopped short of the Joint Committee on Reconstruction's minority report, printed the same day, which encouraged Southern rejection of ratification. Democrats might have preferred a more direct assault on the congressional plan, but the President's response was better than no response at all. Consequently, Democratic spokesmen applauded Johnson's action and claimed his message refuted Republican misrepresentations of his position. There could be no doubt, charged Washington McLean, that the president opposed the amendment and believed "no good will come of its adoption."[17]

Efforts at political reorganization largely dictated Johnson's stance. As Congress concluded its deliberations on the amendment, the movement to provide an organizational basis for administration policy, dormant for over a month, once again gained momentum. One June 11 the President met with several conservative Unionists, including Alexander Randall and members of the National Union Club, Orville Browning, Samuel Fowler, and Senators Cowan and Doolittle. Johnson made clear his desire to seize control of Congress from the Radicals and stated his willingness to contribute money or patronage to secure this objective. The group agreed on the need for a national convention but disbanded without taking action.[18]

In the meantime the Seward-Weed-Raymond triumvirate was developing its own plan. Seward was aware of the sentiment for a convention and had Weed urge Raymond to draft a call. This was a disingenuous maneuver. Not party to the White House conference on reorganization, Seward feared a misstep in the convention might lead to Democratic domination, with its inference of a coalition tainted by treason. He did not want to jeopardize the president's or his own political future. As chairman of the National Republican Committee and a supporter of the proposed Fourteenth Amendment, Raymond could guard against such dangers by issuing a statement of principles that appealed to many moderate as well as conservative Unionists. But while Raymond favored political realignment and increased his attacks on Copperheads and secessionists, he was reluctant to draft the call and deprived Seward of his chance to direct the movement.[19]

Seward's machinations led others to take action. Disturbed by Weed's arrival in Washington, Gideon Welles and Doolittle visited the president and urged the calling of a convention. It was agreed that Doolittle would draft the announcement and that it would be presented to cabinet members for their endorsement. Doolittle did not intend to exclude the Seward faction from the movement but rather to provide a platform broad enough for most conservatives. Accordingly, the Wisconsin senator included a recognition of the indivisible nature of the Union, the abolition of slavery, state control of suffrage, the right of Southerners to congressional representation, and the need for sectional reconciliation. Noticeably absent from the draft was any mention of the Fourteenth Amendment.[20]

The difficulties inherent in the coalition effort were evident when Doolittle turned to other conservatives for advice. Raymond, while approving of a convention, labeled the proposed call "too broad" and implied it would admit secessionists and their Northern sympathizers but exclude many Unionists. He feared the announcement would not bring the needed support. The disclosure of the draft to Welles and the Blairs brought forward another criticism. Welles, after consultation with Dean Richmond and other party leaders, feared the Democrats might prove intransigent if the White House appeared to be under Seward's influence. He decided that the omission of any statement of opposition to the Fourteenth Amendment would be interpreted as such a concession. Francis Preston Blair agreed and promised to join Welles in bringing this to Johnson's attention. But when approached, the president stated the draft was too detailed and avoided an opinion on the congressional plan.[21]

Johnson's failure to attack the substance of the amendment in his June 22 message to Congress reflected his desire to avoid alienating Seward and Raymond. This same attitude prevailed the next evening when Seward, along with Doolittle, Welles, Randall, Browning, Hugh McCulloch, and several others arrived at the White House to complete their plans for the convention. After several hours of discussion the group agreed on Philadelphia as the site and fixed August 14 as the date. Doolittle's draft was approved substantially as written, with no mention of the constitutional amendment. Disillusioned over the outcome, Welles returned home and recorded his dissatisfaction with the president for failing to recognize the importance of cultivating the Democrats. "This call which has been gotten up," he noted, "is Seward's call, the party is to be Seward's party, and it cannot therefore be Democratic." He concluded that "the president is purchasing or retaining Seward at too high a price, too great a sacrifice."[22]

The call was released on June 25 under the authority of the Executive Committee of the National Union Club and included the endorsement of Senators Norton, Dixon, Nesmith, and Hendricks. The omission of Seward's name and the listing of the two Democrats did not prevent the reaction Welles had feared. While there were Democratic regulars who embraced the movement, most were hesitant or strongly opposed. The editorial support of the *New York Times* and the *Herald,* along with continued editorial forays by Raymond and Bennett against secessionists and Copperheads, did not inspire confidence. Nor did the continued presence in the cabinet of individuals who were believed to be in accord with the Radicals. Others thought the convention was designed to create a new party and reacted vigorously against losing their Democratic identity.[23]

Concern over the party's future autonomy came about because there were no statements in the call about the convention's objectives and over support for realignment by a number of conservative Unionists. James Gordon Bennett proclaimed the Philadelphia movement meant dissolution of the Democratic party and the creation of a "broader and stronger and more elastic national party." General Thomas Hart Benton and Iowa conservative Unionists met in Des Moines on June 28, announced the formation of a National Union party, and nominated candidates for state office. Benton and his cohorts exerted pressure on Iowa Democrats to support the ticket and endorse conservative Unionists for Congress. Disturbed over this train of events, one of the local party faithful asked Mason whether organizers of the Philadelphia movement really intended "to obliterate the name of Democracy . . . write its eulogy, and sing its Requiem?[24]

Democratic apprehension was even more marked in states where the party was a major political force. Members of the Ohio State Central Committee, along with a number of prominent editors, met in Columbus on June 27, reaffirmed their support for the Democratic ticket and resolutions adopted in May, and called for the immediate convocation of district conventions to nominate congressional candidates. While it made no pronouncements on the National Union movement, its deliberations indicated an aversion to any tampering with the Democratic organization. Nevertheless conservative ideologues led by Alexander Long sought to capitalize on potential defections among party regulars. In early July these conservatives met in Cincinnati, reconstituted their State Sovereignty party, and condemned the Democrats for catering to Johnson. Faced with the sniping of Long to their rear and possible preemption by conservative Republicans ahead, the Ohio Democratic Executive Committee convened and resolved against sending delegates to Philadelphia.[25]

There was also a strong negative reaction among members of the New York party leadership. At the time the National Union Club issued its pronouncement, August Belmont was considering bringing together the National Democratic Executive Committee to fill vacancies from the Southern states and either holding a national party convention or issuing a declaration of principles. The publication of the Philadelphia call, he confided to Barlow, "takes the wind out of our sails," and raises the question of whether party regulars should join the movement "and thus give up the *National Democratic Organization. . . .*" Barlow's response appeared the next day as an editorial by Marble, who praised the National Union Club but declared "the Democratic party will not merge its existence in the proposed new organization." He concluded that it was too late for the creation of a new party; the mass of Republicans had already detached themselves from Johnson, and the president's only hope for control of Congress lay in working with the Democrats.[26]

National Union organizers needed some demonstration of Democratic support to overcome this resistance. They turned to Democratic representatives on Capitol Hill and sought their endorsement. By early July they secured the commitment of a number of congressional Democrats, who attempted to win over local leaders. On July 5 the effort gained momentum with the publication of an address signed by a large majority of Democratic congressmen. Seeking to allay fears about the aims of the Philadelphia convention, the signers claimed the only purpose of the movement was to preserve the Union, protect the Constitution, forestall further encroachments upon states' rights, and bring together Northerners and Southerners in a common public forum. By implication the address rejected any intention of creating a third party organization.[27]

During the next week other developments clarified the purpose of the movement. The two conservative clubs in Washington agreed to consolidate and create a new National Union Executive Committee, which included Randall as president, Mason as corresponding secretary, Browning, Blair, and several additional representatives from both the North and South. To avoid confusion over the selection of convention delegates, the committee issued a circular specifying there would be four representatives from each congressional district and called for delegates-at-large from each state. The apportionment of Northern delegates was equally divided between those who supported Lincoln in 1864 and those who voted for McClellan. The division significantly guaranteed the preservation of Democrats' party identity and assured them former Unionists would not dominate.[28]

On the contrary, the Democrats began to recognize the possibility of controlling the Philadelphia proceedings themselves through cooperation with Southern delegates. Southern opposition to the call came from a number of old-line secessionists, but many Dixie conservatives endorsed the movement and by early July had launched plans for supportive local conventions in several states.[29] Such a show of enthusiasm strongly influenced the Democrats, who could hardly disagree with those whose interests they professed to protect. More importantly, the National Union Executive Committee, in providing for the selection of Southern delegates, avoided the equal division stipulation imposed upon the North. In so doing it merely recognized the virtual nonexistance of the Lincoln-Johnson ticket in most Southern states. But at the same time it left the way open for the formation of delegations that would, if necessary, side with Northern Democrats.[30]

A major administration reorganization added to the shifting perspective. During the second week in July the National Union Executive Committee, with the president's approval, addressed letters to individual cabinet members requesting their reaction to the call. Seward's reply was evasive, but the attorney general and postmaster general resigned rather than infer even tacit support for the movement. Their departure, along with an additional opening in the Interior Department, permitted Johnson to alter the character of the cabinet by the appointments of Henry Stanbery, Alexander Randall, and Orville Browning. Democrats might have preferred the outright dismissal of all suspected dissidents within the White House circle, including both Seward and Stanton. Yet limited change by indirect pressure was better than no change, and Democrats were gratified to find the same tactics being applied to the lower echelons in the federal bureaucracy.

Thus by mid-July there were definite signs of a reorientation in Democratic opinion. Iowa party regulars, meeting in convention on the eleventh, agreed to split the state ticket with the National Unionists and endorsed the Philadelphia movement. Within the next two days the Rhode Island Democratic Executive Committee issued a call for a conservative assembly, and Ohio party leaders reversed their earlier decision and appointed Pendleton, George Morgan, William Allen, and W. R. Gillett delegates-at-large. Other state party organizations, with varying modes of procedure, joined in the procession of supporters. In Minnesota, for example, the Democratic central committee appointed all delegates after consultation with the conservative Union leadership. A number of states followed the Ohio precedent whereby the central committee appointed delegates-at-large and arranged for the selection of the remaining representatives through district or statewide assemblies. Massachusetts and Connecticut made their official selections at bipartisan state conventions.[31]

Significant support came from prominent figures associated with the former peace wing of the party. William B. Reed of Philadelphia was an early convention advocate who worked to sway his Democratic colleagues in New York and Connecticut. Fernando Wood and the Mozart Hall Democratic organization were also receptive and saw the National Union movement as an opportunity to strengthen party ties at the expense of the ambivalent Tammany Society. In the Midwest, Vallandigham and Henry Clay Dean joined the cause, and Copperhead journals such as the *Dubuque Herald* reversed their earlier hostility. Continued opposition came primarily from doctrinaire states' rightists who were alarmed at the notion of a coalition with former war activists. National Unionism had made too many concessions to an expanding federal government, and they opposed any modification of time-honored Democratic principles. The Philadelphia Convention, one correspondent informed Ohio's William Allen, could only "bolster up an administration whose whole power is lent to exalt the wrong theory and put down the right."[32]

The rising tide of Democratic endorsements was equally unsettling to many conservative Unionists. Having called the convention with the intention of isolating both the Peace Democrats and the Radicals, they now realized that it might be dominated by Democrats, even including some secessionists and Copperheads. Their reaction was to suggest additional criteria for admission of delegates beyond the general principles embodied in the convention call. Shortly after the National Union Executive Committee issued its circular on delegate representation, James Gordon Bennett appealed for a test oath and repudiation of the 1864 national Democratic peace plank. Bennett soon dropped his demands and agreed to an open convention, but other disgruntled Unionists maintained their pressure for tougher guidelines. A delegate to the Indiana National Union Convention spoke for a number of his colleagues when he declared they should not "be made tools in the hands of traitors and copperheads for the overthrow of the Republican party." Similarly an early Connecticut supporter of the Philadelphia movement warned Gideon Welles that he was reluctant to fraternize with Peace Democrats until they "repudiate their war record, declare the Chicago platform, at least, a mistake, and agree to behave in the future."[33]

The problem was particularly acute for Henry Raymond. A loyal supporter of the administration in Congress and through the editorial columns of the *Times,* the chairman of the National Republican Executive Committee's position in his party was increasingly jeopardized as Johnson rejected accommondation with moderate Unionists. The upsurge in Democratic support for the National Union movement compounded his dilemma. At a Republican congressional caucus on July 12, party colleagues took him to task for his early interest in the Philadelphia convention, which they claimed would lead to a Democratic take-over. Raymond's response was ambivalent. He feared Democratic dominance, but when the president appealed directly to him for support, the *Times* editor sought to modify the makeup of the convention by calling for the exclusion of Copperheads and secessionists. Meanwhile, having invited Democratic criticism, he refused to affirm or deny his support of the Philadelphia meeting.[34]

An outbreak of massive race violence in New Orleans on July 30 put many conservative Republicans on the spot. Governor J. Madison Wells of Louisiana, who was aligned with the Radicals against a hostile legislature, attempted to redistribute power in the state by reconvening the 1864 constitutional convention. Conservative forces, led by Lt. Gov. Albert Voorhies and Mayor John Monroe of New Orleans, challenged the movement's legality and charged that the delegates who reassembled could not constitute a quorum. They pressured Gen. Absalom Baird, commanding federal troops in New Orleans, to disband the "rump" conclave and arrest the delegates. A communiqué from the general to the secretary of war, requesting federal guidance, went unanswered. Detachments of New Orleans police converged on the assembly hall, encountered a protective guard of blacks, opened fire, and killed or wounded over 150. Northern Democrats blamed the Radicals for the tragedy, but the propaganda advantage went to the Radicals. They charged that the ex-Confederates were unregenerate and that protection was still a necessity for Southern Unionists.[35]

Northern indignation over the New Orleans riot changed conservative Unionist dissatisfaction with the Philadelphia movement into open rebellion. At the National Union convention held in Wisconsin in early August, one district delegate rejected his election and disclaimed any further association with the coalition. Agreement to establish separate National Union congressional committees kept other potential bolters in line but drew sharp reactions from the Democratic press. There was even more acrimony apparent at the Connecticut convention. The chairman, Gen. James Pratt, opened the session with a letter from an individual protesting the inclusion of his name in the convention call. Following the report naming district delegates, Pratt took exception to the choice of two Hartford Democrats and moved they be replaced. When this failed the general and one of his colleagues marched out of the hall. Less dramatic but similar withdrawals also occurred in other Northern states. Unless these disparate elements could find grounds for accommodation, the Philadelphia convention would fail.[36]

The role of New York at this stage was especially crucial. In no other Northern state were the conservative forces more powerful, influential, and blessed with the requisite numbers for success at the polls. Yet Thurlow Weed was harshly criticized when he issued the call for a conservative convention to be held in Saratoga on August 9. Republicans of Democratic antecedents charged they were being shunted aside by former Whigs, the *New York World* complained the regular Democracts were being ignored, and the Mozart Hall organization took exception to the exclusion of Copperheads. National Union organizers knew that a collapse of their efforts in the Empire State would have a disastrous impact on the Philadelphia convention. By the time of the Saratoga gathering they devised a patchwork formula to keep the membership in line. Raymond, uncommitted and not present, was selected as a delegate-at-large, as was John Dix, the Unionists' choice for the gubernatorial nomination. Sanford Church and Tilden, relatively unscarred by wartime politics, rounded out the list as representatives of the Democrats.[37]

With the New York meeting safely behind, National Union organizers made a last minute effort to clear away remaining problems for the Philadelphia convention. Chief among these was the selection of Copperheads as delegates by local district conventions. Many conservative Unionists made it clear they would not tolerate the presence of Henry Clay Dean, Fernando Wood, or Clement Vallandigham. They also viewed the inclusion of Alexander Stephens as unwise. Forceful removal of these individuals could precipitate a bolt among Democratic regulars. Seeking to steer a middle course, Mason and Randall worked to secure their voluntary withdrawal. Dean and Wood both relented on the eve of the assembly and submitted letters of resignation to their state delegations, and Stephens pleaded illness as an excuse for his absence from the convention floor. But Vallandigham was less obliging and proclaimed his intention to be seated even as the delegates assembled.[38]

The situation was volatile and could easily lead to a disruptive floor fight. The Ohio Copperhead, charging that the attacks on him were irrational and objecting to being made a scapegoat, was able to secure promises of support from the Kentucky and Connecticut delegations. Many Unionists, on the other hand, appeared to be eager for his public humiliation. Mason, looking for a way out, was informed that Vallandigham would withdraw only if the convention's executive committee endorsed a resolution prohibiting any delegate test other than support of the convention call. Mason secured Blair's backing for the proposal but encountered stubborn resistance from Browning. Further negotiations resulted in an alternative solution. The chairman of the Ohio delegation was finally permitted to read a letter from Vallandigham before the general assembly, affirming his right to a seat but also including his resignation upon the advice of friends and consultants. Thus the "Prince of Copperheads" was permitted to have his last word and the crisis was averted.[39]

The remainder of the convention reflected the careful planning of the convention's executive committee. Randall, Blair, Doolittle, Browning, and Cowan, gave major emphasis to the themes of national peace and reconciliation. The procession at the opening session dramatically illustrated the theme of reconciliation, as Northern and Southern delegates entered the hall arm-and-arm and marched to their respective seats. When the applause subsided, John Dix took the platform as temporary chairman, condemned the exclusion of Southern representatives from Congress, and extolled the president's program. The proceedings of the convention reflected the determination of organizers to maintain a tight control and prevent dissension. Doolittle became the permanent president of the meeting, Cowan was designated chairman of the Committee on Resolutions, and Blair the head of the Committee on Permanent Organization. Together they allotted the time each day for general business, determined that all resolutions form the floor be immediately referred to the appropriate hand-picked committees, and guarded against impromptu speeches.[40]

The Declaration of Principles and main address by Henry Raymond were especially important because they defined the issues that united National Unionists and constituted a platform for the fall elections. Both were designed to avoid friction. A preconvention agreement to limit deliberations to reconstruction matters facilitated the process, and the Committee on Resolutions was able to compromise their disagreements on reconstruction policy. In response to criticism from Southern representatives, Raymond deleted a reference to the disruptive impact of slavery on prewar politics and softened phrases relating to treason and rebellion. He modified a section on constitutional revision to avoid inferences of endorsement of the Fourteenth Amendment. A final modification concerned a statement in the Declaration of Principles praising Union veterans, but Raymond rephrased it in a manner acceptable to Southerners and Democrats.[41]

After the delivery of Raymond's address and endorsement of the declaration, the convention adjourned and the delegates departed. They encountered a mixed reaction from the Democracts at home. Copperheads attacked portions of the Declaration they believed conceded too much power to Washington and criticized the assembly for not seating Vallandigham. Most party regulars were enthusiastic over the outcome. The convention had irrevocably divided the Republicans, without jeopardizing Democratic identity or principles. Moreover, it provided a striking disclaimer of the opposition's charges about the South; contrary to Radical propaganda the convention demonstrated Southern leadership to be moderate, rational, and conciliatory. Democrats hoped it would provide the momentum for a conservative victory in the fall elections.[42]

Difficulties surfaced quickly when they carried their campaign to the electorate. The Republican program, developed in Congress and sanctioned by state party conventions, was a hard target to assault. Democrats claimed that ratification of the Fourteenth Amendment by Southern states should not be a precondition for readmission because Southerners had no part in its framing. But Congress had refrained from stating that ratification completed the reconstruction process. If the Democrats challenged there was no final criteria for normalization, they faced the precedent of Tennessee, which Congress had admitted in July after the Tennessee legislature endorsed the amendment. This ambiguity surrounding the congressional plan allowed Republicans to maintain party unity and at the same time keep their options open. It was a maddening situation for Democrats.[43]

Nor did they find an easier way to attack the substance of congressional legislation. Conservatives' criticism of the Civil Rights Act and a reconstituted Freedmen's Bureau Bill (passed over the president's veto in July) seemed misplaced in the wake of the New Orleans riot, and their professions of support for independent state action to protect freedmen appeared weak and ineffective. Democrats could not focus on the section in the Fourteenth Amendment relating to Confederate disabilities without playing into the oppositions' hands. The section redefining the basis of representation provided an easier target and bore the brunt of Democratic criticism. But most Northerners were unwilling to allow expanded Southern power in Congress after the abolition of slavery and insisted a redefinition of representation was mandatory. Consequently Democratic objections to the amendment often appeared trivial.

The Democrats met similar frustrations in their attempt to capitalize on the race issue. Party spokesman were convinced that Republicans wanted universal black suffrage, but they had little tangible evidence to support their belief. Moderate Republicans had forestalled Radical efforts to impose black suffrage on the South, the District of Columbia, or the western territories. Nor was there sufficient evidence of a concerted drive to cast aside black voting restrictions in the North. In the spring the Wisconsin State Supreme Court had ruled that an antebellum referendum entitled Wisconsin blacks to vote and provided the first instance of legal black voting in the Midwest. But Wisconsin Democrats let it stand without serious protest and there was no disposition to make it an issue outside the state. In Michigan, where a movement for a constitutional convention was underway, Charles Walker of the *Detroit Free Press* unsuccessfully challenged the Republicans to admit they were planning a revision of state suffrage qualifications. Similar efforts elsewhere fared no better and Democrats were left with little more than their charges of deceit and duplicity.[44]

Their situation was complicated by the president's decision to engage in an extensive campaign tour of the North in late August and early September. The first stage of the trip, highlighted by a dinner at New York City's fashionable Delmonico's Restaurant, went well. Johnson was among friends and sympathizers in a atmosphere that promoted a dignified and positive public image. As the presidential train sped into Republican upstate New York, hecklers appeared and the former Tennessee tailor began to lose his composure. In the Midwest Johnson's "Swing Around the Circle" degenerated into a fiasco. Republicans seized upon his extemporaneous and unbridled exchanges with local critics, reported his repeated comparison of himself with Christ, and charged he was lowering the dignity of the presidency. Johnson, rather than focusing on the issues dividing the White House and Congress, allowed his speaking style and personal character to become the focal point of the campaign.[45]

Democrats attempted to defend and explain the president's behavior. Johnson's stump-speaking campaign style, they claimed, derived from his frontier upbringing and was a form of democratic social discourse in the honored tradition of a Jackson or a Lincoln. If it degenerated into vituperation, Radical rowdies at the rallies were responsible, and Johnson should not be blamed for his response. In any event, the incidents hardly reflected the president's character and his "courteous and polished manners." While concealing their displeasure, party spokesman privately conceded that the trip had been a disaster. Johnson had provided the Republicans with a fruitful source of political propaganda, and by leaving Washington with key figures in the National Union movement he failed to give leadership and direction at a crucial stage of the campaign.[46]

There were a number of internal administrative problems that surfaced following the Philadelphia convention. In some congressional districts the Democrats had held early conventions and nominated candidates from the peace wing of the party. When conservative Unionists tried to change the tickets, they were repulsed. This kind of infighting was intensified in Pennsylvania, where there was an effort to replace the Democratic gubernatorial nominee. War Democrats and Republican followers of Sen. Edgar Cowan regarded Heister Clymer as a threat to conservative chances for victory in Pennsylvania. Authorized by Washington, the state's National Union Executive Committee offered Clymer a diplomatic post in Spain or Russia if he would withdraw from the race and allow the nomination of Asa Packer. Clymer angrily refused and lashed out at moderate Democratic regulars whom he believed were behind the proposal. Because of this squabble, the gubernatorial candidate's patronage recommendations were ignored, as were his requests for funds from New York conservatives.[47]

There was greater cooperation evident in states where conservatives held their conventions after Philadelphia and where the Republican party was traditionally dominant. In Michigan, for example, regular Democrats allowed conservative Unionists to nominate a War Democrat and former Whig, Gen. Alpheus Williams, for the gubernatorial contest and select a number of veterans to round out the ticket. The Democracts ran individuals under the regular party label in most congressional districts, with the exception of the first and second where they agreed to fusion candidates. Similarly, Massachusetts Democrats merely ratified the results of a state National Union convention, which had eliminated all traces of Copperheadism. In both states the conservative campaign closely conformed to the original design of National Union organizers.[48]

New York posed a problem. John Dix was the favorite of War Democrats and conservative Republicans for the gubernatorial nomination, and his candidacy was given a boost when the Republican convention nominated Reuben Fenton, who was aligned with the Radicals. With Dix as their candidate, conservative Unionists planned to capitalize on resentments created by the Republican ticket and particularly on the discontent of western New Yorkers who believed their interests had been slighted. But many regular Democrats had reservations about Dix because of his wartime violations of civil liberties. Tammany Hall, reorganized and rapidly expanding its power base in New York City, put forward Mayor John Hoffman as their candidate. The Albany

Regency contested the rising influence of Tammany and negotiated with Henry Murphy's Brooklyn organization and other party factions, while keeping its options open. The death in late August of Dean Richmond, nominal head of the Regency and state Democratic chairman, complicated the picture and contributed to rumors of backstage political agreements.[49]

The initial deliberations of the New York National Union Convention, held in Albany on September 11, proceeded smoothly. The delegates agreed upon Sanford Church, a Democrat not publicly associated with any of the rival factions, as chairman, and settled the issue of rival delegations from New York City and Brooklyn without serious contention. But the underlying conflict surfaced early in the afternoon when Democratic regulars, fearing a stampede to Dix, moved for a recess prior to nominations and balloting. When the convention reassembled at four o'clock they attempted to adjourn to the following day. Church ruled the motion carried, despite what appeared to be an overwhelming vote against it. The next morning the chairman formally apologized for his arbitrary ruling, but this did little for the anti-Hoffman forces. Dix allowed his name to be withdrawn under a prearranged agreement and Hoffman received the nomination. If conservative Unionists expected to be rewarded with the lieutenant governorship they miscalculated, for the choice went to John Pruyn of the Regency.[50]

Democrats may have imposed their will at Albany, but their enthusiasm was tempered by news of stunning Republican victories in Maine. These returns, the nomination of Hoffman, and reports of Johnson's western tour caused James Gordon Bennett to renounce National Unionism and advise the president to yield to the Republicans. Henry Raymond showed his dissatisfaction by publicly withdrawing from the congressional campaign, denouncing the Hoffman ticket, and condemning the Democracts for their treachery. Defection of the *Herald* and the *Times,* two of the most widely read newspapers in the country, shocked Democrats beyond New York political circles. By the end of September Democrats were on the defensive, and the *New York World,* revising its earlier call for a conservative congressional majority, now merely hoped for enough gains to sustain the president's vetoes.[51]

Election returns in early October confirmed their worst fears. Heister Clymer, campaigning heavily on racial issues in Pennsylvania, lost his gubernatorial bid by 17,000 votes. Republicans maintained their control of the legislature, and Democratic congressional candidates in Pennsylvania failed to gain a single seat. Indiana, Iowa, and Ohio had similar returns. Democrats noted that the margins of defeat were less than in previous contests and were gratified by the addition of Gen. George Morgan to the Ohio congressional delegation. This solitary victory was small consolation, given the importance of the elections and the decisive Republican mandate. After much soul-searching and efforts to discover the causes for their defeats, Democrats recognized that if this trend were to continue the Republicans on Capitol Hill would be able to carry their program against any White House opposition.

There were reports during the first half of October that Johnson, facing a Republican upsurge, was considering a modificaiton of his position. This possibility alarmed Democrats in New York, Illinois, and other states yet to hold elections. While some were willing to consider the administration's acceptance of a revised Fourteenth Amendment, they generally agreed that discussion should be postponed until after the November returns. In the meantime Democrats urged the President to deny the rumors and bolster the conservative campaign. Orville Browning agreed, drafted a letter assuring several of his Illinois constituents that the president would not compromise, and along with conservatives Stanbery, Cowan, Thomas Ewing, and William Sharkey presented the letter to Johnson for consideration. Johnson agreed, and its publication gave the Democrats some momentary relief.[52]

But there were other problems. White House policy on control and distribution of patronage was one concern. Following the Philadelphia convention, Johnson removed many federal officeholders who were openly hostile to the administration, and for the first time included a number of Democratic regulars among the replacements. Yet party loyalists remained convinced there were legions of bureaucrats still in office whose sympathies lay with the opposition and who, through inaction or covert activities, directly contributed to Republican victories in October. They intensified their pressure on the president to no avail. Johnson resolved to exercise the "greatest caution" in using his patronage powers and stated there would be few additional removals before the November elections.[53]

The Fenians were another vexing problem. There was widespread Irish-American dissatisfaction with the administration after Johnson put down the June raid into Canada, and a faction of the Fenian Brotherhood, led by William Roberts, adopted resolutions condemning the president. Republican politicians grasped the chance to annex a traditional source of Democratic support by identifying themselves with Irish nationalism. Prominent Illinois Radicals appeared at Fenian picnics, Ohio Republicans nominated a Fenian for the state legislature, and the New York Republican press claimed Governor Fenton had rejected Johnson's appeal for state militia to use against the Canada invaders. New York Democrats with their large Irish constituency were particularly concerned when the *Irish American* withheld its support from Hoffman and several Fenian Army officers toured upstate denouncing the National Union ticket. On the defensive, the Democracts put forward their own speakers of Irish extraction, who reminded voters of the Know-Nothing origins of Republicanism, pressured Johnson to release Fenian prisoners, and demanded a forceful foreign policy against Great Britain.[54]

These last minute efforts by the Democrats were not enough to stem the Republican tide. In November the Republicans swept statewide contests and retained control over congressional delegations in Massachusetts, Michigan, Wisconsin, Illinois, and Minnesota. Even more significant were the returns from New York, where the Democracts had hoped to win; although Hoffman and the National Union ticket polled sizeable majorities in the metropolitan area, they were not enough to offset the massive Republican majorities in the northern and western portions of the state. Conservatives in New Jersey still dominated the lower house of the legislature, but Republicans continued to control the state senate. The only dramatic increase in conservative influence was in Maryland, where Democrats secured undisputed power over the legislature and elected four of their five congressional candidates.

The returns signalled the collapse of the National Union grand design. Conceived as a strategy to bind together those favoring the president's restoration program, the movement floundered from internal weakness and failure to win broad public support. Early proponents of the National Union plan had envisioned a new national organization that would include moderate Democratic regulars, Southern conservatives, and Republicans alienated by Radical excesses. However, congressional development of the Fourteenth Amendment caused most Republicans to question the wisdom of any departure from their traditional party alignment. The rising influence of the Democrats in the movement seemed to strengthen conventional party forms. As a result of this change, Johnson's bungling, and other problems, the extent of the National Union defeat closely approximated that of the Democratic defeat two years before.

# 5

## *Miscalculated Strategy*

THE RESOUNDING DEFEAT of the conservatives in the fall elections demanded some careful reexamination of Democratic strategy. The Democratic assumption that public disapproval of congressional legislation would weaken Republican authority was replaced by the realization that the Republicans could now claim support from the electorate for their program. The decision Democrats faced was whether they should modify their position in view of the Northern mandate. A satisfactory solution depended upon an accurate assessment of Southern attitudes, presidential interests, and the motivations of various Republican factions. During the next four months Democrats were divided in their judgements over issues and party policy. But despite this internal discord, the Democrats played a significant role in the proceedings that lead to the adoption of Radical reconstruction.

One conclusion Democrats did not make from the election returns was the need for an apology for their role in the National Union movement, even though Conservative Unionists might condemn them for subverting the movement's initial purpose. On the contrary, the party faithful generally condemned the Philadelphia convention as a misguided venture. Some argued that the coalition movement itself contributed to the conservative defeat by obscuring issues and alienating thousands of Democratic loyalists. Others recognized the returns indicated a deeper and more profound voter reaction. If the Democrats were temporarily out of favor with their Northern constituencies, they should boldly reassert the party's integrity and identity. James Buchanan advised a confidant that Democrats should refuse to bow to the leadership of nonparty trimmers; instead, they should "hold up the principles of Jefferson and Jackson on our banners, and maintain them to the last."[1]

Actions by Democrats confirmed their disengagement from the National Union organization. August Belmont summoned the national executive committee to his home in December, and they agreed to develop the Democratic party in the South by filling in Southern vacancies on the committee. Similarly, Northern state party leaders indicated they intended to direct conservative policy through their party structure. At the Ohio state convention on January 8, regular party leaders pushed conservative Unionists to the sidelines, monopolized the rostrum, and made a private agreement to support George Pendleton for the presidential nomination, Allen Thurman for the governorship, and Clement Vallandigham for the United States Senate. Connecticut Democrats, meeting the same day, likewise offered the best offices to party loyalists.[2]

In the meantime there was a concerted effort to organize a national Democratic convention in the spring. Kentucky Democrats initiated the movement by forwarding a resolution to other state organizations and received official encouragement from both Ohio and Connecticut. As the pressure intensified, Charles Mason and other party leaders in Washington considered the matter and finally decided to issue a call through the National Democratic Association. The response indicated many Democrats wanted a convention but revealed that distrust and dissension still afflicted the party. Western Copperheads wanted to impose their own definition of principle upon the "Democracy," took exception to the National Democratic Association's preemption of the movement, and charged that members of the organization had been instrumental in organizing the National Union fiasco. The association's choice of New York as the convention site merely confirmed their suspicions. Consequently a contingent of Midwest extremists led by Alexander Long decided to hold its own national assembly in Louisville.[3]

The negative attitude of Democrats toward National Unionism was also directed against President Johnson. Regular party members were ready to blame him for their defeat in the fall elections. They claimed that by his weak and erratic policy and disastrous campaign tactics Johnson had damaged the conservative cause and paved the way for Republican victory. Some Democrats believed the president's political future was so doubtful that the only logical solution was a complete separation from the White House. In mid-November Wilbur Storey of the *Chicago Times* openly blamed the administration for the party's failures and called upon his Democratic brethren to disassociate themselves from it. Both principle and expediency, Storey reasoned, dictated that Democrats "cut loose from the Administration of Andrew Johnson, and leave that hybrid concern to float on the sea of public contempt into which it some time entered, and from which no party power can rescue it."[4]

Most Democrats did not agree with Storey and regarded a complete separation from the presidency as irresponsible and destructive to the party. So long as Johnson leaned toward the conservative position, he was their potential check on Radical Republican legislation. Already there was discussion of impeachment, and if the president were driven from office, the consequences would be disastrous for the Democratic party and the country. Democrats who disagreed with Storey's logic argued that the party must come to Johnson's defense. This did not mean they had to support White House policy without reservation, but only as it coincided with Democratic principles. George Paul of the *Milwaukee News* advised that Democrats should "ultimately trust and support" the administration "just so far as it unflinchingly adheres to the right. For its errors and timidity, no party is responsible. For its virtues and patriotism . . . it is entitled to due credit and an equivalent degree of encouragement and support.[5]

Johnson's future position on the Fourteenth Amendment was of special concern to Democrats in early November. Despite Johnson's published opposition to ratification in the Browning letter, there were rumors that the president might suddenly change his stand because of the recent elections. This was a possibility the Democrats could not tolerate. Whatever other disagreements existed within the party, Democratic spokesmen were united in their opposition to the congressional amendment. They assumed that conservatives were still capable of shaping future national policy, regardless of the fall elections. Southern sentiment appeared to be strongly opposed to the amendment, and by mid-November the Texas and Georgia legislatures overwhelmingly rejected it. If the remaining Southern states refused to ratify, along with Delaware, Maryland, and Kentucky, the amendment would be doomed, Democratic opposition justified, and Congress checkmated. If this happened, Democrats could count on the resulting "deadlock" to work to their party's advantage.[6]

Beyond this point, however, the consensus evaporated amid conflicting assessments of Republican motivations and future political projections. Ironically it was the *New York World,* often condemned in the past by Democratic ideologues for its temporizing, that emerged the chief exponent of an uncompromising policy. According to Manton Marble, most moderate Republicans would not dare endorse Radical demands for dissolution of the existing Southern state governments and direct imposition of black suffrage by federal dictum. "Congress," he reasoned, "having already done its utmost against the South, that section has nothing to fear in consequence of these elections beyond what it already suffers." The proper role for Southerners and the president was a quiet but persistent acceptance of the status quo. In time, Northern public opinion would become impatient and turn against the Republican party for its failure to resolve the conflict. Then the Democrats would come to power and restore the Union on conservative terms.[7]

Marble's strategy was not universally accepted by his Democratic colleagues. Some objected to the suggestion that conservatives and the president adopt a position of passive defiance and called for aggressive warfare against the Radicals. Others disagreed about tying conservative fortunes to future elections with the South still unrepresented. William Cassidy, for example, called upon Johnson to endorse a compromise in the amendment which would require representation based on the number of voters rather than population. The *Argus* editor's analysis questioned Marble's assumption that Congress would not be provoked into adopting more radical measures if the current amendment were rejected. Conservatives should use what leverage they had to extract concessions, but they should avoid alienating moderate Republicans.[8]

Wilbur Storey carried Cassidy's logic one step further. From his perspective the eventual adoption of black suffrage was inevitable. The only question was how it should be achieved. Storey was certain that if conservatives continued their resistance, Congress would eventually impose universal black enfranchisement on the South. The only sensible course for Democrats and

Southerners would be to adopt the principle of "impartial" suffrage by independent state action. By openly rejecting race as a criteria for voting, they would preserve the doctrine of states' rights and leave the way open for property and literacy qualifications that would indirectly exclude large numbers of landless and illiterate freedmen. Thus Storey perceived impartial suffrage as a means of maintaining conservative domination of Southern politics, securing the South's admission to Congress, excluding racial issues from the public forum, and allowing Democrats to concentrate on Republican economic policies.[9]

Storey's call for impartial suffrage generated widespread reaction from the Democratic press. The *Davenport Democrat* and the *Boston Post* supported the proposal, but most major party newspapers were critical and condemned the plan on pragmatic grounds as well as on principle. Should the Democratic party accept property and literacy qualifications, they charged, it would disavow its own long-standing commitment to equal suffrage for all adult white males. Actually there was little likelihood the plan would be implemented, since racial prejudice was national rather than sectional in scope. Even if impartial suffrage was brought before Congress, there was no reason to assume Republicans would accept this as a basis for settlement or refrain from demanding voting rights for all black males. In this case, Democrats would have lost their change to capitalize on a backlash among the nation's white constituencies.[10]

Charles Mason viewed impartial suffrage as a practical short-term solution to the reconstruction dilemma but disagreed with Storey's tactics. Mason wanted Republicans to take the initiative with a new constitutional amendment; Democrats and Southerners would accept the proposal under protest and thereby preserve the right to use the race issue in the future. To implement the plan, he solicited the support of the governor of Alabama and Horace Greeley of the *New York Tribune*. Salmon Chase, concerned about the impact on the nation of a confrontation between the president and Congress, also began to use his influence for compromise. In mid-November the chief justice visited Johnson and urged an accord with Capitol Hill. Chase reasoned that if the president did not endorse the Fourteenth Amendment as constituted, he should request the sections on representation and Confederate disqualifications be replaced with impartial suffrage and universal amnesty.[11]

By the end of the month there were numerous press reports of missions similar to Chase's and speculation over Johnson's possible reaction. The prospect of a dramatic reversal in presidential policy and his acceptance of a compromise was taken seriously by Democrats who desired an extended deadlock. A Washington reporter for the *New York World* wrote Marble he feared Johnson might capitulate in his annual address to Congress. If this were so, the reporter continued, he had arranged with Samuel Cox to launch "some sort of thunderbolt immediately on the reading of the message. . . ." If Johnson was unwilling to stand up to the Radicals, then Democrats must be prepared to fight them both. "We must have a fight with them *anyhow,*" he concluded, "and if they fall back on the message, we must either dislodge them from their stronghold or *blow it up*."[12]

But this fear was unfounded. When Johnson sent his address to Congress in early December, he reviewed the process of reconstruction since the conclusion of the war and noted the South had fulfilled presidential policy requirements. The failure of Congress to seat Southern representatives remained the sole barrier to national unity. But in urging admission of the Southerners, he avoided a direct verbal attack on the congressional Republicans or inferences that the legislature was illegally constituted. Nor did he allude to the pending constitutional amendment or suggest a need for additional compromise. Democrats who had favored a revision of the conservative position did not comment. Other party regulars praised the president for his devotion to principle, and the only serious criticism came from those who wanted Johnson to be more militant.[13]

Few critics could be found among the Democratic congressional leadership. Discussion in the Democratic caucus was consciously moderate as a matter of policy. They reasoned that with the president apparently opposed to the constitutional amendment and the South likely to defeat ratification, Republicans would find themselves in an impossible situation. Any attempt by Republicans to move toward more radical measures or grant further concessions could lead to a dangerous intraparty quarrel. Democrats should refrain from any intervention that might force the opposition to unite or provide an excuse for punitive legislation. One prominent Democratic leader confided to a Washington reporter that Democrats would "give the radicals all the rope they want, hoping that they may hang themselves."[14]

The course pursued by Republican congressmen in the three weeks between the opening of the session and the holiday recess confirmed Democratic assessments of the opposition's dilemma. A House bill to convene the next Congress in early March brought little debate; Democratic representatives labelled it an effort to limit presidential patronage powers, declared they had no personal interest in the matter, and offered only token resistance as it passed by a party vote. Nor were they aroused by the sudden adoption by the House of a proposal to repeal wartime legislation that granted the president authority to pardon individuals engaged in the rebellion; as in the case of the bill on the opening of the next Congress, the Senate did not press the issue, and Democrats did not see how it could interfere with general pardoning powers conferred by the Constitution. They also tended to view such maneuvers as a sign of timidity. Despite the bluster of the Radicals and their threats of impeachment and territorialization, Republicans appeared reluctant to push measures directly concerned with reconstruction.[15]

Republicans did try to test the crucial issue of Negro suffrage. Shortly after the reassembling of Congress, the Senate resumed its deliberations on the District of Columbia voting bill, carried over from the first session. During a press debate over a compromise Southern settlement based on impartial suffrage, the inclusion of literacy qualifications for District voters was suggested. Dixon's proposal of this amendment revealed the sharp division of opinion among Senate Democrats. Thomas Hendricks, speaking for those Democrats who favored accommodation, agreed to overcome this dislike of literacy tests and support the Dixon amendment. Although Hendricks was joined by Senators Buckalew, Nesmith, and George Riddle of Delaware, Garrett Davis and Willard Saulsbury were staunchly opposed. But the Republicans were not as divided as the Democrats anticipated; moderates and Radicals voted down literacy qualifications and passed the bill by a vote of thirty-two to twelve.[16]

Encouraged by their victory, Senate Republicans the next day introduced a proposal for Nebraska statehood, amended to require Nebraskans' acceptance of black suffrage. The intent was clear. Having successfully carried the black suffrage issue in the District of Columbia, the Radical leadership looked to Nebraska to provide a precedent for congressional imposition of suffrage requirements on all new states admitted to the Union. If they were successful, the way would be open to disband existing Southern state governments and extend federal control over voting rights as a basis for reconstruction. Democrats, in reaction, charged Republicans with violating their campaign pledges and contradicting their own pending constitutional amendment that left control of suffrage to the states. Hendricks and Reverdy Johnson, seeking compromise, argued that the proposed amendment to the Nebraska bill precluded the option of Nebraskans establishing literacy or property qualifications.[17]

Democrats were not as yet alarmed. When the Republicans passed the District suffrage bill, they were unable to muster the two-thirds majority necessary to override a presidential veto. Certainly they would encounter even more resistance to the Nebraska bill, which involved fundamental constitutional questions, and this assumption was confirmed when the Senate adjourned for the holidays without voting on the issue. Southerners remained firm in their opposition to the constitutional amendment, and by the time Congress recessed five additional states had overwhelmingly rejected ratification. Most Democrats reasoned that they had cornered the opposition and that their deadlock strategy had worked.

The Supreme Court decision on December 17 in the Milligan case strengthened this conviction. The Court ruled in behalf of Milligan by a five to four vote and declared unconstitutional the trial of civilians by military tribunals when civil institutions were functioning normally. Jubilant Democrats saw the decision as a vindication of their wartime campaign against martial law. At the same time it provided legal justification for their opposition to congressional reconstruction. They claimed that by logical extension the Freedmen's Bureau and Civil Rights Act would be rendered inoperative. They also predicted that the Court on its own would soon rule unconstitutional the existing state test oaths, and that any attempt by Congress to enforce a Radical reconstruction program would be doomed to failure. With the president now joined by the Court against Congress, a deadlock appeared certain.[18]

Johnson, too, was emboldened by the Supreme Court's action. When

Congress reassembled in early January, the president drafted a veto of the District suffrage bill and received the encouragement of every department head except Stanton. The tone of the veto message was markedly different from his annual message. He reviewed the attitude of District residents expressed in the 1865 referendum, denounced the enfranchisement of a large mass of ill-prepared people, and chided Republicans for legislating in the District what their constituents refused in their own states. Finally, he lectured Congress on the separation of powers as a schoolmaster would address a classroom of unruly students. The president asserted that it was the legislative branch, pressured by an hysterical public, that was most to be feared in any drift toward despotism and subversion of the republic.[19]

The reaction of Congress was swift and direct. In the House there was no question as to the outcome, and the bill passed over the president's veto without debate. The absence of any protest by Democratic congressmen might have indicated a sense of futility, but inaction by Democratic senators suggested the existence of more subtle and complex strategies. Only Reverdy Johnson spoke in behalf of the veto. Johnson argued that the bill conflicted with the wishes of District residents and asserted the president had been ill-advised in inferring that Congress was guilty of usurpation. When the vote came for the final adoption of the bill, Senators Johnson, Hendricks, and Nesmith joined with seven conservative Republicans to vote in the negative. The remaining Democratic senators abstained and allowed the veto to be overridden by a slim margin.[20]

Although the Democrats were willing to saddle the opposition with the problem of black suffrage in the District, they were not prepared for subsequent actions by Congress. On the day the Senate concluded its deliberations, House Radicals introduced a resolution to investigate the president's conduct for possible impeachment and secured its passage by an overwhelming majority. Three days later, following another defiant speech by Johnson at an anniversary celebration of the Battle of New Orleans, the Senate approved the earlier House decision to establish a March date for convening the next Congress. Suddenly it turned to the Tenure-of-Office Bill, that had been in committee since the beginning of the session. Under its provisions the president would be severely restricted in his power to remove or appoint all federal officials except cabinet members. Significantly, in view of the recent House resolution, Senate Republicans added an amendment that declared any violations to be a high misdemeanor and therefore grounds for impeachment.[21]

The militant attitude of Republicans was evident in their rapid action on black suffrage in the West. On January 9 the Senate majority overwhelmingly voted for a bill guaranteeing black suffrage in the territories, and the next day the House added its consent. At the same time they renewed their deliberations on statehood for Nebraska. The Senate Democrats acted as they occasionally had before and voted with the Radicals to defeat an amendment providing for a black suffrage referendum in Nebraska. To the Democrats' dismay a number of moderate Republicans joined the Radicals and passed a new amendment that made statehood dependent on black enfranchisement without an expression of opinion by territorial residents. Almost immediately the Senate adopted a similar proposal for Colorado, and within a week both bills received the sanction of the House.[22]

For the first time Democrats began to question their own negative assumptions about the effectiveness of Republicans. The sudden shift of many moderate Republicans toward congressional control over suffrage was reason enough for concern, but the swift action and size of the vote on the impeachment resolution was even more disturbing. Manton Marble confessed that "contrary to our former impression, we incline to think that the Radicals are in dead earnest, and the President will be impeached and put on trial." Though Marble and his friends doubted that the Senate would convict Johnson, they worried whether this question was relevant. If the president were suspended from office pending the outcome of his trial, the Republicans could restructure the Supreme Court and remove any judicial threat to their reconstruction legislation.[23]

Fortunately, moderate Republicans had second thoughts about impeachment proceedings against the president. The business community seemed apprehensive about the impact of another political crisis on the nation's economy. And new signs of discord surfaced among Republicans over the direction of future Southern policy. Thaddeus Stevens, pushing for a Radical solution, demanded the dissolution of existing Southern state governments and the introduction of universal black suffrage. But on January 16, Republican John A. Bingham of Ohio launched a bitter attack on Stevens's position, charging it contradicted the work of the Joint Committee on Reconstruction and violated recent campaign pledges by Republican candidates. What Bingham wanted was the adoption of the amendment upon ratification by three-fourths of the Northern states and the admission of individual Southern states as each endorsed it.[24]

Bingham's position reflected a flickering hope among moderate Republicans that the Southern governments might still be induced to ratify the amendment. During the preceding month Gov. Robert Patton of Alabama had stumped his state to marshall support for its reconsideration by the legislature. Perhaps Patton and moderate Republicans believed that the impeachment investigation and other action by Congress might persuade Johnson to support the amendment. They found some encouragement from Johnson's quiet behavior after his speech commemorating the Battle of New Orleans. But speculation over whether the president would support the amendment was renewed when a prominent Alabama conservative telegraphed the White House on January 1 requesting a clarification of his views. Johnson's terse response indicated his continued opposition to the amendment and effectively ended any hope of a change in attitude by the president. On the same day that he replied, a Washington newspaper associated with the administration asserted Johnson would not be intimidated and would take forceful action against the Radicals if necessary.[25]

At this juncture the president began preparations for an alternative proposal and invited a number of prominent Southerners, including the governors of South Carolina, Florida, and Alabama, to Washington for consultation. After a week of intensive deliberations they agreed on the outlines of what was called the "Southern Plan." The proposal directed Southern legislators, led by North Carolina, to sponsor a new constitutional amendment patterned after the current amendment but with several important modifications. They would omit the section prohibiting prominent ex-Confederates from holding office while including a direct repudiation of secession. The sponsors agreed that Southern legislators should adopt a separate provision in their state constitutions, basing suffrage on literacy and property qualifications but exempting anyone previously entitled to the ballot. On February 3 the plan was forwarded to a number of Southern state capitols, accompanied by letters indicating Johnson's approval.[26]

The Southern Plan drew a mixed response from Northern Democrats. Wilbur Storey, ignoring the virtual exemption of all white adult males from the franchise qualifications, welcomed the compromise formula as supportive of his plan for impartial suffrage. William Galloweigh of the *Boston Post* and Cassidy of the *Argus* joined Storey in his endorsement. Other party regular were more guarded, raising no objection to qualified suffrage if the South adopted it voluntarily. Yet they had serious reservations about approving the congressional position on representation. Finally there were Democratic spokesmen who flatly rejected any concession on black suffrage; when James Dixon introduced the plan in the Senate, Willard Saulsbury took the floor, asserted he was speaking in behalf of the Democrats, and angrily dismissed the suggestion that limited black enfranchisement should be the price paid for Southern admission to Congress.[27]

Republicans were impatient over the drift of national political affairs. On February 2, while rumors circulated about the Southern delegation's deliberations, the House reversed a decision made the previous day and voted to include cabinet officials under the restrictions of the Tenure-of-Office Bill. Within the week the Joint Committee on Reconstruction reported a bill that would place the South under direct military rule. According to its provisions the Southern states would be divided into five military districts, each under a commander appointed by the general in chief of the army. The bill suspended habeas corpus and authorized commanders to institute trials by military tribunals. So despite recent Supreme Court rulings and maneuvers by Southern conservatives, the committee spoke for a growing Republican conviction that more drastic measures for the reconstruction of the South be undertaken.[28]

When the House began to debate the reconstruction bill there were indications that many Republicans hoped for a last minute compromise with the president. Nathaniel Banks and Henry Raymond objected to an immediate vote on the grounds that the bill lacked specific conditions for Southern restoration. Both spoke of the need to secure the cooperation of the president, if possible, and Raymond referred to the Southern plan as being worthy of support. On February 12 Congressman James Blaine proposed an amendment to the bill; any Southern state would be admitted to Congress once it ratified the Fourteenth Amendment and altered its own constitution to provide for impartial suffrage. Significantly, Blaine did not call for black participation in the revision of state constitutions and expressly excluded disfranchised ex-Confederates from the impartial suffrage scheme.[29]

The House deliberations provoked rumors of private negotiations between Republican representatives and the president and reports that Johnson would no longer automatically oppose plans embodying the constitutional amendment. The *New York World,* on the basis of such "private intelligence," sharply criticized the White House for even considering capitulation. "The President cannot justify himself either morally or logically in keeping everything at loggerheads for so long a period," Marble warned, "if the quarrel is to be settled at last by Congress having its own way." Marble would allow Johnson no option other than the deadlock strategy; the president "should either not yield at all," he concluded, "or have yielded earlier and saved all this gratuitous mischief."[30]

But would congressional Democrats accept the movement for accommodation? When Blaine attempted to get the bill and his amendment referred to the Judiciary Committee with instructions for its immediate report, Democratic representatives sharply divided. On a successful preliminary ballot to force a vote on Blaine's motion, eighteen Democrats joined Republican moderates in the affirmative and fifteen sided with the Radicals in opposition. On the subsequent roll call to refer the bill, five Democrats and a much larger number of Republicans reversed their positions and voted in the negative. The shift killed the motion and the House passed the unamended bill by a large majority. Incensed by the outcome, Raymond in the *New York Times* charged the Democrats with complicity in a Radical program for the South.[31]

Democratic representatives who voted against the Blaine amendment may have hoped that the Senate would either kill the reconstruction bill or extend deliberations long enough to allow a pocket veto. When the upper house took the bill under advisement, the determination to resolve the conflict quickly was evident. Reverdy Johnson, responding to the Republicans' mood, offered a proposal similar to Blaine's, except that revision of Southern suffrage provisions would include all adult male citizens. Thomas Hendricks suggested that the amendment be altered to allow for impartial suffrage, a move angrily denounced by Willard Saulsbury. However, the rapid shift in Senators' altitudes became fully evident when several of Saulsbury's colleagues, including Garrett Davis, spoke in support of Hendrick's position.[32]

Senate Republicans drafted their own response in a committee selected by their party caucus. The plan, reported by John Sherman, provided a substitute for portions of the pending bill. Basically it was a new compromise with significant concessions to both conservatives and Radicals. Under the substitute the South would be placed under military rule, but the president would appoint district commanders and the writ of habeas corpus was guaranteed. As in the Blaine proposal, individual Southern states would secure representation by adopting the Fourteenth Amendment and guaranteeing black suffrage. The Sherman substitute called for the extension of the ballot to all black males and required their participation in the drafting and ratification of the new state constitutions.

The unanimity displayed by Senate Republicans allowed the Democrats to insert the principle of impartial suffrage, but it lost on a voice vote. A roll call was moved on Sherman's proposal; Republicans obviously intended to pass a reconstruction bill before adjourning, and most Democratic members decided they were better off with the Sherman substitute than without it. Consequently only three Democrats—Senators Buckalew, Davis, and Saulsbury—cast negative votes, Hendricks voted aye, and the remaining party regulars abstained. They made one last attempt at revision by proposing that universal black suffrage in the South be withheld for a five-year period as it was with all foreign applicants for citizenship. The Senate defeated this effort and passed the unamended bill by nearly a three-to-one majority.[33]

Many Democrats did not agree with the Senate Democrats that the Sherman substitute was the best alternative. Manton Marble charged the proposal contained enough contingencies "to keep the Southern States out of the Union until doomsday" and called upon House Democrats to postpone the issue for two days so that the president could use his pocket veto. Charles Eldridge and Francis LeBlond were assisted by Radical Republicans when they attempted to act on Marble's advice. Thaddeus Stevens hoped that another delay would allow consideration of a more comprehensive measure. Stevens moved the rejection of the substitute amendment and permitted Democrats to dominate the debate in the evening session. On the morning of the nineteenth the House Democrats joined with the Radicals and adopted Steven's motion.[34]

When the Senate received notice of the House action, it refused their request for a conference committee and insisted upon acceptance of the Sherman substitute. The bill subsequently came back to the Representatives in time to settle the issue before the deadline permitting a pocket veto. Once again Democrats joined the Radicals in dilatory tactics. Discussion was diverted from reconstruction to an army appropriations bill and other legislation. When pressure mounted for a resolution of the reconstruction issue, Democratic floor leaders stalled with a series of roll calls until the House finally adjourned. The next morning, with the deadline passed, Radicals broke with the Democracts and offered their own revision that called for an expansion of officeholding disqualifications for ex-Confederates and extensive restrictions on Southern white voting rights in the construction of new state constitutions. Republicans coalesced behind the Radical amendments and passed the enlarged bill by a sizable majority.[35]

Senatorial concurrence in the House report was largely a formality, with the notable exception of Reverdy Johnson. The Maryland Democrat surprised onlookers when he announced his support of the amended bill. Johnson declared that his first preference had been for the immediate admission of the Southern states, but with this rejected he was unwilling for Congress to disband without providing for their readmission. Republicans, delighted over Johnson's statement, praised the senator for his devotion to the public welfare. Conservative critics were less charitable, and there were those who implied his decision was influenced by the pending confirmation of his son-in-law as a federal district attorney.[36]

Though most Democrats would not actively support the reconstruction bill, the unexpected revision by the House and subsequent concurrence by the Senate caused further division among party regulars. Fernando Wood, spokesman for those who championed a policy of resistance, advised the president to pocket veto the plan and continue to fight in the next Congress. Yet other influential party spokesmen had second thoughts about the deadlock strategy. Manton Marble and Charles Walker, in a sudden reversal of their previous positions, argued there was little to be gained in prolonging the conflict. They reasoned that the new Congress would be even more radical; thus Southern interests could be better served if the president returned the bill with his veto and allowed the current congressional majority to enact it into law.[37]

The president agreed and on March 2 forwarded his message to Congress, accompanied by a veto of the Tenure-of-Office Bill. In accordance with a prearranged agreement with the president, Charles Eldridge announced that Democrats would vote against military reconstruction but would not attempt to prevent a resolution of the issue. Congressmen Sydenham Ancona, Benjamin Boyer, and Francis LeBlond took exception and called on Democratic representatives to use whatever parliamentary tactics were necessary to defeat the reconstruction bill. They were outmaneuvered when the House suspended the rules and overrode the president's veto. The Senate's discussion made clear the division among Democrats and the results were the same. Congress then enacted the tenure-of-office proposal that expanded restrictions over the president's powers of appointment and removal.[38]

Conservative and moderate Republicans implied that if features of the Radical reconstruction program were excessively harsh, Democrats had only themselves to blame. The Democrats had prevented the adoption of a moderate plan by encouraging the South to reject the Fourteenth Amendment, blocking adoption of the Blaine amendment to the reconstruction bill, and allowing the Radicals to legislate extensive white disfranchisement and universal black suffrage for the South. The Republican critique ignored the diversity of opinion among Democrats and the extent to which some members of the minority party were willing to compromise. Nevertheless, because most Democrats had adhered to the deadlock strategy, Democratic spokesmen could not deny that their own basic miscalculations and political maneuvers had contributed to the acceptance of the new congressional plan.[39]

# 6

## *Accommodation and Resistance*

THE ENACTMENT OF congressional reconstruction found Democrats disillusioned by their past actions and divided over their future course. When the various factions assessed their party's failures, they drew conflicting conclusions and became increasingly suspicious of each other. For those elements long critical of the party hierarchy, the March second act strengthened their convictions about the ineptness of national Democratic leadership and the folly of any modification of conservative principles. For others, past experience seemed to call for flexibility and moderation. So it is not surprising that during the spring of 1867 a division developed within the Democratic party between the advocates of resistance and accommodation. Dissension and renewed intraparty warfare were the result.

Meanwhile the president attempted to reduce Northern tensions over reconstruction. He weighed the possibility of administrative opposition to the congressional program against the failure of his compromise plan and finally chose the path of least resistance. He avoided known conservatives in his selection of generals to command the Southern districts and appointed several who were reputed to be Radicals. Johnson made it clear in an interview with a Virginia delegation and through editorials in the *National Intelligencer* that for Southerners, discretion was the better part of valor; in short, the reconstruction act represented the best hope for the South, and Southerners would be wise to cooperate. He tried to divert the nation's attention by stressing economic issues. In an interview with Charles Halpine of the *New York Citizen* he proclaimed the death of the old aristocracy based upon slavery and condemned the rise of a financial aristocracy whose power increased in direct proportion to the national indebtedness. Unless checked, this new aristocracy would plunge the nation into economic ruin.[1]

In early March Johnson encountered little opposition to his position and some support from an important segment of the Democratic hierarchy. Conservatives generally favored the selection of Generals William T. Sherman, George G. Meade, Winfield S. Hancock, William S. Rosecrans, and Lawrence Rousseau to command the Southern districts. Johnson's choice of Philip H. Sheridan, John Pope, Edward O. C. Ord, and Daniel E. Sickles obviously fell short of the Democrats' preferred list, and the inclusion of John M.

Schofield, a reputed conservative, did little to offset the dominantly Radical outlook of the Southern military governors. Yet the *New York World* allowed Johnson's appointments to pass without comment. New York party leaders soon endorsed the president's views in the *Citizen.* In the period immediately following the publication of Johnson's conversation, Charles Halpine discussed the interview with a number of important Democrats. "Marble, Sam Tilden, and Seymour are highly pleased with it," he wrote the president, "and say it makes out a strong case against the Radicals—all the stronger because so quiet."[2]

This endorsement of Johnson's position by the New York leadership was motivated by their independent assessment of the existing political situation. When the deadlock strategy failed, there appeared to be no hope for the party from either the president or the Supreme Court. Should Johnson decided to block the administration of the congressional program, his efforts would be checked by the Tenure-of-Office Act, the early convocation of the Fortieth Congress, the two-thirds majority of the congressional opposition, and the continued threat of impeachment. Conservatives controlled the Supreme Court by a slim margin, but legislation adopted the previous summer reduced the Court's eventual membership from nine to seven and threatened a reversal in its political outlook. In any event, there was little likelihood of securing a test case before the Southern governments established by Johnson were dismantled. Once this took place, the Court would be powerless to secure their reinstitution.[3]

The only possible recourse for conservatives was the electoral process and the 1868 congressional and presidential contests. Marble cautioned that it would be foolish to seek a solution based solely on the prospects of a Northern Democratic victory. Overturning legislation required more power than preventing its passage, and while Northern Democrats might gain control of the House of Representatives and the presidency, they had no immediate prospect of securing a Senate majority. Added support must come from the South, and this could only be achieved if Southern conservatives accepted the congressional program and dominated the reconstruction process. To do so they would have to recruit some of the freedmen's votes. Marble concluded that blacks could be influenced to vote Democratic by their former masters, whom they supposedly regarded with affection. If successful, these tactics would permit Southerners to cast a conservative vote in the 1868 elections because the March 2 act promised restoration of normal political relations upon compliance. The alternative, the *World* proclaimed, was continued political turmoil and social disintegration.[4]

Northern Democrats had a part in the new policy. First of all they had to still public fears over their position on Negro rights. The *World* speculated about extending the vote to blacks disfranchised under New York law. Noting that existing suffrage restrictions had been adopted under Whig auspices, Marble argued that New York Democrats could compete for the black vote if they would expand it in their forthcoming state constitutional convention.

More importantly, this would neutralize the race issue which had brought Republicans to power. Having disposed of this issue, Marble called upon Democrats to "waste no time with its carcass, but promptly clear the decks" for the "new issues"—the economic difficulties besetting the nation. Recognizing that Marble's position would create a row within the party, August Belmont called the national committee to his home on August 12, discussed convening a national convention, and decided against it.[5]

The policy guidelines suggested by the New York Democratic leadership were dependent upon congressional restraint in any supplemental legislation to implement the March 2 act. They kept a close watch on the Fortieth Congress as it began its deliberations for construction of the new Southern state governments. Though a number of congressional Democrats were conspicuous for their frequent absences during the session, Thomas Hendricks, Reverdy Johnson, and Samuel Marshall spoke for those attempting to make the legislation acceptable to the South, and conservatives who favored Southern participation under congressional reconstruction were partially satisfied with the final product. The revised bill directed military commanders to implement the reconstruction process but did not grant them additional powers to interfere with existing governments. It also established September 1 as a terminal date for completion of voter registration, providing some protection against prolonging the process indefinitely.[6]

Other aspects of the legislation were less satisfactory. Marble and his colleagues feared that requiring a majority of registered voters to initiate a constitutional convention or ratify its final product could cause lengthy delays, and they claimed the Radicals included these provisions in order to postpone reconstruction. In addition, the section relating to white disfranchisement was vague and failed to specify what constituted rebellion or whether presidential pardons allowed recipients to participate in governmental reorganization. The *World* chose to interpret the section in a manner beneficial to Southern conservatives and criticized the president's veto message for implying the bill disfranchised a majority of the white population.[7]

Still the New York Democratic leadership concluded that the supplemental act of March 23 might not check their strategy, and they looked to the South for the reaction of Southern conservative spokesmen. They found two groups in South Carolina, led by Governor James Orr and Wade Hampton, moving in a similar direction; of the two, Hampton's had the most influence. Following the enactment of the supplemental bill, Hampton wrote a Northern Democratic editor that Southerners could not wait for the Democratic party to save the South, since "it was *that* party that led us to our ruin and forsook us." Because the March 23 act removed from Southerners the onus of instituting reconstruction, they should use the opportunity to "direct the negro vote." Accordingly, Hampton and his South Carolina allies arranged biracial meetings in which both blacks and whites appeared as speakers, free barbecues were provided, and blacks helped police the proceedings.[8]

There were encouraging signs in other states. Governors Francis H.

Pierpoint of Virginia, Robert Patton of Alabama, and Jonathan Worth of North Carolina endorsed the plan to divide the black vote, and the movement was backed by such prominent Southerners as Robert E. Lee, Joseph E. Brown, James Longstreet, Alexander H. Stephens, John Forsyth, and P. G. T. Beauregard. Estimates of cooperation in Mississippi ran as high as three-fourths of the white population. Conservatives warned blacks at rallies throughout the South that they were being deceived and swindled by the Radicals and called for the rejection of agitators who would divide the races. And there was evidence that these tactics had some appeal. A black convention in Nashville adopted resolutions supporting the conservative congressional candidate and condemned the opposition for trying to silence freedmen who would not vote the Radical ticket. Elated over the turn of events, Manton Marble proclaimed the South was "gradually giving in to the situation, and preparing to follow our advice."[9]

Marble got additional support for the *World*'s policy guidelines in Northern Democratic newspapers. During the first half of March Wilbur Storey adopted a conciliatory tone toward the congressional reconstruction program, and after the passage of the supplemental bill and the Wade Hampton movement in South Carolina, he openly endorsed cooperation. Storey acknowledged that Southern compliance would incite certain Radicals to demand additional legislative restrictions. But he also believed that many Republicans endorsed the reconstruction program in good faith. Therefore cooperation would not only defeat Radical ambitions in the South but would divide the opposition. The editors of the *Boston Post* and *Davenport Democrat* concurred, once they were convinced of the possible recruitment of the freedmen's vote. Even the *Detroit Free Press,* not always noted for liberal tendencies, asserted that Southerners would be fools not to take advantage of "an element of power in negro suffrage."[10]

Other Northern Democrats remained unconvinced, and militant opponents of cooperation publicly condemned those who would modify conservative principles on the race issue. Editor C. Chauncey Burr of the *Old Guard* proclaimed Johnson's policy made the president an "object of contempt," an assessment heartily concurred in by Washington McLean. In New York, critics of cooperation claimed that Democratic supporters of this view were a clique of "chronic and incurable sneaks" motivated by a drive for "the spoils and plunder of office." James Robb of the *Philadelphia Age* warned the South that if it followed the "whimpering blandishments" of the New Yorkers it would lose "fame and honor and manhood." The editor of the *Columbus Crisis,* in a more strident tone, labelled cooperation as "something more than dishonor," and Washington McLean viewed it as nothing less than treason.[11]

For many opponents cooperation was bad politics as well as a betrayal of principle. It was folly, they argued, to assume Republicans would allow the South to organize under conservative leadership. Should Southerners successfully dominate the reconstruction process, Congress would simply impose new conditions to prevent them from participating in the 1868 elections. They preferred the South to remain under military rule and await the outcome of the elections. Meanwhile right-thinking Democrats needed to keep the reconstruction issue before the public. During the spring opponents of cooperation predicted land redistribution would follow the establishment of black governments in the South, accused Republicans of conspiring to foster black suffrage in the North, and dared the congressional majority to launch impeachment proceedings against the president.[12]

Although they agreed on strategy, anticooperationists divided on tactics. The editors of the *Philadelphia Age* and the *Cincinnati Enquirer* advised Southern conservatives not to participate in the construction of the new governments and by inaction deny their legitimacy. The South should initiate a series of court cases to show its disapproval. If litigation succeeded, so much the better. If not, it would dramatize the South's plight and revive conservative sentiment in the North. Only a victorious Democratic party could save the South from congressional reconstruction, and to achieve that objective James Robb of the *Age* called on Democrats to solicit the support of conservative Unionists. Robb did not favor a revival of National Unionism, but he believed that those conservative Republicans and War Democrats willing to accept the authority of the regular Democratic organization should be rewarded with positions of power and influence.[13]

Many Copperheads took sharp exception to this reasoning. C. Chauncey Burr rejected proposals to test the constitutionality of congressional reconstruction as a diversion from the main task of conservative reorganization. A diversion of this kind would probably add judicial sanction to the legislation. But rather than advocate total passivity on the part of Southerners, Burr asserted they had "a God-given right to kill every wretch who would consent to be a tool of our tyranny." This appeal to physical violence was not supported by most Copperheads, but Burr agreed with his colleagues in their opposition to War Democrats and conservative Republicans being given positions of power within the Democratic party. Rather than follow such a policy, Democrats should turn out of office the existing party leadership. In pursuit of this goal Burr, Alexander Long, Henry Clay Dean, and other prominent Copperheads pressed for a conservative convention in Louisville to give the party new direction.[14]

All Democrats looked to the New England spring elections for public reaction to the congressional reconstruction program. Republicans once again carried New Hampshire, but the Democrats polled 3,000 more votes than in the previous year. Noting that a similar increase elsewhere could bring several key states into the Democratic column, party spokesmen looked to Connecticut for a resounding rebuke of Radical policy. James English had proven his state-wide popularity in the last gubernatorial campaign when he lost to Joseph Hawley by a slim margin, and easily secured renomination. The campaign was a repeat performance of the earlier contest, with the important exception that Hawley could no longer claim administration backing or deny his support of Radical measures for the South. Thus Democrats charged the governor with duplicity in his relationship with the president and in his position on national policy.[15]

While the Connecticut Democrats directly attacked Republicans in their state platform for conspiring to prevent sectional reunifications, they refrained from condemning black suffrage. This allowed them flexibility on an issue that divided New England Democrats. Prominent speakers imported into the state either used or ignored the racial question, depending upon time and circumstance. But the racial problem tended to receive more emphasis as the campaign progressed. During most of March, for example, Alfred Burr of the *Hartford Times* paid little attention to black suffrage. Yet in the closing days of the campaign he concentrated on the theme that Radical reconstruction was but a preview of what the opposition had in mind for the country at large—the congressional imposition of universal black suffrage.[16]

When the returns were in, English won the governorship, and the Republican majority in the state legislature was reduced to one in the senate and ten in the assembly. Democrats analyzed the outcome with great care. Many moderate regulars and conservative Unionists stressed the selection of candidates untouched by association with former peace advocates as significant. Others emphasized their choice of a straight Democratic ticket. Conflicting viewpoints surfaced on the role the reconstruction issue played in the campaign. Proponents of Southern cooperation noted the moderate nature of the Connecticut platform and warned Southerners not to misinterpret the election as a mandate to defy Congress. Opponents of accommodation, on the other hand, argued the returns dictated a determined stand against black suffrage.[17]

Copperheads in particular seized upon the Connecticut contest as a vindication of their partisan purism. They joined those Democrats who would maintain a firm position against the "villany and corruption of mongrelism" and argued the victory confirmed that Democrats should divest themselves of the "dead weight" of the National Union movement. Ohio Copperheads acted to guard the party against any drift towards expediency. In April Clement Vallandigham reminded the Ohio state central committee that it had not implemented the party's earlier call for a national convention. He requested a postponement until July 4 but insisted that it be held even if the Ohio central committee and those of other states ignored the movement. On April 13 State Sovereignty Democrats from Ohio, Kentucky, Indiana, Illinois, and Alabama met in Cincinnati and endorsed Vallandigham's proposal. This did not influence many Democrats, and in late May proponents of a western convention in Louisville cancelled their plans because of lack of support.[18]

The failure of the Louisville convention stemmed primarily from distrust of its leadership, for developments during the late spring favored the position of party hard-liners. Those Democrats who opposed cooperation but hoped for a judicial remedy were disillusioned by deliberations of the Supreme Court. When Mississippi sought an injunction against the president to prevent enforcement of the reconstruction acts, the Court agreed with Johnson's attorney general, who argued the president could not be made a defendant. Democrats seeking the injunction reacted bitterly to the administration's intervention but hoped to achieve their goal in another case by Georgia against the secretary of war. Georgia chose two distinguished lawyers—Charles O'Connor and Jeremiah Black—who avoided the Court's objections to involving the president, but they fared no better than Mississippi. In mid-May the Court supported a brief by the attorney general that the case involved political questions outside the justices' purview.[19]

The rulings by the Supreme Court's strengthened the case of Democrats who favored Southern participation in the reconstruction process, but cooperationists soon were discouraged. Republicans, alarmed over conservative efforts to divide the black vote, pursued their own political interests. Radical Congressman and protectionist "Pig Iron" Kelly of Pennsylvania and Senator Henry Wilson of Massachusetts toured the South to win over the freedmen. The Union League proved an effective organizer of black recruits for the Republican party. Southern blacks appearing before local registrars generally encountered a friendly reception. Whites did not fare as well. The registration boards in a number of Southern districts followed a loose interpretation of the reconstruction acts, disfranchising former petty officials, Southerners who entered Confederate service under compulsion, and those holding presidential pardons.[20]

Democrats were offended and angered by the intervention of the military commanders. They not only set registration guidelines that supported Republican objectives but engaged in more serious offenses against Southern civil officials. When the appearance of "Pig Iron" Kelly sparked a disturbance in Mobile, General Pope deposed the mayor, police chief, board of aldermen, city council, and other officials, and between March and mid-July made over 150 political appointments in the three states under his jurisdiction. In the Fifth District, General Sheridan ousted a New Orleans judge, the mayor of the city, the state attorney general, and governor of Louisiana, while also threatening to remove the governor of Texas. Even General Schofield, whom Democrats considered the least objectionable of the generals, made appointments to vacant Virginia offices, although this was done on a modest scale. When Generals Pope, Sheridan, and Sickles issued orders governing the civil activities of the general population in their districts, they lent substance to the conservative charge of military despotism in violation of the Constitution.[21]

The aggressive action by Republicans checked conservatives' plans to dominate reconstruction. General Sheridan in Louisiana pressed for a rapid completion of registration, and estimates of potential Republican majorities ran as high as 20,000. What a similar trend might bring in other Southern states gave cooperationists reason for misgivings. Samuel Tilden warned Manton Marble that it was "extremely inadvisable" for the *World* to commit itself further on reconstruction in the immediate future, a warning Marble heeded. During May and June the *World* changed its editorial policy of endorsing cooperation to a noncommittal stand on black suffrage. Meanwhile, the editors of the *Boston Post* and *Chicago Times* moved in a similar direction.

Although there were occasional signs of Democratic liberalism on black suffrage by early summer, the characteristic attitude of moderate party spokesmen was an ambivalent one.[22]

Clarification of their position depended in part on the direction the administration chose to take. As inquiries poured into Washington about registration procedures and the role of the military commanders, Johnson's Attorney General Stanbery began presenting his views on reconstruction legislation. In early May several Southern delegations visited Washington and left with the impression Stanbery would adopt a thoroughgoing conservative position. His first formal opinion, drafted on May 24, covered the reconstruction issue and fell short of moderate Democratic expectations. He ruled that men who entered Confederate service under compulsion would not be disfranchised and registrars could not investigate the veracity of oaths, but he ignored the status of lesser officials and Southerners who received presidential pardons. This decision obscured rather than resolved the future outlook for Southern politics; white enfranchisement had been expanded, but Democrats were uncertain whether it was sufficient to ensure conservative domination.[23]

Stanbery had not ventured an opinion on the functions of military commanders. On June 12, after a delay sharply criticized by Democrats, the attorney general handed down his ruling. The reconstruction acts created two forms of government, but until the reorganization was completed the existing civil governments were sovereign and military authority was merely auxiliary. The commanders had no power to remove, suspend, or replace civil officials, nor did they possess legislative authority. The decision, presented to the cabinet on the eighteenth and announced two days later, drew an enthusiastic Democratic response for various reasons. Washington McLean declared that the ruling effectively blocked the Radicals' main objective and therefore would nullify the reconstruction program. William Galloweigh of the *Post,* on the other hand, welcomed the protection of civil officials but insisted that Stanbery's decision should not be construed as impairing the reconstitution of the Southern governments.[24]

Republicans did not share Galloweigh's assessment and immediately reconvened Congress to draft supplemental legislation. Manton Marble, aware that Southern reorganization might be delayed indefinitely, supported the move and warned Johnson and the Democratic representatives to avoid opposition that might result in "fruitless postponement." Congressional Democratic leaders agreed that while they would try to temper proposed legislation, they would reject obstructionist tactics. Again it was the Senate that provided the best forum for such a strategy. Buckalew of Pennsylvania introduced a proposal for a system of proportional representation based upon cumulative voting in Southern congressional districts. Buckalew's amendment, the most novel idea introduced during the session, attracted an enthusiastic response from Northern conservatives but lacked the support of border-state Democrats and Senate Republicans. Despite this failure, Senate conservatives successfully deleted a number of House sponsored proposals from the bill.[25]

The final bill was far from acceptable. The third reconstruction act, passed on July 19, stipulated that civil officials were "subject in all respects" to the military commanders and the paramount authority of Congress. The generals had authority to make removals, and registrars could question prospective voters and conduct independent investigations. The conclusions of such investigations were binding, irrespective of contrary opinions by civil officials. Congress broadened the scope of disfranchisement and denied that presidential pardons could restore political privileges. Democratic spokesmen considered the legislation a breach of faith. It created new conditions for the South and its objective was Republican domination of the South rather than improvement of the freedmen's condition.[26]

The strategy of accommodation also encountered difficulties other than those generated by political trends in Congress and the South. A major cooperationist assumption held that Republicans' unity and power depended almost solely upon their attitudes about the role blacks would play in the postwar society. If Democrats shifted debate to economic policies, the Republicans would fragment into discordant factions. This strategy would not concentrate exclusively on the economics of congressional reconstruction but would emphasize issues only indirectly related to reconstruction. The tariff and national financial policies offered attractive alternatives, and cooperationists, with few exceptions, made free trade, liquidation of the national debt, reform of the banking structure, reduction of taxation, and a restoration of hard money key aspects of their program. To broaden their appeal, they endorsed selected internal improvement projects, including promotion of a Niagara canal, Mississippi levee repairs, and expansion of the transcontinental railroad system.[27]

Although Democrats perceived widespread differences among the opposition on economic issues, the crucial question was whether their own party could unify on a platform free from racial considerations. The answer was they could not. On the question of internal improvements, Ohio valley and border-state Democrats opposed funding of a northern Pacific railroad and, joined by others interested in competing routes, also opposed the Niagara project. As for the tariff, important segments of the Democratic party had reason to make exceptions to free trade doctrine; Ohio party spokesmen applauded congressional passage of a wool tariff as beneficial to western interests, and Pennsylvania Democrats, capitalizing on congressional failure to enact a general tariff bill raising iron duties, indicted Republicans for betraying manufacturers.[28]

And there was discord over the demands of workingmen. Postwar labor leaders, drawing upon expanded organizational strength, focused on the goal of an eight-hour day, and politicians from both political parties responded to the campaign. Indiana Democrats supported the proposal in the 1866 state platform, and Congressmen William Niblack introduced legislation covering the hours of federal employees. John Morrissey, fighter and flamboyant Tammany Hall stalwart, used his support of the movement to get elected to

Congress, and Connecticut Democrats attributed the election of James English—at least in part—to his endorsement of an eight-hour day. During the first half of 1867 New York, Illinois, Missouri, Connecticut, California, and Wisconsin all passed similar bills with some measure of Democratic support. In Pennsylvania and Ohio, Democrats led a drive for additional legislation to regulate the hours of labor.[29]

Cooperationists regarded the movement as a dangerous perversion of economic principles and misguided political strategy. They identified with the established commercial interests and hoped to attract conservative businessmen to the Democratic standard. The eight-hour day proposal embodied the seeds of class conflict and economic disruption detested by those who prized order and predictability. Manton Marble conceded that workingmen had cause for dissatisfaction but argued the reason lay in protective tariffs, fluctuating currency, and high taxes; in endorsing the eight-hour day, Democrats not only helped deceive laborers but violated established party doctrine. Wilbur Storey reminded Chicago workingmen that wages and hours were ordained by natural law and were not subject to legislative fiat. When Chicago laborers struck to make the Illinois eight-hour day law binding on employers, Storey branded the leaders demagogues and applauded the collapse of the effort.[30]

The divisions over internal improvements, the tariff, and labor policy were insignificant when compared to those generated by financial issues. When the New York leadership shifted its attention to economic concerns, it had visions of repeating Jackson's successful attack on the national banking system. Early in 1867 the *World* endorsed a bill by Samuel Randall that would substitute Treasury notes for national bank currency and provide for additional contraction of greenbacks. Marble supported the plan because it would mean a restoration of specie payments and a curtailment of national bank operations. By February the program had run into difficulty, as Randall's bill was weakened in committee by rumors about a concentrated banking lobby. From the perspective of some bank opponents, Democratic bank stockholders were their party's own worst enemies.[31]

Bankers had other concerns besides the Randall bill. Of particular importance, early in 1867, was the problem of handling $140 million in compound interest notes due for redemption during the year. Because these notes were used by national banks to meet reserve requirements, their contraction threatened a reserve squeeze while liquidating a profitable source of interest. Bankers reacted with a bill that allowed the Treasury Department to redeem the compound interest notes with 3½ percent loan certificates and permitted use of the certificates as part of the banks' reserves. An amendment by Thaddeus Stevens in late February provided for the redemption of compound interest notes in legal tender. Coupled with a section directing the Treasury to forestall further greenback withdrawals, Steven's proposal threatened to halt resumption of specie payments and stimulate currency inflation.

Democratic reaction reflected the intraparty conflict over financial policies. Initially House Democrats divided along nonsectional probank and antibank lines. Intrusion of Steven's amendment altered the division, with western representatives favoring the inflationary proposal. Faced with the Greenback movement, eastern members united in support of a final compromise measure that redeemed a limited number of compound interest notes in loan certificates, lowered interest rates on the certificates, permitted their use in meeting reserve requirements, and allowed the Treasury to continue currency contraction.[32]

The sectional division reflected disagreement within the party over the handling of government securities held by private investors. The amount of private investment in compound interest notes was relatively small, but their redemption had important ramifications for the large number of government bonds. Nearly 83 percent of the bonds were owned by eastern creditors and this had a disproportionate sectional influence on politicians. Thus an influential segment of the Democratic hierarchy and the *New York World* were willing to attack the national bank system but excluded the bondholders in their indictment. To do otherwise would antagonize influential party contributers and potential recruits from the business community.[33]

Midwest Democrats were less hesitant. Midwestern Copperheads had already begun a lengthy campaign against bondholders and the federal banking system. They detested the national debt because it was incurred by an unjust war, and they saw little moral or legal legitimacy in the bondholder's claims on the government. Wisconsin's "Brick" Pomeroy in an 1866 pamphlet captured the prevailing sentiment in Copperhead circles when he depicted eastern "nabobs" drawing high interest rates on tax-free government bonds, while widows, farmers, and others were heavily taxed to pay the bondholder. Pomeroy and other Copperheads were irritated by bondholders' demands that bonds purchased during the war with depreciated currency be redeemed in gold. At the April 1867 State Sovereignty Convention in Cincinnati, Henry Clay Dean summarized the Copperhead position when he argued the government was under no obligation to pay the debt and claimed repudiation would give bondholders what they deserved.[34]

By spring the bond issue became a matter of public debate. Ohio was the center of the protest and Washington McLean its leading propagandist. Although the *Enquirer*'s editor was identified with the peace wing of the Democractic party, he was uncomfortable with the rigid views of the State Sovereignty faction. Like most Ohio Copperheads, McLean resented the dominance of Allen Thurman in state party circles and the power of the New York hierarchy in the national Democratic party. Earlier in the year he had tried to enhance his own status and that of his Ohio colleagues by pointing to new issues to round out their opposition to congressional reconstruction. Initially this included a proposal to bring Louis Kossuth, the European revolutionary leader, to the United States, as well as attacks on the national banks, the tariff, and the Treasury's currency contraction policy.[35]

In April McLean concentrated on the financial issue. Shortly after the

State Sovereignty Convention in Cincinnati, McLean published an editorial entitled "A Popular Plan to Pay Off the National Debt." In it he took sympathetic note of agrarian sentiment for a new issue of legal tender to redeem government securities. During the next few months, McLean's views were often fluctuating and ambiguous. He implied the proposal should extend to all bonds but never dealt with the legal requirement that the interest on the five-twenty bonds and both principal and interest on other bonds be paid in gold. Moreover, a sudden redemption of the debt in greenbacks would obviously stimuate inflation, but he played down this aspect of the proposal. Instead, he emphasized that the main goal would be to relieve taxpayers from heavy interest payments to bondholders. Whatever inflation occured as a byproduct was incidental but beneficial and would stimulate business revival.

McLean's program failed to convince the more moderate Democrats. On the one hand it verged on repudiation by implying the redemption of all government securities in greenbacks. On the other, it violated conservative tradition by threatening wholesale currency inflation. Democrat George Hunt Pendleton of Ohio, in search of the presidential nomination, sought to capitalize on the Greenback and bond issues raised by McLean and attract the support of a wider audience. During late summer Pendleton formulated his position in a series of speeches, beginning in St. Paul and ending in Milwaukee. He guarded against the charge of repudiation by limiting his greenback redemption plan to the five-twenty bonds where no gold payment was required. Pendleton claimed the entire debt could be liquidated in sixteen years by a sinking fund without stimulating inflation or new taxes. He urged that the time be shortened, thereby providing for mild currency expansion as a concession to the inflationists.[36]

Crop failures and a continued currency shortage created by payments on sectional balances helped spread the Greenback movement to other midwestern states. The administration was alarmed and denounced the inflationary clamor but temporarily curtailed its policy of monetary contraction. Democratic cooperationists readily acceded to the Treasury Department's change of policy, but demands by McLean that they take a stand on the merits of the "Ohio Plan" were practically ignored. Hard-money Republicans who sought to capitalize on the negative eastern reaction to greenbackism were challenged by Democrats who recalled Thaddeus Steven's proposal to redeem compound interest notes in greenbacks and charged the movement was of Republican origin.[37]

Democratic division over economic issues increasingly undermined cooperationist strategy, already jeopardized by Southern and congressional action, and by midsummer Democrats showed a greater semblance of unity in their opposition to the form as well as the substance of congressional reconstruction. Irate over the role of the military, they encouraged the president to remove Generals Pope, Sickles, and Sheridan, revoke the orders of generals intervening in civil affairs, and the reinstate ousted civil officials. They called on Johnson to straighten out his cabinet and reorganize the War Department.

Initially, the Democrats had reason to be optimistic about the attorney general's interpretation of the early reconstruction acts and Johnson's sharply worded veto of the July supplemental legislation. But when the president did not proceed with more concrete action party regulars berated him for his lack of courage. Angered by this charge, Johnson replied that the criticism was unreasonable and attributed it to Democratic annoyance that they could not control him.[38]

In large part Johnson's hesitance arose from the fear that he might alienate his general of the army, Ulysses S. Grant, whose importance had increased after the passage of the Third Reconstruction Act. Conservatives generally had reason for concern. During July and early August they sought to counter Republican overtures to the general and hoped to keep him neutral or enlist him in the conserative cause. Charles Eldridge, a minority member of the House Judiciary Committee, reported that Grant's testimony in committee hearings indicated his agreement with the Democrats, and Montgomery Blair publicly called for the president to appoint Grant his secretary of war. A group of New York Democrats led by "Sunset" Cox tempted Grant with the prospect of a presidential nomination. But these efforts were hampered by the intransigence of party hard-liners. Taking note of this movement, Washington McLean denounced Grant as an exponent of "unbridled and arbitrary power" and characterized him as notoriously unfit" for public office.[39]

Meanwhile Southern political affairs took a dramatic and adverse turn for the Democrats. In the August elections in Tennessee blacks participated for the first time under state legislative enactment, and the Republicans won a major victory. Radical incumbent governor "Parson" Brownlow, depicted by Democrats as "the most profane, extreme, unreasonable, malicious, and crazy headed creature that ever bore official honors," secured reelection by a lopsided margin and his followers swept the congressional contests. Noting that the black vote went overwhelmingly to Republicans, conservatives projected a dismal future for other Southern states. Final rejection of the accommodation strategy by Wade Hampton and other Southern cooperationists confirmed their apprehensions. With white registration minimal and little evidence of a division among blacks, Republican control of the South under existing congressional guidelines seemed a certainty.[40]

Influenced by these events, Johnson finally began his reorganization of the War Department. He approached Grant with an offer of Stanton's post, and the general, aware of conservative claims that the Tennessee election ruled out any possibility of his presidential nomination by Republicans, overcame his initial reluctance and consented. Stanton proved less amenable, refused to resign, and confronted Johnson with the alternative of dismissal and a test of the Tenure-of-Office Act. The president, reluctant to openly defy Congress, turned to a temporary solution. In mid-August the attorney general suggested that Radicals in Congress and the Bureau of Military Justice might have solicited perjured testimony against the president. Stanton's loyalty to his superior was in doubt, and Johnson suspended the secretary of war and appointed Grant ad interim to the cabinet post.[41]

Democrats applauded the decision, although some were disappointed that Johnson had not simply removed Stanton. They intensified their pressure for additional changes in the cabinet and military, a general amnesty proclamation, and the reopening of Southern registration lists. Johnson responded by replacing General Sheridan on August 17 and General Sickles ten days later. Early in September he extended presidential amnesty to all but several thousand ex-Confederates. Aware that the proclamation might imply bestowal of political as well as civil rights, the Democracts waited for Johnson to postpone Southern convention elections and demand enfranchisement of the pardoned whites. But the president balked. The Louisiana election went forward as scheduled at the end of the month, while Johnson lamely refused to interpret his own proclamation and left the enfranchisement issue to the courts.[42]

Continued factionalism among conservatives and renewed doubts about Grant's allegiance weakened the political support needed for bold executive action. Johnson was willing to consider changes in the treasury, state, and postal departments, but disagreement among Democratic regulars, former Unionists, inflationists, and hard-money advocates made the selection of replacements exceedingly difficult. Johnson was unsure that an endorsement by an important segment of the Democratic party could be won on any terms. On August 1, Albany Regency chieftain William Cassidy wrote Montgomery Blair that he was concerned over the administration's inaction and was inclined to disclaim any association with Johnson. Cassidy's statement implied a repudiation of Johnson by the forthcoming New York Democratic convention. Montgomery and Frank Blair sought to improve relations between the administration and the New Yorkers. They discussed appointments with the president and then asked Cassidy and Tilden to name a Democrat to replace Secretary Seward. Cassidy's choice of Henry Murphy was disingenuous. On the one hand, the Brooklyn party boss was known as a fervent wartime supporter of the Union and had some diplomatic experience as a former minister to the Netherlands. If Johnson was seriously considering a change in the State Department, the nomination of a prominent Irish-American during a period of delicate negotiations with England would have created obvious difficulties. Discussion over the replacement of Seward quickly collapsed, and the Blairs were once again unable to conciliate the conservative factions.[43]

Despite protests that the administration had acted in bad faith, Cassidy and his political cohorts probably anticipated the outcome. The party had much to gain by encourging Johnson to move against the development of a Republican South. Political endorsement of the president was another matter. Johnson's declining prestige meant that Democratic identification with the administration could become a distinct liability. Election results in early September strengthened the assumption that the Democrats had more to offer Johnson than the president did the party. California Democrats, polling heavy majorities in San Francisco and Sacramento, took over the governor's chair, the legislature, and two of the state's three congressional seats. Democrats gained in Vermont and registered a sizable increase in Maine. Party spokesman, exuberant over the returns, rejoiced that the nation's voters were returning to the Democratic fold.[44]

One day after the Maine contest the *New York World* warned that Johnson should not take credit for the results. Democrats were reminded that identification with the White House would make their party responsible for "blunders and mismanagement perpetrated against its judgement and in contempt of its wishes." The editorial generated criticism from conservative Unionists and those Democratic regulars who claimed that the administration's support was vital. It also brought action by the White House. An alarmed Johnson asked Lewis Bogey, a member of the National Democratic Committee from Missouri, to negotiate a settlement with the New Yorkers. The conference, held at Mayor John Hoffman's residence, ended in an ambiguous agreement. Johnson's emissaries claimed the Democrats had indicated they would publicly endorse Johnson, while the New Yorkers denied any such understanding.[45]

Johnson tried again to bolster his position with the Democrats. Using Lewis Bogey as intermediary, he suggested replacing Seward with Horatio Seymour. The proposal, supported by some conservatives, was received with little enthusiasm by the New York leadership. Seymour was a prime candidate for the Democratic presidential nomination and his association with the administration might jeopardize his political career. Some speculated that Seward may have initiated the proposal to hamper the Democratic nomination of Seymour for the presidency. The *New York World* responded that the president would be hard pressed to find any Democrat of political stature willing to accept a cabinet position. Marble predicted that the only hope for the country was in Democratic success at the polls and any coalition with Johnson would hold the party back.[46]

The October elections provided a test of Marble's analysis. The major contest in Pennsylvania involved the selection of a state supreme court judge. Pennsylvania Democrats nominated George Sharswood, a court incumbent from Philadelphia, and adopted a platform that condemned black suffrage but ignored the Johnson administration. Conservative Unionists were irate over the rebuff and threatened a separate ticket; the president, anxious to mollify the Democrats, scuttled the proposal and cultivated the support of Jeremiah Black and Samuel Randall. Aided by limited patronage concessions, Pennsylvania Democrats entered the campaign planning to capitalize on the race issue and economic discontent. The financial quesiton assumed major importance, and Sharswood's wartime opposition to redeeming state bonds in greenbacks became the center of attention. While his hard-money views may have hurt Democrats in western Pennsylvania, they were an asset in the eastern part of the state. The Democrats made substantial gains in Philadelphia and carried the supreme court contest by a narrow margin.[47]

The Ohio election was even more significant. There the Democrats, continuing their estrangement from conservative Unionists, nominated Allen Thurman for governor on a platform that ignored the administration and strongly condemned congressional reconstruction. Passage by the Republican legislature of a proposed black suffrage amendment to the state constitution made race the foremost issue in the campaign. Plans by the legislature to disfranchise Union veterans who left the army before being officially mustered out caused Democrats to argue that Ohio was a test case of Radical efforts to extend reconstruction into the North. The imagined social consequences of black political power brought wagonloads of young girls in white carrying banners proclaiming, "Fathers save us from negro equality." Democrats knew how effective these scare tactics were; faced with widespread hostility to black suffrage, the Republican state executive committee distributed a circular assuring citizens that voting for the constitutional amendment was not a test of party loyalty.[48]

Other issues played an important role in the campaign. Thurman was reluctant to attack business interests and gave economic issues a low priority. Pendleton, Vallandigham, and McLean tried to ease the financial difficulties of farmers and laborers to the party's advantage. They charged the opposition was led by bondholders, bankers, and brokers whose policies were detrimental to the general welfare. They claimed that Republican gubernatoral candidate Rutherford B. Hayes, while serving in the House of Representatives, "was so intent upon protecting the growers of black wool he has no . . . consideration for those who raised white wool." The Republican legislature's refusal to enact an eight-hour day and attempts to change Ohio's suffrage requirements demonstrated its contempt for white mechanics. Finally, by rejecting greenbacks to relieve public indebtedness the Republican state convention showed voters "they have nothing to expect from this party, which does nothing but legislate for the negro."[49]

Comparison of the Ohio and Pennsylvania returns provided a perspective on Democratic options. Economic issues worked to the party's advantage at the local level, but the merit of the Ohio Plan as a viable national platform was questionable. Greenback advocates, attributing Allen Thurmans's defeat to his unenthusiastic response to their proposal, claimed that general returns from Ohio indicated soft money was the key to future success. The Pennsylvania contest demonstrated that greenbackism could hurt eastern Democrats. The racial question worked well for both sectional wings of the party; Pennsylvania Democrats successfully exploited Negrophobia, and Ohio voters rejected their black suffrage amendment by a large majority and gained control of the legislature. Moreover, the elections aided those Democrats who claimed the party could succeed without making major concessions to former Unionists.[50]

The New York Democrats held their state convention immediately after the Ohio and Pennsylvania victories. Chairman Horatio Seymour called for full redemption of all public securities and put down an incipient greenback movement among the delegates. The racial theme became the focal point of the campaign. The convention condemned "negro supremacy" in the South as "an outrage upon democratic principles, and an attempt to undermine and destroy the Republic." Proceedings of the New York constitutional convention provided an opportunity for political exploitation of this racial issue. Noting that the Republican-controlled convention had adjourned until after the fall elections, Democrats suggested that Republicans were trying to forestall any public reaction against a change in the state's suffrage requirements and demanded that the question of black suffrage and the revised constitution be ratified separately by referendum.[51]

Noticeably absent from the platform was any mention of Johnson or the national administration. Johnson's supporters considered the omission a deliberate rebuke, and the president was dismayed. New deliberations over cabinet reorganization were begun as prominent Democrats converged on Washington, some by Johnson's invitation and others on their own initiative. One group, led by Daniel Voorhees of Indiana, encouraged the president to change his advisors and include Democrats in his administration before November. The New York leadership viewed this proposal with consternation. The New Yorkers made their point at an informal Democratic gathering in the nation's capital, and the group agreed not to assume any responsibility for Johnson's policies. Angered by this action, Johnson publicly declared that he would not be pressured by the Democratic party and claimed the Ohio election implied a rejection of "extremists" like Allen Thurman as well as Radical Republicans.[52]

The New York Democrats, having achieved their objective in Washington, returned home for the remaining two weeks of the campaign. Their initial concern over public apathy influenced their effective use of the race issue to arouse voters' interest. The *New York World,* completely reversing its position in the spring, warned that republican institutions would be threatened by the bestowal of suffrage on "millions of stupid and ignorant people of an inferior race." Marble advised Southerners to defeat the new state constitutions by refusing to participate in ratification referendums. Elsewhere passivity would force Congress to deny recognition of black-dominated Southern governments. Henry Raymond of the *Times* charged that Marble had rejected making any demands on the South. Marble denied the claim and insisted that Democrats would consider alternative proposals to the congressional program. He did not elaborate, and there were few expressions of moderation during the remainder of the campaign. Democratic speakers at the election-eve rally at Cooper Institute repeatedly condemned congressional reconstruction and rejected the extension of black suffrage in the South and New York.[53]

The suffrage issue played a similar role in other state contests. Party spokesmen throughout the North, but particularly in the border states and Ohio valley, devoted considerable rhetoric to the spectacle of black domination of the South, with its supposed social, political, and economic evils. Local developments in a number of states emphasized the racial issue. Wisconsin Democrats pointed to a Republican legislative enactment disfranchising Union "deserters" and charged the opposition with unjust discrimination against Wisconsin whites. In Michigan, conservatives used the constitutional convention's deliberations over racial restrictions on suffrage as their target. Minnesota submitted a resolution to strike the word "white" from the state constitution to a referendum. Democrats conceded that the opposition's claim that enfranchisement of the small number of blacks would have little or no impact on Minnesota politics, yet they called for its defeat in order to register their disapproval of congressional reconstruction.[54]

Exploitation of racial fears and concern over economic problems produced some victories for conservative forces in November. In the mid-Atlantic region, Democrats reasserted their control over Maryland and dislodged Republicans from power in New Jersey and New York. The triumph in New York was gratifying, as the Democrats compiled a 65,000 majority in New York City, reduced the normally heavy Republican upstate margin, and claimed nine additional state senators and nineteen assemblymen in the new legislature. Party regulars were elated that the voter reaction appeared to be nationwide because of gains in Massachusetts, Michigan, Kansas, Minnesota, and Illinois. Republicans claimed the returns indicated approval of congressional reconstruction, but Democrats pointed to the defeat of the Minnesota constitutional revision as a sign of continued white resistance to black suffrage and dissatisfaction with Radical rule. Democrats took heart; the long-awaited day of reunion on Democratic terms might soon be at hand.[55]

Democratic unity on reconstruction in the fall of 1867 contrasted sharply with the previous policy conflict during the spring and early summer. Influential moderate party spokesmen having failed to modify reconstruction legislation, attempted to recruit Southern blacks and divert attention to economic issues. Few blacks were won over by the conservatives, and congressional Republicans tightened their program so that conservatives were unable to control the new state governments. Advocates of accommodation also found concentration on economic issues to be counterproductive when Midwestern Democrats supplemented their resistance to congressional reconstruction with a soft-money campaign that had a strong regional appeal. By fall the Democratic division over reconstruction policies had ended, but the currency question remained as a source of intraparty factionalism that would have serious implications for the party in the months to come.

# 7

## *Defiance And Confrontation*

DEMOCRATS, in their exuberance over the outcome of the fall elections, looked forward to carrying the presidential and congressional contests and nullifying Radical reconstruction in the South. The conservative trend reflected in the election returns once again threatened Republicans with conflicting pressures and intraparty conflicts that could weaken their party organization. Moderate Republicans, apprehensive about Northern voter reactions, would be inclined to resist new Radical demands. Radicals, on the other hand, would press ahead with military reconstruction to guarantee the formation and admission of Republican governments in the South prior to the 1868 presidential elections. Democrats could try to divide the opposition and alert the public to Republican activities in the South. Nevertheless, most Democrats realized that their fate and that of the nation rested in the hands of others, and especially with the president and the Supreme Court.[1]

During the fall the Northern Democratic press continued to counsel noncooperation in the military reconstruction program. This advice was couched in general terms and lacked tactical details. Dixie conservatives, unclear about what form of political action to follow, contributed to the uncertainty. The collapse of the cooperationist movement in the South brought agreement to delay the organization of new state governments, but there were several strategies possible under existing reconstruction legislation. Elections for delegates to the constitutional conventions divided Southern conservatives who met the registration requirements into those who abstained from participation or voted against the convention calls. Although the tallies met the legislative stipulation that a majority of registered voters had to participate to be considered a valid election, the better organized white Republicans and blacks claimed a majority of the actual votes cast and directed the calling of constitutional assemblies.[2]

After initiation for constitution-making passed to the South, Manton Marble of the *World* once again tested the possibility of a compromise settlement. The New York editor was aware that Democrats could not count on much Southern support in the next presidential election. Democratic leaders should enlist the aid of those conservative and moderate Republicans who, in reaction to the recent Northern state contests, might be inclined towards conciliation. Marble advised compliance with the Republican demand that freedmen be guaranteed their civil rights and called upon Democrats to acknowledge this concession. Beyond this, he suggested a compromise suffrage formula that accepted the gradual enfranchisement of Southern blacks; freedmen would be prohibited from voting until after 1868, then granted the franchise with a property qualification, and finally there would be universal suffrage for all descendants of slaves. The suffrage proposal was accompanied by a provision for universal amnesty for all ex-Confederates and a limitation on the tenure of the presidency to a single six-year term.[3]

Marble's plan was acceptable to some conservative Republicans and won a tentative endorsement once again from conservative Wade Hampton and his South Carolina contingent. In general the Democratic response was unfavorable. W. N. Halderman of the *Louisville Courier* agreed that the issue of black civil rights should be removed from politics and urged repeal of the Kentucky law prohibiting admission of black testimony. Yet after the recent Northern elections, few party spokesmen were willing to modify what they considered their advantageous position on the racial issue. At best, they advised that Democrats postpone discussion of compromise plans until after the party had been restored to power. Those less charitable condemned the *World* on the basis of principle or expediency, and some Copperhead purists openly proclaimed that Marble and his cohorts were traitors and subject to expulsion from the party.[4]

Northern Democrats remained committed to a policy of defiance. Disunity among Southern conservatives may have resulted in Radical constitutional conventions, but these still held some prospect for party advantage. Alabama constitutional convention delegates met in early November, followed by conventions in other Southern states, and Democratic propagandists hoped to capitalize on their activities. Supremely confident that the spectacle of black political power would produce a wave of revulsion among Northerners, Democratic spokesmen cited the convention proceedings as evidence of Southern black ineptitude. The Alabama deliberations, claimed William Galloweigh of the *Boston Post,* served as "a perfected demonstration of what is to be the result of the entire experiment. It is nothing more or less than trying to make water run up the hill, to make a pyramid stand on its apex, to make ignorance serve the tune of intelligence, and, in fine, to make black white."[5]

Democrats advised Southern conservatives to adopt a position of political noninvolvement and allow the revolution to run its course. Such a strategy did not mean acquiescence in Radical reconstruction but questioned its legitimacy and provided for its ultimate failure. Southern white passivity would deny Republicans political propaganda and elicit the sympathy of the Northern electorate. A conservative voting boycott of the new constitutions, coupled with the anticipated division among Southern Republicans and personal considerations that might keep others from the polls, could prevent an endorsement of the state constitutions by a majority of the registered voters and cause their rejection. The South would suffer from nonrepresentation in Washington, but this would not last indefinitely and was preferable to the alternative of black domination. C. Chauncey Burr argued that "the Southern States have only to just stand still—resolutely, suddenly still—and they will not be *reconstructed,* but *preserved* as free and honored members of the Union."[6]

The policy of passive defiance gave added importance to the military commanders. Initially, Democrats perceived the reconstruction program as posing a choice for Southern conservatives between continuing the existing state governments without congressional representation or adopting new governments with representation. The persistent intervention of the military in Southern civil affairs violated this perception; the military could create new de facto governments even if Southerners rejected the work of the constitutional conventions. Given this framework, Democratic leaders assumed that noninterference in the affairs of governments sponsored by Johnson was necessary for Southern rejection of the Radical constitutions. The supplemental legislation adopted during the summer authorized extensive military rule, but this could be checked through a change in personnel. Thus Democrats anticipated that Johnson's suspension of Stanton and the removal of several commanders in the Southern districts would benefit their party strategy.

Their expectations seemed about to be realized when General Winfield Hancock assumed command of the Fifth District, including Louisiana and Texas, in late November. Hancock, using his discretionary powers, issued an order proclaiming the district's tranquility and affirmed the supremacy of civil law. A series of decisions followed that identified him with the conservative position. Hancock repealed Sheridan's instructions to local registrars that benefitted Radicals, reopened the registration lists, and annulled Sheridan's order permitting blacks to serve on juries. And he reappointed government officials removed by his predecessor. In response, Democrats hailed Hancock as a patriot, gloated over the reversal of Radical policies, and suggested the general be considered for the party's presidential nomination.[7]

However, they soon realized that the success of their conservative military policy depended on the cooperation of the acting secretary of war. Grant, as ad interim member of the Cabinet, was still a political enigma. There were Republicans who regarded Grant's disagreements with Johnson over reconstruction issues as evidence that Grant might become the standard bearer for their party. Copperheads, distrustful of all things military, were happy to concede the hero of Vicksburg and Appomattox to the opposition. A moderate Democrat like Montgomery Blair considered Grant a conservative and a possible Democratic nominee. Confused by the public tug-of-war over the general's alledged loyalties, Alfred Burr expressed the frustrations of rank-and-file party regulars. If Grant was to be the candidate of either party, he proclaimed, "all this *finessing* must cease. He must show his *colors*. He must either endorse or *repudiate* Radicalism and its negro suffrage."[8]

The House Judiciary Committee's report in late November reduced the apprehensions of Burr and other conservatives. The report included extensive testimony by Grant during the summer that convinced Democrats that the general agreed with the administration's Southern policy and opposed Radical reconstruction. Moderate party spokesmen cited the report as evidence of Grant's loyalty to the president, and, after Hancock's actions in Louisiana, characterized Grant as a decided improvement over Stanton. But an undercurrent of suspicion remained. Republicans who had personal ties with the general continued to claim Grant as their own, and rumors persisted of continued friction between the War Office and the White House. If it came to a showdown between the president and Congress, Grant's ultimate allegiance was still to be tested.[9]

The decision of the House Judiciary Committee to begin impeachment proceedings against President Johnson was a reminder of the dangers in such a confrontation. Though the newly accumulated evidence favored Johnson, a Republican committee member shifted his position at the last moment and provided a majority favorable to impeachment. Samuel Marshall and Charles Eldridge, Democratic members of the committee, dissented on the grounds that the conflict was primarily between the president and the party that elected him. They held that under the impeachment powers conferred by the Constitution, Republicans would be unable to substantiate the charges. However, most Democrats knew that if the opposition were determined to remove Johnson they would not be dissuaded by constitutional scruples. Nor would Republicans be deterred by a possible Senate decision against conviction; if the House concurred in the committee's recommendations, Radicals could gain time and power by suspending Johnson's executive authority during an extended impeachment trial.[10]

What was crucial, Democrats admitted, was public reaction, and there was every reason to assume it would be negative. Democratic party strategists anticipated that if the Radicals persisted in their impeachment efforts, the effect would be to strengthen the conservatives. Washington McLean was convinced that the Democrats would benefit if impeachment proceedings continued, and he openly invited the opposition to press ahead. "The public trial and removal of the President," he declared, "would sink the Radicals lower than plummet ever sounded in political waters." Jeremiah Black, one of the inner circle of White House advisors, counseled Johnson that his political future and place in history would be assured if he dared the Radicals to go ahead.[11]

The advice reinforced the President's own views. Late in November John Coyle of the *National Intelligencer* publicly expressed the White House mood by advising Southern conservatives to stand firm, demanding repeal of the reconstruction acts, and suggesting that impeachment was simply political bluster. Johnson asked Jeremiah Black to formulate the administration's position for a draft of the president's annual message to Congress. Johnson submitted this draft of impeachment-related questions to the cabinet. Their response convinced the president he had his department heads' support in resisting any attempt to restrict or suspend his executive functions prior to a Senate conviction. This display of unanimity prompted Johnson to send the message to the press and Congress.[12]

The reaction was predictable. Republicans considered the publication of the message by the press before its congressional reading an insult and resented the inference in the title page that Congress's extended summer session was illegal. They were distressed by the president's branding of reconstruction acts as unconstitutional, his attack on black suffrage, and his threatened use of force if Congress attempted to suspend him from office. Democrats praised the message and relished the distress it caused Republicans. The one negative reaction by conservatives came from Copperhead purists, who admitted the address was admirable but reminded Johnson that he had helped create the reconstruction problem by his earlier imposition of terms upon the South.[13]

Johnson's defiant attitude raised the question of whether the Radicals could muster support for a concerted counterattack. A preliminary count in the majority caucus indicated they could not. Democrats relished the suggestion that moderate Republicans were frightened by the fall election returns and feared an extension of the impeachment controversy might embarrass or alienate Grant. They fully expected to capitalize on the Republican division when the House Judiciary Committee's recommendation came to the floor for debate. The Radicals attempted to postpone consideration of the report, but minority congressmen joined moderate Republicans in opposition. The final roll call defeated the committee proposal by a two-to-one margin and Democrats were pleased to predict that radicalism was on the wane.[14]

The outcome stiffened Johnson's resolve. Five days after the House vote, the president sent the Senate his reasons for Stanton's suspension. Johnson asserted that the secretary of war had concurred in the administration's policy during Johnson's first year in the White House. But in the New Orleans riot Stanton was primarily responsible for the unfortunate bloodshed for which Johnson had been blamed. The relationship steadily deteriorated after the adoption of military reconstruction and finally forced the suspension. Johnson registered his disbelief in the constitutionality of the Tenure-of-Office Act. He pointed out that the act did not cover Stanton and that the secretary of war had concurred in this opinion himself when the legislation came up for consideration in the cabinet.[15]

After making Stanton's duplicity a matter of public record, Johnson went on to other matters that enraged the Radicals. In mid-December he urged Congress to adopt a resolution commending Gen. Winfield Hancock for his devotion to "law and justice throughout the country." Any remaining doubts about the presidential intentions to refashion the Southern military command along conservative lines were dispelled at the end of the month. Increasingly exasperated over General Pope's high-handed methods, Johnson issued orders for his replacement and the removal of the subdistrict commander in Alabama.[16]

Democrats were delighted with the president's strong stand, but party spokesmen made it clear that in applauding Johnson they were not embracing him as one of their own. The editor of the *St. Paul Pioneer* characteristically noted: "The Democratic Party has no sympathy for Mr. Johnson, personally, and it repudiates all responsibility for his official acts as well as for every omission of duty charged against him." Certainly this questionable support should have made the president wonder whether the Democrats were to be trusted. An exchange on the House floor in mid-December should have heightened his suspicions. Congressman George Woodward, in his discussion of the impeachment issue, asserted that officials could be deposed for offenses not indictable under criminal law. Radicals, delighted that their constitutional arguments had been endorsed by one of Pennsylvania's most prominent Democratic jurists, publicized the speech and were strengthened by an editorial endorsement of Woodward's statement by Washington McLean.[17]

Those conservatives who believed Grant would support Johnson if there were a confrontation between the president and Congress soon were disillusioned. On December 17, four days before the legislators were due to adjourn for the holidays, Grant responded to a request from Congress to forward his correspondence on reconstruction. Republican Congressmen found and read several letters showing disagreement between Grant and Johnson. In a letter written to Sherman prior to the adoption of military reconstruction, Grant acknowledged widespread civil disorder in the South and the need for martial law. In another, Grant protested the removal of Stanton as a violation of the Tenure-of-Office Act and asserted that Stanton's and Sheridan's forced departures were more than "loyal men" could tolerate. The House ordered the letters printed and within a day they appeared in the press.[18]

Montgomery Blair, who had been grooming Grant for the Democratic nomination, wrote Samuel Barlow that he was "astounded" by the revelations and believed his task was "hopeless." Other Democratic advocates of the general came to a similar conclusion. Nevertheless, party moderates refrained from a full scale partisan attack on the popular military hero. It was conceivable that future developments might still prevent Grant's endorsement by the Republicans; it would be foolhardy for the Democrats to identify him with the opposition. Consequently the Democratic press put the best construction it could by claiming the general's protest of Sheridan's removal stemmed from their close personal ties and that the fall election returns had probably changed Grant's attitude on reconstruction.[19]

Good news from another quarter cheered the conservatives. When the Supreme Court met in December for its winter term, Jeremiah Black appealed a lower court's decision against William McCardle, a Mississippi newspaper editor tried and convicted by a military commission for publishing articles critical of the army. On January 10 Black argued that this case could test the constitutionality of the reconstruction acts and requested that it be advanced for an early hearing. Technical difficulties prevented an immediate decision on Black's motion. Nevertheless, the Court implied that a ruling would soon be forthcoming. Jubilant Democrats rejoiced because they assumed that a majority of the justices favored accepting jurisdiction and were probably inclined to find the reconstruction acts unconstitutional.[20]

They were hardly prepared for the swift Republican response. On January 13 the chairman of the House Judiciary Committee called for a suspension of the rules to consider an amendment to a Senate bill on Supreme Court quorum requirements and requested that the bill and amendment be referred back to committee. When the movement for suspension failed, the House proceeded directly to consideration of the proposed legislation. Democratic leaders Samuel Marshall, John Pruyn, and George Woodward immediately took exception to the amendment, which stipulated that future Court rulings on the constitutionality of laws would require a two-thirds majority. The amendment and bill passed by a strict party vote, despite a protest that this action threatened the federal concept of a separation of powers. Many Democrats were shocked and called the House decision one of the most dangerous and flagrant perversions of the Constitution yet undertaken by the opposition.[21]

Others thought the dubious honor belonged to a bill introduced the same day. Encouraged by the Grant correspondence and incensed over Hancock's operations in Louisiana and the removal of Pope, Republican members of the Committee on Reconstruction demanded a change in the army's command system. The general of the army, under the new supplemental reconstruction bill, was empowered to remove and appoint both civil and military officials in the Southern districts, and any attempt to interfere with his authority constituted a high misdemeanor subject to fine and imprisonment. James Brooks in the minority report claimed the bill was designed to secure Grant the presidential nomination. Moderate Republican support for the bill and the obvious discomfort it created for Radical leaders reinforced this view. Despite the apparent division in Republican ranks, the proposal passed the House by an overwhelming majority after a week of extensive debate.[22]

Developments in the War Office weakened Radical resistance to the bill. On January 10 the Senate Committee on Military Affairs, after a review of Johnson's reasons for Stanton's suspension, recommended nonconcurrence in the president's decision and called for the secretary of war's reinstatement. Johnson discussed the situation with Grant the following day and reminded the general of an earlier promise either to continue in the office and force Stanton to appeal to the courts or resign and allow the president to make another appointment. Grant, distressed by his predicament, was unwilling to subject himself to the penalties of the Tenure-of-Office Act, but under pressure from Johnson he apparently agreed to confer with the president on the thirteenth. The general failed to keep his White House appointment. Instead, hearing that the Senate had concurred in the committee's report, Grant quietly allowed Stanton to reoccupy his office in the War Department.[23]

During the mid-January crisis Democrats appealed to Johnson to press the issue with Congress and to use force if necessary. When it became evident that the president was willing to ignore Stanton and the Senate was reluctant to pass the supplemental reconstruction bill or agree to the House Supreme Court amendment, the rhetoric became less threatening. Democrats conceded Grant to the Republicans but continued to use their disagreements with Grant for propaganda purposes. Seizing upon information released by Johnson to the *World* and the *National Intelligencer,* the conservative press criticized Grant for his treachery and deceit. Each new revelation appeared to tarnish Grant's public image. Democrats were content to allow the relationship between the president and Grant to deteriorate in the hope that the general would damage his prospects for the presidential nomination.[24]

Subsequent events confirmed the wisdom of their strategy. By the end of the month journalistic coverage of the Stanton affair and Grant's rejection of Johnson's plan to ignore the secretary of war had strained the relationship to the breaking point. Sensing there might be material to support another impeachment attempt, congressional Radicals in early February called for pertinent correspondence between the president and the general, moved that all impeachment evidence be referred to the House Reconstruction Committee, and launched a subcommittee interrogation of witnesses. Release of the correspondence created an immediate sensation. Democrats were delighted. They insisted the letters substantiated conservative press coverage of the affair, confirmed Grant's duplicity, and convicted him of insubordination. There could no longer be any doubt, one editor noted, that the Radicals had manipulated the general of the army "into a course of conduct that has greatly lowered him in the estimation of his countrymen . . . ."[25]

By mid-February the political situation appeared to favor the conservatives. Both Ohio and New Jersey rescinded their ratification of the Fourteenth Amendment, raising anew the possibility of its defeat. The Supreme Court affirmed its jurisdiction in the McCardle case and prepared for a scheduled hearing of the evidence in early March. In the South, Alabama Radicals failed to win the necessary majority of registered voters for ratification of their constitution, and Northern Democrats, elated over the outcome, advised Southern conservatives elsewhere to follow the Alabama example. The congressional opposition seemed unable to solve its dilemma. Senate Republicans balked at passing a bill to expand Grant's appointment and removal powers when the general's own negative reaction was made known. Nor were they willing to act on another bill that stipulated a simple majority of votes cast would be sufficient to ratify Southern state constitutions. Meanwhile, a new effort to bring impeachment proceedings against the president was defeated in both House and Senate committees.[26]

The possiblity of impeachment continued to cloud the Washington atmosphere. While political observers watched for some dramatic event that might precipitate a final confrontation between president and Congress, the Senate concluded its deliberations on the credentials of Phillip F. Thomas of Maryland. Thomas had been elected by the Maryland legislature to join Reverdy Johnson on Capitol Hill but had been temporarily denied his seat because of alleged disloyalty in providing his son with a small sum of money when the young man joined the Confederate Army. Democrats protested that the act hardly constituted support of the Confederacy, asserted other charges against him were superfluous, and maintained the Republican attack rested on flimsy claims of unproven motivations. However, in the Senate, where a single vote could make the difference in an impeachment trial, the issue of Thomas's loyalty certainly was not the only consideration. On February 19 the Senate moved to reject his claim by a vote of twenty-seven to twenty.[27]

The decision came as Johnson made his final plans to remove Stanton. By the end of January the president had decided to replace the secretary of war and began looking for a suitable successor. Next to Grant, William Tecumseh Sherman was the most popular and influential figure in the military, but he was leery of Washington politics, unwilling to quarrel with Grant, and refused the post. In mid-February the president once again tried to win over Sherman by nominating him general by brevet and ordering the creation of a new Department of the Atlantic, with headquarters in Washington. When this second attempt to bring Sherman to the capitol failed, Johnson decided to act without Sherman's protective presence. On the morning of February 21, the president signed the papers for Stanton's removal and appointed Adj. Gen. Lorenzo Thomas secretary ad interim.[28]

Johnson's move coincided with the arrival of members of the National Democratic Committee in Washington to select a site for the party's convention. Speculation that the president hoped to get the party's endorsement for his removal of Stanton was reinforced by his simultaneous nomination of George McClellan as Minister to England. If this was his intention he miscalculated. August Belmont heard about Stanton's removal in the afternoon when the president's message arrived in the Senate. Dumbfounded, he contacted several Democratic senators, only to find they too had not been informed. Their dismay increased during the next several days as Thomas's efforts to occupy the War Office bordered on the ludicrous. Thomas backed off in his initial meeting with Stanton but boasted he would take the War Office by force if need be. Suddenly, he found himself under arrest. Brought before a district judge, Thomas agreed to post bond and was discharged. Consequently, Johnson missed a choice opportunity to apply for a writ of habeas corpus, and to bring the issue of the Tenure-of-Office Act before the Supreme Court.[29]

Democratic leaders were appalled and made no effort to hide their displeasure. They let the president know they were offended by his failure to inform them before he acted, and they called the handling of the Stanton affair "misadvised." The national committee, in an obvious snub, concluded its scheduled business in Washington and adjourned without any formal statement in behalf of Johnson. Nor was the president successful in a belated effort to reconcile party leaders; in a formal gathering at the While House in early March, only six Democratic Congressmen and one Senator made an appearance. The Democratic press repeated what was becoming a familiar partisan refrain: Johnson was neither the titular leader of the Democrats nor should the party be held responsible for his sins of omission or commission. Thomas S. Bayard, an influential Delaware Democrat noted: "I do not think he has a particle of personal weight with the party who yet . . . look to him mainly for the preservation of the form of our Government. . . .[30]

Democrats were worried that Johnson's removal of Stanton would cause reactions that might threaten the very nature of our constitutional government. Republicans closed ranks when they heard the president's order and prepared to meet the challenge. In an executive session on February 21, the Senate passed a resolution declaring Johnson had acted illegally in removing Stanton from his cabinet post. The House Reconstruction Committee ignored a standing rule against committee meetings while the House conducted business, and voted the following morning to begin impeachment proceedings. Two days later the House voted in favor of the committee report by an overwhelming margin. The Senate on the following day effectively destroyed the conservative Southern strategy of passive defiance and passed a House bill that stipulated ratification of Southern constitutions must be by a majority of the actual votes cast. Their worst fears seemed to be realized. Now the Republicans would probably depose Johnson during the trial, place the Radical Ben Wade, President pro tempore of the Senate, in the president's place, and launch an attack on the Supreme Court.[31]

Despite their low regard for Johnson, Democrats could not stand by and allow a Republican takeover of the government. The president may not have been a man of their choice, but he stood firmly in the way of Radical ambitions. Like it or not, Democrats were bound to support and defend the administration. Speaking in support of the constitutional authority of the president, if not for the man who held the office, House Democrats provided most of the rebuttal on the House Reconstruction Committee's resolution. Throughout the nation Democrats sponsored mass rallies and circulated petitions in support of the president. The heirs of Jefferson and Jackson seemed ready to take strong measures if necessary; Congressman James Brooks threatened in House debate that any attempt to depose Johnson during the trial would be resisted by force, and in Pennsylvania the influential Keystone Club reconstituted itself into a paramilitary organization.[32]

Democratic threats of a resort to arms quickly faded when it appeared that the opposition had reservations about an immediate deposition of the president. There was also a growing conviction that the Democrats stood to benefit by the impeachment trial. As the debate proceeded in the House on the impeachment resolution and subsequently on the Articles of Impeachment, the congressional majority focused its attack almost exclusively on Johnson's attempt to replace Stanton with Thomas. This issue gave Democrats a chance to charge that the Republicans were acting from strictly political motives. James Brooks and Samuel Randall, spokesmen for the conservatives, asserted that Johnson directed Stanton's removal in order to obtain judicial review of the Tenure-of-Office Act. In so doing, the president adopted a course of action well established by historical precedent. Republican efforts to keep the issue out of the courts merely confirmed their own doubts about the legislation's constitutionality.

Those who would impeach the president were on dubious grounds within the context of the act itself. The Republican claims were based on the stipulation in the law that any violation of its provisions would constitute a high misdemeanor; Johnson's action clearly constituted an impeachable offense. Democratic Congressmen George Woodward, George Morgan, and others argued that Republicans would be hard pressed to demonstrate that the president had actually broken the law. According to the first section of the legislation, presidents were restrained from removing cabinet officials they appointed without senatorial consent. Stanton had been appointed by Lincoln, and was not covered by the Tenure-of-Office Act; he held his position solely at Johnson's sufferance. Even if the law could be stretched to cover Stanton, he still occupied the War Office, and the Senate had not confirmed a successor; thus for all intents and the purposes he had not been removed.[33]

The logic of the Democratic position created difficulties for the Republicans. The House committee responsible for drafting the articles, mindful that the congressmen had previously voted against impeachment on other grounds, limited its indictment to Johnson's alleged violation of the Tenure-of-Office Act. The conservative assault may have caused Republicans to question the tenuous nature of their charges. Benjamin Butler sought to expand the indictment by a new article citing the president for offensive acts dating back to the National Union movement. Although Butler's article was rejected, the proposal gave Democrats the distinct impression that those in favor of impeachment were hard pressed; so Democrats looked for the impeachment controversy to have a major impact on the spring elections.[34]

During the pretrial deliberations of the Senate, the Democratic press charged that a resolution condemning Johnson for his attempted removal of Stanton was evidence of prejudice that disqualified judges or jurors in a court of law. When a select committee reported its recommended procedural rules for the trial, controversy emerged over whether the Senate had actually transformed itself into a judicial body. Early in the debate, a Radical took exception to the committee's use of the term "high court." Reverdy Johnson responded that historical precedent and the constitutional requirement of an additional oath for senators clearly implied the Senate would become a court. The Senate at this point appeared to concur in Johnson's reasoning and refused to alter the committee's terminology. However, on March 2, the last day of discussion on procedural guidelines, several Republicans shifted their position and voted to strike all mention of a "high court" from the rules.[35]

The issue had a direct bearing on the powers of the chief justice as presiding officer. According to the committee report Chief Justice Chase was to decide all questions of law and evidence, unless overruled by a majority; by inference, he would be entitled to cast his vote as a member of the "court." Chase's status as a possible Republican presidential nominee, his presence on the tribunal that was expected to cast judgement on the McCardle case, and rumors of his defection from the Radicals created doubts about his authority. This caused Republican senators to divide over modifications of the rules for the presiding officer. A change was made that weakened Chase's authority but avoided a commitment on his right to vote.[36]

Democrats demonstrated as much uncertainty and confusion during the debate as the Republicans did. Nevertheless, Thomas Hendricks emerged as one of the principal spokesman against any restriction of the chief justice's powers. The Indiana senator insisted that the Senate would become a court and that Chase should decide procedural issues that arose during the trial. Henricks stopped short of claiming Chase was entitled to vote and raised a troublesome question about the Senate's mode of operation. Since the Senate would actually become a court, he noted, it could not adopt rules as a legislative body when Chase was not the presiding officer. Hendricks was unable to sway a majority to his point of view, and on March 2 the Senate passed the rules as amended.[37]

Two days later Chief Justice Chase created a sensation with his terse letter to the Senate endorsing Hendricks's position. But Republicans ignored Chase's opinion and received the impeachment articles from the House. That evening the president and his daughter created added excitement by their appearance at a reception held in the Chase residence. The press reports the following morning were filled with speculations about its implications for the impeachment proceedings.[38]

Democrats, now aware they might have an unexpected ally in this former Radical, eagerly awaited the chief justice's scheduled appearance in the Senate. When Chase arrived late, accompanied by an associate member of the Supreme Court, Democrats regarded this as a tacit rebuke for the Republican majority. Subsequent maneuvers reinforced this conclusion. Chase's judicial colleague administered the oath to the chief justice, establishing Chase's position as a full-fledged member of the Senate tribunal. After the chief justice administered the oath to the senators, Hendricks objected to including Benjamin Wade, the President pro tempore and Johnson's successor if Johnson was removed, on the grounds that his addition to the "court" entailed a conflict of interest. Republicans tried to dispute Hendricks's charge, but Reverdy Johnson reminded them that they had opposed John Stockton's vote in his 1866 contested election on similar grounds. A motion to adjourn was challenged by a Radical who objected to terminology, and Chase used this choice opportunity to impose his will and forced a vote on the motion as constituted.[39]

Wade's status was discussed the following day, and the Radicals attemped to cut off debate by using one of the trial rules. Chase responded that the rule did not apply because the Senate had not yet organized for the trial. The Radicals tried to appeal the decision, but moderates and conservatives united to sustain the chief justice. Hendricks, in accordance with a possibly prearranged agreement, withdrew his objection but reserved the right to renew it when the court was fully organized. With his own position strengthened by the Democratic maneuver, Chase administered the oath to Wade.[40]

The inclusion of Wade was not without its benefits for the minority. During the controversy generated by the impeachment movement, Phillip Thomas had resigned his Senate seat and cleared the way for the Maryland legislature to name a successor. The conservatively inclined legislators hurriedly selected George Vickers, arranged for an ice breaker to bring him through the frozen Chester River to Baltimore, and rushed him on a special train to Washington. Vickers arrived in the capital at the right moment. Senators supporting Wade had just argued at great length that he should be seated to ensure each state equal representation. Thus the Senate was hardly in a position to deny a seat to Vickers, even though the Maryland conservative had two sons who were Confederate veterans. In this dilemma, Charles Sumner tried to have Maryland's government ruled nonrepublican. The Senate refused to support the Sumner proposal that would have removed Reverdy Johnson as well as Vickers from the assemblage and allowed the senator-elect to be seated.[41]

The Democratic successes in early March came to an abrupt end on the eleventh. Returns from New Hampshire were disappointing to conservatives and heartening to Republicans. The next day the chairman of the House Judiciary Committee reported a seemingly innocuous Senate bill, passed by the upper house in early January, that expanded the Supreme Court's appellate jurisdiction in trials involving customs and revenue officials. A Republican congressman introduced an amendment to repeal the Court's authority over cases arising from the Habeas Corpus Act of 1867. Charles Eldridge, the ranking Democrat on the committee, had been called from the floor and returned just as the amendment was offered. He was uncertain what was happening and hurriedly questioned Samuel Marshall, a committee colleague, who was also confused. By the time Eldridge reached the Speaker's desk to read the proposal it had been voted on. From there it was sent to the Senate, which concurred in the House revision without debate. Only then did Democrats realize that Congress had acted to forestall a Supreme Court decision in the McCardle case.[42]

Other problems followed. On the thirteenth the president's counsel appeared before the impeachment court and requested forty days to answer the charges. The members of the court allotted ten. The absence of Jeremiah Black from Johnson's legal defense indicated an additional problem. The president was anxious to have a Democrat on his legal team, and selected Black over Allen Thurman, Charles O'Connor, and Samuel Tilden. Though some conservative Unionists objected, his choice reflected the confidential relationship existing between the two men during the past year. But in mid-March Black was involved in a quarrel with Seward that threatened a break with the administration and his resignation as one of the president's lawyers.[43]

The controversy centered on the obscure guano-rich Carribbean island, Alta Vela. Black and his son were lawyers for a Baltimore firm that had secured leasing rights from Santo Domingo, only to be dispossessed in favor of another American corporation. At the time of his appointment to the president's legal staff, the Pennsylvania Democrat had urged the administration to send a warship to the island and enforce his client's claim. He was angered when Seward ruled against him and Johnson refused to reverse the decision. Because Thurlow Weed was involved with the competing firm, Black questioned the impartiality of the secretary of state. Accordingly, he protested to Johnson that "Mr. Seward's little finger . . . is thicker than the loins of the law" and resigned. The publicity aroused suspicions about the administration that were only partially alleviated when several of the impeachment managers were also implicated in the Alta Vela affair.[44]

There were also some unexpected reverses in the Southern reconstruction process. Arkansas was the first state to hold elections under the March 1868 reconstruction act, and at first Democrats believed that the conservatives had won a majority of the actual votes cast and defeated the constitution. Late returns put the outcome in doubt, and by the end of March it was obvious that Congress would become involved in the controversy. The answer to how Republican Congressman would handle this problem came on the twenty-eighth when the House passed a bill for the admission of Alabama. In so doing, the Republicans conceded that a majority of registered voters did not vote for the constitution; thus it did not meet the original congressional provisions established for ratification. Republicans answered that state civil authorities had intervened improperly and proposed that the constitution and the newly elected officials be recognized as a provisional government.[45]

Frustrated by the opposition, Democrats looked to the Supreme Court for relief. Late in March they anticipated a ruling by the Court to the effect that the recent legislation about the judiciary did not cover the McCardle case, and the Court could proceed to render a verdict. When the justices considered the issue on the thirty-first, they merely postponed final judgement until their December term and put off several reconstruction cases not based solely on pleas for writs of habeas corpus. Angered by the delay, Democrats berated the Court for "timidity" and "moral cowardice" and charged them with acting in collusion with congressional Radicals.[46]

These developments weakened the President's position, and when the impeachment trial began at the end of the month most Democrats feared that conviction was virtually inevitable. Under those circumstances, their best line of defense was to emphasize the specious nature of the charges and the partisan motivations of the impeachers, and hope for a division of the opposition. The emergence of Benjamin Butler as chief spokesmen for the prosecution provided a convenient target. The Democratic press attacked his opening argument in order to substantiate their claim that the managers were politically motivated. Butler's speech renewed the dispute over the presiding officer's role, fostered factional divisions among Republicans, and illustrated the underlying political forces involved in the trial.[47]

The issue surfaced when the managers presented their evidence. During the interrogation of a witness, the president's counsel objected to a question. Chase ruled the testimony competent and affirmed his right to make preliminary decisions on points of law. This was objected to by the managers and they moved that the senators retire for consultation. The resulting vote ended in a tie that allowed Chase to claim another prerogative by casting the deciding affirmative vote. In the conference that followed, Radical efforts to restrict the chief justice's authority were defeated, as was a similar motion on the following day when the court resumed it deliberations. Democrats were delighted with the outcome, praised Chase for his independence, and circulated rumors that he might agree to a dismissal of the indictment.[48]

The speculation on dismissal derived mainly from evidence presented by the prosecution. When the managers completed their case after only one week, Democratic onlookers concluded there was little in the testimony that was not known beforehand and no proof of criminal intent by the president. They held that subsequent examination of Lorenzo Thomas by the defense fully dispelled claims of criminal conspiracy. Under skillful interrogation, the secretary of war ad interim admitted his threats to remove Stanton by force were idle boasts not sanctioned by Johnson. Conservatives reasoned that Thomas's testimony confirmed the president's contention that he had acted merely to secure a judicial test of the law, not to defeat it.[49]

They looked to Connecticut to determine the impact of impeachment on the electorate. On April 6, just after the prosecution closed its presentation, Connecticut voters went to the polls, reelected the incumbent Democratic governor by an increased majority, and added several Democrats to the state legislature. Democratic spokesmen claimed that only the state's "rotten borough" apportionment prevented their control of the assembly and characterized the outcome as an indictment of those who favored impeachment. At the same time they sought to exploit any factional tendencies the election might create for the opposition by warning Republican moderates that Johnson's conviction would allow Wade to staff the bureaucracy with Radicals, force his own nomination as vice-president, and ruin Grant's political prospects.[50]

The attempt to turn Grant against impeachment was not successful. On the contrary, the *New York Tribune* reported that the general believed Johnson's conviction was vital to the country's security; since Grant did not repudiate the claim, conservatives concluded the statement was made with his consent. Radicals and Republican moderates appeared equally opposed to using Grant's past relationship with the president in the trial. When Johnson's counsel sought the admission of testimony involving cabinet discussions, Chase made a preliminary ruling that the evidence was pertinent. Republicans immediately voted to countermand the decision, and the conservative press charged the move was designed to damage the president's defense and save Grant's reputation.[51]

This display of Republican unity looked bad for Johnson. When the court finished taking testimony two days later, most observers concluded he stood little chance of acquittal. The chief justice remained the conservatives' one bright hope for an acquittal. Chase had expressed dissatisfaction with courtroom procedures. He soon began to divulge his personal views on the merits of the case. On April 20, for example, he called John Pruyn into his chamber at the Supreme Court. During a conversation with the New York congressman, he commented that Johnson was correct in seeking judical action on the

Tenure-of-Office Act and claimed there was no evidence to warrant a conviction. Nor was Pruyn the only individual to share his confidence, for there were rumors in the press of similar conversations. Democrats looked to Chase to instruct the Senate before the final verdict and possibly influence the outcome of the trial.[52]

Positive developments during the next two weeks inspired a reevaluation of the president's prospects. During the closing arguments William Groesbeck delivered an incisive refutation of the impeachment charges, and conservatives believed it had a marked impact on the Senate. Another member of Johnson's counsel created a flurry of excitement by suggesting that a number of Republicans, including four of the managers, had sought to influence the president in the Alta Vela affair after the impeachment proceedings had begun. Sensing an opportunity to embarrass the opposition, James Brooks introduced a resolution in the House instructing the managers to explain their involvement. Republicans voted down Brooks's resolution and also squelched a subsequent attempt to form a select committee of investigation. But conservatives could find some consolation in the suspicions this incident raised about the prosecution.[53]

President Johnson acted to bolster his position. On April 24, after a discussion with some of his advisors, he forwarded the nomination of Gen. John Schofield as secretary of war. The move had obvious political implications. In making his choice, Johnson chose to nominate an individual who had supported congressional reconstruction and was acceptable to Grant. Schofield's appointment could enlist the support of moderate Republicans who had reason to distrust Stanton and who were alarmed that Wade might become president. At the same time this action could reduce concerns over the course Johnson might pursue if acquitted. Implicit in the nomination was a possible compromise solution to the impeachment crisis; Johnson would refrain from future intervention in Southern reconstruction if allowed to retain his office.[54]

A handful of Senate Republicans were amenable to this kind of compromise. By the end of April, South Carolina, North Carolina, Georgia, and Louisiana adopted constitutions that provided for black suffrage and restricted the voting rights of ex-Confederates. These states, along with Arkansas, represented a victory for the congressional program and guaranteed the Republican party a reasonable chance for success in Southern politics. Consequently, Republican moderates wondered whether the gains from Johnson's conviction would offset its possible disadvantages. Several contacted Reverdy Johnson, who acted as liaison to the White House, and admitted they favored acquittal if the president would publicly disavow further "excesses." Reverdy Johnson believed that the completion of congressional reconstruction under Andrew Johnson was preferable to turning the process over to Benjamin Wade. But he advised that it was too much to ask the president to make the requested public statement. He resorted to an alternative solution and arranged a meeting in his home between the president and Iowa Senator James Grimes, in which the specified assurances were made in private. Grimes, in turn, relayed the agreement to three wavering colleagues.

Other Democrats used similar tactics. One of Johnson's trial strategists wired Samuel Cox to come to Washington and call upon Senator John Henderson, a close personal friend, whose position on the trial was as yet undetermined. Henderson acknowledged that he was under intensive pressure to vote for the president's conviction but had determined to follow his conscience. With Cox's encouragement, he stated his decision in a telegram, which Cox brought to the White House. Johnson was in a despondent mood, but the news cheered the president and gave him renewed hope.[55]

Republican maneuvers attested to the improvement of Johnson's prospects. On May 8, the House adopted a bill to admit Arkansas over minority protests of undue haste. Three days later the senatorial court alloted each member time to state his opinion on the impeachment before a final vote. Buckalew of Pennsylvania tried unsuccessfully to include the views of the chief justice, but this setback was more than compensated for by the discussion that followed. It soon became evident that there were enough Republicans leaning towards acquittal to sustain a verdict of not guilty. Thus House Radicals hurriedly reported a bill for the admission of North Carolina, South Carolina, Louisiana, Georgia, and Alabama. At the same time senators favoring conviction caucused and discussed ways of strenghtening their position.[56]

The following afternoon the court postponed voting for four days because of the illness of Jacob Howard of Michigan. Democrats called the extension a ruse designed to prevent acquittal. They charged the Radicals were using dilatory tactics to secure new recruits from the reconstructed states. In addition, they were attempting to pressure their wavering Northern party brethen. There were rumors during the adjournment that the leaders advocating impeachment had gotton together a million dollar slush fund to either bribe or set up demonstrations to influence the count.[57]

When the court reassembled on May 16, a motion was passed to vote on Article XI, an inclusive proposal charging the president with a series of misdemeanors. It was with this article that the Radicals hoped to muster the necessary thirty-six votes to depose Johnson. Conversely, the president needed only ten Republicans along with nine Democrats for acquittal. As they progressed through the roll call, several whose attitudes had been in doubt voted against conviction, providing Johnson the nineteen votes necessary for victory. Shocked by the result, the Radicals pushed through over Chase's objection a motion for another ten-day delay before proceeding with the remaining articles.[58]

Once again Republicans acted to influence the court. The House managers launched an investigation of the Senate deliberations and attempted to link Daniel Voorhees, Samuel Cox, and other conservatives with a conspiracy involving a professional gambler to improperly influence the outcome of the trial. When the Democrats failed to place one of their congressmen on the committee, they conducted their own investigation to check the Radical offensive. No firm evidence was uncovered to substantiate the charges of corruption against those who voted not guilty, but there were new inferences of misconduct by senators who favored conviction. Nor did the Radical effort to secure the immediate admission of Arkansas and to use the Republican National Convention to support their position succeed. When the court resumed voting on the remaining articles on May 26 it confirmed Johnson's acquittal.[59]

Georges Clemenceau, an observer of the American political scene, concluded "that the Democrats [were] almost as disappointed as the radicals" in the final verdict.[60] This assessment reflected a general suspicion, particularly evident among conservatives identified with Johnson, that Democrats privately hoped for the presidents's conviction. After all, Democrats had urged Johnson to take the actions that led to his impeachment, and during the crisis they refused to give their political endorsement. On more than one occasion they had speculated publicly about the political advantages that might come to them from his removal. Yet they knew that Johnson with all his defects was preferable to a Ben Wade in the White House. Actually, they regarded Johnson's acquittal as the confirmation of their constitutional arguments and hoped the final verdict would create new divisions among Republicans. Thus most Democrats were not disappointed by Johnson's victory.[61]

# 8

## *Search for Leadership*

DEMOCRATS began preparing for the presidential contest even as Congress struggled with reconstruction legislation and the impeachment proceedings. The previous fall elections had seemed to indicate a conservative trend in the country that might produce a new direction in the federal government. But Democrats recognized that success depended heavily on candidates and platform proposals with broad public appeal. They would consider both with care because their decisions involved the future of the party and the nation. The task would have been simplified had Johnson fulfilled their early expectations. He had not, and the search for a replacement threatened a disruptive internal conflict that could jeopardize the conservative cause.

George Pendleton was clearly the leading candidate for Democratic standard bearer as the year began. Youthful, vigorous, and dignified, "Gentleman George" had the manner of a born statesman. As a wartime member of Congress, he had chosen a middle-of-the-road position in the Democratic party. He had supported appropriations maintaining the Union cause, while disagreeing with the Lincoln administration on emancipation, the infringement of civil rights, and the creation of a Union coalition party. His devotion to party orthodoxy earned him the vice-presidential nomination in 1864. During the campaign he won the respect and friendship of many influential Northern Democrats. His personality, experience, and the proven appeal of his greenback plan, gave him a solid political base and advantage for his presidential bid. In January and February Democratic state conventions in Ohio, Indiana, Minnesota, Nebraska, Iowa, Kentucky, and West Virginia endorsed greenbackism and demonstrated their preference for Pendleton. In Illinois a group of influential party men adopted a resolution supporting his candidacy, as did the Springfield *Illinois State Register* and the *Chicago Times.*[1]

Many Democrats remained unconvinced of the merits of his candidacy. While few were personally antagonistic towards Pendleton and most recognized his good character, there were serious reservations about his financial plan. This skepticism dominated New England and the Middle Atlantic states, where there was strong sentiment against the Ohio Plan. The *New York World,* despite some success by soft-money candidates in the fall elections, continued its opposition to redemption of government bonds in greenbacks and asserted that further contraction of the currency and a return to specie payments was necessary to revive the economy. Nor was this sentiment confined to affluent members of the party. In early December the Tammany Hall ticket led by John Hoffman scored a victory in New York City municipal elections over candidates backed by Mozart Hall who were known to favor Pendleton. Elsewhere, New Hampshire and Connecticut Democrats prepared for their spring contests by either rejecting greenbackism or ignoring it altogether.[2]

Although these sentiments reflected conflicting sectional interests, it was doubtful whether the Ohio Plan could attract sufficient recruits, irrespective of section, to ensure national success. The best potential ground for Democratic gains lay among conservative Republicans disenchanted with congressional reconstruction. Generally, they were sound-money advocates who abhorred greenbackism, and their warm support for Johnson's message to Congress favoring further contraction showed little flexibility on the issue. Radical Republicans, on the other hand, were more susceptible to the soft-money appeal, and in Ohio and Indiana they successfully incorporated greenback proposals in their party platforms. Meanwhile, Benjamin Butler of Massachusetts and Thaddeus Stevens of Pennsylvania, two Radical stalwarts, championed currency inflation in Congress.[3]

A special January congressional election in Ohio demonstrated the Radicals' ability to capitalize on the greenback issue. The Republican candidate vying for the Dayton district seat adopted a forthright inflationary position and supported the congressional reconstruction program. Since the contest would be viewed as an indicator of political trends, Ohio Democrats devoted much time and energy to the campaign. But the Democrats were disappointed. Their candidate lost, and hard money advocates like James Gordon Bennett of the *New York Herald* claimed the defeat was a rebuke to the Pendleton forces. If Republicans could so easily preempt greenbackism, its viability as a campaign issue was questionable. One Pittsburg Democrat surmised: "The Radicals through the West are astride Pendleton's horse, so I don't see how that race is to be won."[4]

Eastern Democrats used the Ohio contest to associate greenbackism with the Republicans. Manton Marble charged the Lincoln Administration with responsibility for the emission of unbacked paper currency and declared that "If there be any glory in greenbacks, it all belongs to the Republicans. . . ." The Republican press might denounce Pendleton's scheme as hairbrained, but the New York editor considered the Ohio Plan to be a logical deduction from Republican financial principles; if it was legitimate to pay private creditors in greenbacks, public creditors should be given the same privilege. Marble found Pendleton's plan to be "moderate and cautious" compared to those of most Radicals. But he concluded that the Ohio election demonstrated it was not profitable for Democrats "to water a tree of which their adversaries so easily gather the fruit."[5]

The spread of soft money sentiment across party lines was an additional problem for Pendleton. In December, Republicans in the House of Representatives sponsored a bill that directed the secretary of the treasury to stop currency contraction. The proposal passed by a vote of 127 to 32 and went to the Senate, which endorsed it with the addition of a minor amendment. A resolution of the differences between the two legislative bodies delayed final passage of the bill until late in the month, and Johnson allowed it to become law without his signature. Although the anticontraction law fell short of the demands of the inflationists, it prevented the administration from achieving an early resumption of specie payments and helped curb the clamor for greenbacks.[6]

The halting of contraction, the divisions among Democrats on the greenback question, and the ability of Republicans to outflank them on the issue caused members of the Democratic leadership to doubt the merits of Pendleton's platform. In early February William Bigler wrote Samuel Tilden that although Pendleton was a "good man," he "started an issue on which we cannot unite; at all events it cannot be made the leading issue." Tilden heartily concurred. The major focus of the Democratic campaign, he asserted, should be reconstruction, and financial issues should be relegated to a subordinate position by emphasizing the cost of the congressional program. Charles Mason wrote a fellow Iowa Democrat that the party should endorse a greenback platform only if the Republicans came out unequivocally for paying government bonds in gold; otherwise the Democracy "ought not to raise it."[7]

Conflict over the convention site and date chosen by the Democratic National Committee illustrated the aversion of many Democrats to Pendleton. Cincinnati seemed to be the favored site after the fall elections, but the opposition began to mobilize their forces and Pendleton supporters suspected a conspiracy against their candidate. Washington McLean took exception to the committee's appointment of members from the Southern states as a device to expand the anti-Pendleton forces. Anti-Pendleton midwesterners pressed for St. Louis as an alternative location, and the Johnson administration joined Pennsylvania Democrats in lobbying for Philadelphia.[8]

Rumors surfaced in early January that August Belmont and other financiers wanted New York, but a concerted drive in behalf of the city did not begin until just prior to the meeting of the national committee late in the month. Belmont wrote Tilden, chairman of the subcommittee on convention arrangements, and requested an outline of the advantages of New York over other possible sites. Tilden complied, and the committee finally agreed on Belmont's choice. The committee dealt Pendleton an additional blow by resolving to hold the convention on July 4, a delay generally deemed harmful to his candidacy.[9]

The movement against Pendleton gained momentum in state conventions in the early spring. While California and Oregon Democrats endorsed greenbackism and instructed their delegates to vote for Ohio's favorite son, neither state had enough clout to influence national trends. The Pendleton forces dominated the Illinois meeting, but only after unexpected opposition from the powerful Cook County contingent. On the East Coast, the New York leadership successfully squashed attempts to bring a greenback plank before their convention, and the platform notably avoided the issue. The New York outcome was no surprise to Pendleton's supporters, who hoped to offset it by a win in Pennsylvania. Despite early predictions, they were unable to overcome the influence of state party leaders William Bigler and William Wallace and won only a small fraction of the delegates chosen to attend the national conclave.[10]

Pendleton's financial plan only partially accounted for the opposition he encountered; his wartime image was a major factor. Although he could not be classified a Copperhead extremist by his congressional voting record, conservative Republicans and War Democrats were suspicious. A conservative Unionist wrote Marble that Pendleton could not dispel distrust by turning attention from war-related issues to financial matters. The opposition was too clever to be diverted by the "smoke created by the Greenback humbug" and would confront Unionists with the argument that a vote for Pendleton was an admission they had been "wrong" on the war. The result would be certain defeat at the polls.[11]

To avoid this, conservative Unionists launched their own movement to influence the Democrats. War Democrats believed that they might become the "predominate element in the party." Conservative veterans were contacted and urged to organize the state conventions so they might influence the platforms and choice of candidates. The White Boys in Blue, a veterans's organization formed in Ohio during the fall elections, received special attention. Units appeared in other states to act as a moderating influence within the Democratic party and to check the political activities of the Republican-oriented Grand Army of the Republic. Plans were made for a national soldiers' and sailors' convention in New York to coincide with the national Democratic convention.[12]

The major objectives of these activities, urged one War Democrat, was "to manifest to the country that the Democratic Party is not a Copperhead organization." He shared a common concern with conservative Republicans and moderate Democratic regulars, who feared the fall elections would make the Democrats overconfident and revitalize their Copperhead image. James Gordon Bennett publicly questioned Pendleton's war record and denounced the appearance of prominent Copperheads in the New Hampshire campaign. Manton Marble reminded his readers that the fall victories were primarily caused by the crossover votes of conservative Republicans who were repelled by extremists in both parties, and he warned that a resurgence of the Peace Democrats could drive these allies back into the ranks of the opposition.[13] This concern influenced the operations of the national Democratic leadership. Samuel Randall, chairman of the Washington Resident Committee, arranged for conservative Republicans and War Democrats to dominate the podium at the annual Jackson Day Banquet and helped organize the White Boys in Blue. The new Resident Committee, selected in February with James Doolittle as chairman and moderate Democrats and conservative Republicans making up most of the membership, had a similar orientation. August Belmont, chairman of the national executive committee, solicited advice from disaffected Republicans and in early April wrote an open letter encouraging Democrats to recruit such individuals to the party.[14]

Belmont and other moderates were cheered by the outcome of the senatorial contest in Ohio. Democrats, in control of the legislature, moved to fill the seat held by Benjamin Wade. Clement Vallandigham believed he had an agreement with state party leaders that the appointment would be his in the event of a Democratic victory. Allen Thurman took exception to Vallandigham's claim. Thurman, who had been narrowly defeated in his gubernatorial race, let it be known he wanted the Senate seat and his supporters began a spirited campaign in his behalf. The major obstacle to Vallandigham's appointment was his prominence as a wartime Copperhead, which could keep him from being seated by the Senate. When the legislature finally acted in mid-January, Thurman won the election by a two-to-one majority. Vallandigham was embittered by the setback and not surprisingly refused to attend a reception in Thurman's honor.[15]

The New Hampshire election returns aided the moderate party faction. The Democratic ticket was headed by John Sinclair, who had Copperhead connections but was not an extremist. The campaign assumed major national importance and many prominent conservatives from outside the state made appearances, including former Unionists Montgomery Blair and James Doolittle. Moderates viewed former Copperhead leaders Henry Clay Dean and C. Chauncey Burr as unwelcome intruders. Their involvement in the campaign focused attention on the Democratic party's wartime record and created apprehensions that Sinclair's victory might cause the party rank-and-file to speak or act in a provocative way. Consequently those who wanted to rid the party of the taint of treason found solace in the New Hampshire defeat and a rationale for avoiding candidates like Pendleton.[16]

The Connecticut contest substantiated this view. Democratic moderates and conservative Unionists renominated James English for the governorship, opposed the Pendleton plan, and prevented prominent Copperheads from playing a major role in the campaign. They initially had expectations of a resounding victory. But the New Hampshire returns made them reconsider their strategy, and by late March the Democratic canvass was not going well. Yet English managed to double his previous majority and conservatives nearly won control of the state legislature. Surveying the Connecticut scene, James Gordon Bennett attributed the outcome directly to the avoidance of the peace wing of the party.[17]

Many conservative Unionists believed the Democratic party could win the presidency if it would nominate a man from their own ranks. One individual willing to accept the nomination was General Frank Blair of Missouri. Although he had tried to win Grant over to the Democratic party, Blair soon recognized that the Republicans had captured Grant as their candidate. Blair, a former Republican with a successful army career and an unblemished war record, could count on favorable consideration by War Democrats and conservative Republicans. To offset the fears of Democratic regulars, he strongly opposed congressional reconstruction and threatened to use force to control the Radicals should he become president. Blair counted on his Midwest affiliations to aid him if Pendleton faltered, and he carefully avoided any open confrontations with the Pendleton forces. In the meantime he tried to win support from eastern Democrats by his opposition to Pendleton's financial plan.[18]

Blair's strategy dictated a subtle and low-keyed campaign until just prior to the national convention. The movement to nominate Winfield Hancock was open and aggressive. Hancock's name first appeared among the list of presidential hopefuls because of the favorable reaction to his general order, issued late in 1867, that called for the supremacy of civil law in the South. Johnson's subsequent message to Congress commending the general for his patriotism suggested a White House endorsement of his candidacy. Hancock continued to maintain a high public profile during the winter and early spring. He implemented his general order by setting aside military tribunals, negating his predecessor's directives on the selection of jurors, and removing a number of Radicals from the New Orleans city council. This last action involved him in quarrel with Grant that prompted his resignation as district commander.[19]

Although Hancock's Southern policy stimulated enthusiastic support from the conservative press and serious consideration of his presidential prospects, there was criticism of his candidacy. The allegation that he was directly responsible for the arrest and execution of Mary Surratt was unfair, but he could not explain away this threat to his reputation as a defender of civil liberties. Rumors that he was under the tutelage of Johnson and Seward did little to endear him to the powerful New York Democratic hierarchy. More importantly, critics questioned whether Hancock could compete with Grant for the large and powerful veterans' vote.[20]

Hancock remained a contender. He had significant support from his native Pennsylvania, including that of Senator Buckalew. Doolittle of Wisconsin and Voorhees of Indiana favored him, and the *Boston Post* strongly endorsed his candidacy. His record as a military commander in the Fifth District enlisted the aid of a number of prominent Southerners. However, War Democrats provided the crucial support in his bid for the presidency. In late April the executive committee of the conservative veterans' organization met in New York to plan for their forthcoming soldiers' and sailors' convention, agreed upon Hancock as the best nominee, and sent a delegation to confer with upstate New York leaders in his behalf. Charles Halpine of the *New York Citizen,* the self-styled organ of the War Democrats, called for Hancock's nomination and threatened to bolt the party if Pendleton were chosen.[21]

Grant's Republican alignment prompted some conservatives to look for a candidate with a more prominent military record than Hancock's. General George B. McClellan certainly had the distinguished reputation they sought, but after his defeat in 1864 he had continued his travels abroad. He was still the favorite of many Democrats and especially of the New York leadership. Johnson had tried to use McClellan's popularity and assure Democratic support at the time of Stanton's removal by proposing his nomination as ambassador to England. The president was aware that Senate confirmation would tie McClellan to the administration and jeopardize McClellan's presidential nomination. But New York Democrats disapproved, and McClellan requested that his name be withdrawn. Thereafter McClellan was occasionally mentioned as a presidential possibility, but he resisted any organized movement in his behalf.[22]

After his failure to enlist McClellan for the War Department, Johnson turned to Gen. William Tecumseh Sherman and invited him to Washington. Discussion about the general's political prospects followed. James Buchanan and William Bigler agreed that Sherman was the only person with sufficient military stature and conservative outlook to defeat Grant. Overtures were made, but Sherman rejected Johnson's offer, and his Ohio in-laws who carried on the negotiations reported he had no desire for office. In early March Bigler concluded that Sherman had a "strong dislike" for Stanton and little admiration for Grant but remained a confirmed Republican who distrusted most Democratic leaders. Obviously, his nomination was "out of the question."[23]

When the effort to win over Sherman collapsed, another military figure came under consideration briefly. In March Bigler explored the candidacy of Adm. David Farragut and reported there were conservatives who believed he would be a strong candidate. James Gordon Bennett concurred and suggested that after the New Hampshire election the Democrats should turn to the Navy if they could not come up with a suitable army man to run against Grant. He advised Belmont to move the national convention ahead to May and rally conservatives behind Farragut, but the admiral refused, and the movement quickly collapsed without his support.[24]

A major difficulty facing any military figure was the Democratic suspicion of those who had held position of command in the armed forces. Copperheads resisted any party decision in this direction and showed their disapproval in no uncertain terms. The editor of the *Columbus Crisis* argued that Hancock deserved condemnation for his war record and for implementing Radical reconstruction. C. Chauncey Burr agreed but felt condemnation too mild a penalty and suggested that Grant and Hancock be executed for treason. "Brick" Pomeroy pointed out that previous attempts at compromise had ended in failure and claimed justification in demanding the party search for "a civil rather than a military candidate—for principle rather than policy."[25]

Many moderate party regulars shared his distrust of the military. The suspension of civil law and the power of military tribunals promoted reservations about placing any individual from the armed forces in the White House. Unlike the Copperheads, they could make accommodations to ensure a Democratic victory at the polls. The question was whether a military candidate would guarantee victory. The selection of Hancock could create problems for a campaign based upon the necessity of maintaining constitutional government and would weaken the case against Grant. If Grant were the Republican leader, a Democratic military candidate might lose more votes from party ideologues than he would gain from veterans and disaffected Unionists.[26]

The questionable assets of a military nominee convinced Democrats who had reservations about Pendleton that they should consider other prominent civilians. The editor of the *Oneida Democratic Union* suggested Horatio Seymour, whose selection had obvious merits. Seymour had proven administrative abilities as a former governor of New York, and his wartime record attested to his party fidelity. If his actual position on the war differed little from Pendleton's, his image as a supporter of the Union was less assailable. He had remained in private life since the end of hostilities and was untouched by internal party conflicts over reconstruction and financial issues.[27]

Seymour was reluctant to enter the race. He wrote an open letter disclaiming interest in the presidential nomination and cited personal reasons for his decision. He confided to Samuel Tilden that he needed to "save what little property" he could and hoped that he would be "left alone" after his disclaimer. He was not so fortunate. William Cassidy and Sanford Church, upstate political chieftains, urged him to reconsider his position. William Bigler wrote Tilden that there was strong support for him in Pennsylvania and he regarded Seymour's refusal "as merely a manifestation of his personal desires and not as denying his name and services to the country." Nor were these sentiments confined to the East. A Nebraska Democrat confided to Cassidy that Seymour was "powerful all through the West" and that many Pendleton supporters considered him an attractive alternative. Disturbed by the response, Seymour wrote an open letter disavowing any interest in the presidency and denied that he wanted to win the nomination by subterfuge.[28]

Ill health and repeated disavowals of interest in the nomination temporarily removed him from the public limelight. In March interest in his candidacy suddenly revived. The selection of New York City as the national convention site enhanced the influence of the New York delegation, and upstate confidants reported that Seymour's health was no longer a restricting factor. Seymour confirmed this report by agreeing to make a major speech before the New York state convention. His address attracted national attention. He attempted to compromise on the tough financial question by calling for taxation of government bonds and an economic program designed to bring the greenbacks to full face value. Additional greenbacks could be issued to take care of business needs. Seymour hoped that the program would avoid either dangerous contraction or inflation of the nation's monetary supply.[29]

The speech was acclaimed by the Democratic press and even by some editors who supported Pendleton. The Springfield *Illinois State Register* reported that the address indicated a "real accord between Mr. Pendleton and Mr. Seymour", and the *St. Paul Pioneer* claimed their financial programs differed only in detail. Nor did these indications of favorable sentiment dissipate when Seymour clarified his position to include the payment of government bonds in gold. But his address, contrary to reports, did not imply a reconsideration of his candidacy. Over the protests of his New York promoters, he requested and secured the status of delegate to the national convention, a move certainly not characteristic of one seeking the presidential nomination. He also continued to disclaim any interest in the White House, and his closest confidants on the eve of the national convention insisted that his position remained firm and unwavering.[30]

When it was evident that Seymour was not interested, those who had favored him began looking for other alternatives. In March several New Yorkers, including Seymour himself, publicly praised Sen. Thomas Hendricks of Indiana. Like Seymour, Hendricks was a civilian, a regular party man, and a man whose wartime political image was less controversial than Pendleton's. Although he had endorsed the Ohio financial plan, he was known to be a pragmatic moderate disposed toward compromise. At the Indiana state convention, where he received the party's gubernatorial nomination, Hendricks condemned universal and immediate black suffrage but inferred he supported gradual and restricted enfranchisement. He was the only Senate Democrat to support James Doolittle's proposal for qualified voting for Southern blacks, and he publicly disagreed with James Bayard and Garrett Davis, who stoutly resisted all efforts to moderate the implementation of congressional reconstruction.[31]

The pragmatic attitude of the New Yorkers was calculated to draw support from dissident Unionists and determined their position on Southern strategy. For example, the question of whether the Democrats should allow Southern conservatives full participation in the party's councils was a touchy one. Despite the reservations of some that this would be mean the recognition of the reconstructed state governments, August Belmont extended membership in the National Executive Committee and opened the door for Southern delegates to attend the national convention. This decision ran a risk that ex-Confederates' involvement in Democratic deliberations might alienate Northern voters. But exclusion of the South would virtually concede the section to Republicans once it was readmitted to the Union, an event that was nearly completed in June when Congress recognized seven of the new state governments.[32]

Samuel Barlow attempted to avoid a conservative Unionist reaction against Southern participation in the national campaign by advising prominent Southerners to follow a policy of moderation. He urged that their state conventions adopt resolutions acknowledging the abolition of slavery, the indivisibility of the Union, and the payment of the federal war debt. But his correspondents, while expressing sympathy for these proposals, claimed it would be difficult to secure their adoption. Nor was this resistance confined to the South. C. Chauncey Burr asserted that any Democrat who endorsed acceptance of the South's defeat would in effect be repudiating his party, and the editor of the *New York Day Book* argued the endorsement of such a "rigamarole platform" would "embarrass and probably swamp us altogether. . . ." However, most of the opposition to Barlow's proposal called for the omission of any reference to the war rather than an overt repudiation of its consequences.[33]

Black suffrage was of more immediate concern and far-reaching in its implications. Southern conservatives had failed in their earlier attempts to solicit the black vote and generally remained opposed to qualified or universal suffrage. But there were notable exceptions. In early April South Carolina Democrats led by Wade Hampton recognized the difficulty of gaining power in a state where blacks outnumbered whites and adopted a resolution favoring qualified suffrage. Embittered by this, another group of conservatives held their own convention and repudiated Hampton's platform.[34]

Wilbur Storey of the *Chicago Times* pointed out that the conservative division over Hampton's proposal showed that qualified suffrage was no solution to the Southern problem. Since Storey had earlier endorsed a similar proposition, his rejection of compromise was evidence of the reactionary attitude of most Northern Democrats. Connecticut conservatives condemned both black Southern political power and efforts to broaden the franchise in their own state, and they perceived their victory in the spring as an indication that the racial issue was a major influence on the electorate. A Michigan referendum held on the same day as the Connecticut election reaffirmed this conclusion. Michigan voters rejected a new constitution that included black suffrage by an overwhelming margin. The editor of the *Detroit Free Press* expressed the attitude of many party regulars when he claimed the returns rebuked "those so-called Democrats" who previously "snuffed Negro votes in the breeze. . . ."[35]

This semblance of unity on the suffrage issue was tested by rising interest in the political aspirations of Chief Justice Salmon P. Chase. Speculation over Chase's prospects as a conservative presidential candidate began in the spring during his disagreements with Radicals over the impeachment trial. Initially much of the pressure for his nomination came from independents and disaffected Republicans. In mid-March Charles Dana of the *New York Sun* wrote a series of editorials suggesting Chase's nomination. As the trial drew to a close, James Gordon Bennett dropped his support of Farragut and called upon Chase to head a new conservative party. A small group of Pennsylvania conservatives interviewed Chase, were encouraged by the discussion, and arranged for a meeting of his supporters in early June.[36]

Alexander Long of Ohio joined the movement. Long and Chase had travelled sharply divergent paths since the early days of their association in law and Ohio legislative politics. Chase's antislavery principles had led to the Republican party, where he became the spokesman for Radicals disenchanted with Lincoln's moderate policies. Long emerged as a vehement critic of the Union war effort who denounced the Democratic party for its preoccupation with compromise and eventually launched his own doctrinaire State Sovereignty party. Their previous positions at opposite ends of the political spectrum made their political affiliation improbable. But Long had his reasons for seeking an accord. The collapse of his State Sovereignty party and estrangement from the Ohio Democratic leaders created doubts about his political future. An alliance with Chase would capitalize on Copperhead resentment over the rejection of Vallandigham's Senate bid and bring vindication at the expense of Thurman and Pendleton.[37]

Long contacted the chief justice in early April and suggested his possible nomination. Chase responded that he shared the Democrats' objections to military reconstruction but still supported universal manhood suffrage. He counseled the wisest course for the party would be the endorsement of black rights as a fait accompli. This platform, coupled with universal amnesty, would get his support, encourage the defection of other nominal Unionists, and assure a Democratic victory in the fall elections. Chase denied any presidential ambition but noted he could not prevent the suggestion of his name by others. But Chase was obviously intrigued by Long's suggestion and during April his personal secretary visited Long in Cincinnatti and discussed the promotion of the chief justice's presidential prospects.[38]

These early efforts of Long and others received little support and much criticism from the vast majority of Democrats. Editors of the party press lauded Chase for his role in the impeachment trial but denied any political endorsement. Conservatives vividly remembered his wartime Radicalism and judicial sanctions of undesirable legislation. Midwestern Democrats took special exception to Chase's actions as secretary of the treasury in the creation of the national banking system and government bonding program. If Chase were to seek the Democratic nomination, it would confirm his unprincipled and self-serving ambition.[39]

In late May the Chase movement gained new recruits because of the outcome of the Republican National Convention. Since late winter political observers believed Grant had the inside track on the Republican nomination. But many Radicals distrusted him and unforeseen developments might prevent his selection. When Republican delegates met in Chicago, the maneuvers of the anti-Grant forces came to nothing. The Republican platform strengthened the general's nomination. The convention steered between the rival factions on the financial issue; government bonds were to be redeemed according to the letter and spirit of the law, without stating whether this meant in gold or greenbacks. The plank on political enfranchisement called for federal guarantees of black suffrage in the South but left it to state control elsewhere.[40]

The moderate nature of the platform suggested Republicans were relying heavily on Grant's popularity to carry the campaign. Democrats would not find it easy to run against a military hero. Pendleton had supporters in the party but would be no match for Grant in a popularity poll. However, "Gentleman George" remained the frontrunner among conservatives who demonstrated any interest in the Democratic nomination. In early May he failed in an all out effort to secure a binding endorsement from the Michigan Democratic Convention but counted on significant support within the delegation selected to the national assembly. This same pattern occurred in several other states, including Missouri, where he won a fifth of the delegates despite the candidacy of Frank Blair. Pendleton could not sustain the momentum needed for a first ballot victory, but he continued to gain strength and led in the delegates either committed to him or leaning in his direction.[41]

Eastern Democratic moderates and especially those in New York were disturbed. None of the other conservatives seeking nomination appeared to generate much public enthusiasm, and with Pendleton as the party's nominee they believed Grant's election was virtually assured. The possibility of Chase's conversion to the Democratic party provided a choice opportunity. The chief justice was one of the major figures of the era. If he could be induced to join the Democrats, the impact on the Republican organization could be divisive. His popularity among blacks might also influence the Southern black vote. New Yorkers concluded they had little to lose and much to gain by courting Chase for presidential nominee.

John Dash Van Buren, a young New York engineer and former aid to Seymour, wrote his Democratic mentor prior to the Republican convention and urged the nomination of Chase on a platform of universal amnesty and universal suffrage. Seymour needed little prodding; he joined Democrats in the Albany home of William Cassidy to discuss the chief justice's candidacy. Reports circulated in the press of Seymour's support for Chase, and other prominent New Yorkers also became involved. Samuel Barlow privately urged prominent conservatives elsewhere to consider Chase, and the *New York World* began testing public opinion on his behalf. Not only state party leaders were involved. Charles Halpine of the *Citizen* endorsed Chase, and several ward bosses inside Tammany Hall did so as well.[42]

The chief justice's position on black suffrage was the main obstacle to his nomination. Late in May Chase wrote August Belmont about political matters and reaffirmed his support for black voting rights. Chase's position was firm; so Chase's nomination depended upon Democratic concessions. In early June Manton Marble proposed a compromise solution. Since reconstruction was virtually completed in most of the Southern states, the wisest course for the party was merely to claim suffrage a subject for state control. Such a platform inferred recognition of the new Southern governments and pledged nonintervention in their internal affairs in the future. However, it came out against any changes in the suffrage by a Republican-controlled Congress.[43]

The New York campaign was a limited success. Some conservatives responded favorably, but the overwhelming reaction from Democratic regulars was negative. Senator James Bayard of Delaware expressed the party faithful's outlook that black suffrage was the vital issue separating Democrats from Republicans; concede this and it would make little difference who became president. Montgomery Blair concurred and labeled the *World's* platform impractical and immoral. On the basis of the results of recent state referendums, he condemned any attempt to dismiss a major issue that could restore the party to power. Threats of a third party movement, if the national convention conceded black suffrage and nominated Chase, lent additional weight to such counsels.[44]

The torrent of criticism raised by the *World's* proposal forced Marble to clarify his position. He explained that he wrote the editorial to determine Democratic attitudes on black suffrage prior to the convention and to test the feasibility of Chase's nomination. In so doing, he had not asked the party to subscribe to the chief justice's views but merely to ignore the race issue. Should the Democrats concur in Marble's platform, they would not necessarily be committed to Chase. Marble predicted that Democrats would eventually have to accept black suffrage but conceded that the reaction to his editorial indicated the time had not yet arrived. Marble concluded that "if a large part refuse to recognize negro suffrage as a *fact,* there need be no more breath or ink wasted on a candidate who represents it as a *principle.*"[45]

Marble's explanation troubled Chase's promoters, but they could not ignore its logic. Obviously further Democratic consideration of the chief justice necessitated some concession on his part. Chase already entertained such a possibility. He wrote John Van Buren that an appreciable number of Democrats might accept the principle of universal suffrage if left under state control. Chase recognized that these individuals were probably a minority in the party and would have limited influence at the national convention, but he appeared willing to test the proposal in the public forum. The day after the appearance of Marble's explanation, Chase wrote a letter for publication containing his revised platform.[46]

The letter kept consideration of his political prospects alive during the remaining two weeks before the convention. Even if Chase were not the nominee, his support of the ticket could have a significant impact on the campaign. Those who continued to court him knew they had to avoid the appearance of manipulation for their own partisan gain. Cassidy wrote Seymour: "Mr. Chase must not be left to think he as been trifled with." Their strategy was of necessity subtle and low-keyed. Marble wrote several editorials favorable to Chase and suggested that Democrats adopt a moderate position on black voting. Wilbur Storey supported this pragmatic advice by resuming his advocacy of impartial suffrage. Meanwhile, arrangements were made for Tilden to visit Chase, and on June 25 Seymour spoke at Cooper's Union in support of the chief justice.[47]

While Chase had his difficulties with Democrats on black suffrage, he faced another obstacle from conservatives allied with Johnson. The president had scrupulously avoided involvement in the preconvention maneuvers during the impeachment proceedings but became active when the trial ended. On May 16 Bennett of the *Herald* reported rumors of negotiations between Johnson and Chase supporters to create a coalition against Grant. One of Tilden's confidants went to Washington for an interview with Postmaster General Alexander Randall. Randall spoke of the President's desire to defeat the Republicans and suggested that Chase and Hancock would make the best conservative ticket. The Negro suffrage issue could be resolved if Democrats simply left the question to state determination.[48]

By early June Johnson's political lieutenants had revised their position.

It may have been that their earlier efforts were designed to influence the chief justice and the Senate in the closing stages of the trial. With the trial behind them, they took issue with the *World's* editorials on black suffrage. Gideon Welles criticized Marble for advocating acquiescence in the imposition of black political power on the South. John Coyle of the *Intelligencer* claimed that the New York editor should not be considered a spokesman for conservatives. Marble retorted that this criticism stemmed from Johnson's fears the proposed platform would eliminate him as a candidate; if so, it was of little consequence to the Democrats.[49]

Subsequent actions by Johnson's supporters substantiated suspicions that he wanted the nomination. With the impeachment trial over, there were several ways to promote the president's candidacy. The power to confer amnesty was one, and Johnson's supporters extended the promise of a general amnesty to entice Southern delegates. They solicited Northern Democratic support by reviving discussions of cabinet changes. They played down their differences with New York party regulars, approached Seymour with thinly veiled offers of a cabinet position, and through Samuel Cox attempted to persuade the *World's* staff to give the President "a just and fair hearing." They were encouraged by Seymour's response, but most Democrats were unwilling to ignore previous problems with the administration and were incensed that Seward was not among the cabinet members considered for removal. Johnson could expect little support from the large and powerful New York delegation.[50]

The president completed the list of prominent conservatives interested in the nomination. Of these, Pendleton came closest to representing the main stream of the Democratic party, and this in large part accounted for his strength. But conservative Democrats saw his war record as a negative factor, and his Ohio Plan hurt him in the East. Johnson, Hancock, Blair, and Chase opposed greenbackism, but their war records were unacceptable to many party regulars. Hendricks' sectional identity, party fidelity, and pragmatism offered a possible compromise between the major conservative factions. However, Hendricks was no match for Grant. Republicans had drafted their platform and selected a ticket with minimal acrimony. The preconvention squabble among Democrats was not the united position they needed for victory in the fall.

# 9

## *Seymour and Blair*

By JULY 1 Tammany Hall had completed arrangements for the Democratic National Convention to be held in a newly constructed building off Union Square. Democratic delegates from the country, supporters of candidates, and spokesmen for special interest groups began to converge on New York. As the convention-goers passed through Washington, Philadelphia, or elsewhere, representatives of the candidates stepped up their efforts to gain the delegates' support. On the eve of the convention, reports and rumors of last minute strategies and predictions about convention actions increased.

A contingent of Pendleton supporters, routed through Pennsylvania in an attempt to influence delegate opinion in that state, arrived in New York on June 30 and checked in at the Fifth Avenue Hotel. Although some predicted the nomination of Ohio's favorite son on the first ballot, most observers gave little credence to such reports. Washington McLean offered a more plausible estimate when he suggested "Gentlemen George" would receive 170 votes on the first ballot. McLean based his estimate on good Southern support and a strong endorsement from the Midwest. He knew his projected total fell thirty-five votes short of the total necessary for nomination if the convention adopted the traditional two-thirds rule, but it constituted a comfortable majority that could turn into victory for his candidate. Consequently McLean hoped for Pendleton's selection by the third ballot.[1]

Pendleton needed to maintain and solidify control over delegations that had indicated an early preference for him. Observers found latent midwestern sympathy for Hendricks, and there were rumors of an impending bolt by Indiana and Illinois from the Pendleton column. The threat was alarming, for it virtually guaranteed the defeat of the greenback champion. Already suspicious of Hendricks, whom they viewed as a stalking horse for New York interests, Pendleton's aides let it be known that they would not take these defections lightly. On July 1 they breathed easier after Senator Hendricks sent a letter to his delegation declining to be a candidate. The Indiana and Illinois delegates caucused and agreed to support Pendleton until Ohio changed its position.[2]

The Pendleton forces were less fortunate in the Wisconsin and Michigan delegations. Although the Wisconsin contingent had instructions to support a greenback platform, it had no similar mandate on the presidential nomination. Its uncommitted status motivated August Belmont and other Pendleton opponents to offer the convention's temporary chairmanship to Henry L. Palmer of Milwaukee. In a preliminary caucus, highlighted by an impassioned plea from a War Democrat, the Wisconsin delegates defeated a resolution for Pendleton by a vote of nine to seven and agreed to support James Doolittle initially. Similarly, Michigan Democrats resolved to save their strength for the later stages of balloting by concurring on a complimentary vote for Senator Reverdy Johnson.[3]

Unexpected aid for Pendleton came from Missouri and Frank Blair. Blair trailed far behind in committed delegates, so he sought additional interest in his candidacy by writing about his political views to James Broadhead, the chairman of the Missouri delegation. The letter, released to the press, revealed the general's belief that the reconstruction acts were unconstitutional and called for the president to order the army to "undo its usurpations at the South." The move was an obvious attempt to win the sympathies of doctrinaire Democratic regulars, many of whom were pledged to Pendleton. As a further effort in this direction, the Missouri delegation caucused and resolved to support Pendleton on the first ballot. Blair hoped to pick up future strength from the Pendleton column if and when the Ohio politician faltered.[4]

Blair sought at the same time to infiltrate the Southern bloc of sixty-five votes. There he ran into stiff competition from representatives of the other major contenders. Southerners were gratified by these solicitations but noted that they raised a troublesome problem. If Northern Democrats were divided between eastern and western factions, the South could exercise the balance of power and determine the eventual nominee. Were they to do so, they would almost certainly provide the Republicans with effective propaganda, and Southerners decided their best strategy would be to keep a low profile. Johnson's amnesty proclamation, issued on the first day of the convention, provided a way out. Although the president's amnesty fell short of the South's expectations in excluding ex-Confederates under indictment, it was still a welcome gesture. Dixie delegates, believing Johnson had little chance of gaining additional Northern support, resolved to vote for him on the first ballot.[5]

The Southern decision elated Johnson's strategists, and they hoped that a deadlock between the major candidates would eventually bring him the nomination. But there were frustrations in laying the necessary groundwork. After preliminary reports of the president's intention to deliver a blanket amnesty, the limited nature of the proclamation came as a disappointment to some Northern Democrats, and the failure to have it read before the convention diluted its impact on others. Johnson's advocates also faced a problem with the local press; after drafting a letter for the *World* favoring the president's candidacy, they found Marble unwilling to publish it. Nevertheless, they looked to the president's ability to influence Northern Democratic congressmen and information at Johnson's disposal to exert a favorable influence.[6]

The political orientation of the South and Midwest meant that the northeastern delegations occupied a crucial position. Although some from this section leaned towards Pendleton, he was opposed by the leadership who could not agree on a suitable alternative. Their immediate concern was to weaken Pendleton, and they resorted to sponsoring a number of favorite son candidates. Maryland, with Blair temporarily withdrawn from contention, decided to back Reverdy Johnson. Connecticut decided to support Gov. James English, and New Jersey rallied behind Joel Parker. Pennsylvania, an important state because of its large delegate bloc and electoral vote, agreed to support Asa Packer, the wealthy railroad magnate and former congressman from Carbon County, and averted a divisive conflict between Pendleton, Hendricks, Hancock, and Chase.

The New York delegation was enmeshed in last minute deliberations. Seymour was clearly the favorite and speculation held that his Cooper's Institute speech in late June indictated he might accept a draft. However, he reasserted his opposition to nomination in a caucus of the state's delegates, and the New Yorkers agreed to abide by his wishes. In addition, Seymour agreed to serve as permanent convention chairman and provided confirmation of his unwillingness to enter the presidential race.[7]

Seymour's stated preference was Chief Justice Chase, who remained under pressure to modify his position in accord with that of rank-and-file Democrats. On July 1 the Chief Justice took an another step in this direction by releasing a proposed fifteen-point program. He restated his preference for universal suffrage under state control but opted for flexibility on the financial issue with the reservation that creditors should not be favored in the interpretation of federal law. He attempted to broaden his support by calling for the withdrawal of troops from the South, except where necessary to maintain order. When Chase was pressed for a date for removal, he responded that it should begin immediately. This was as far as he would go. Conservative appeals to rule the reconstruction acts unconstitutional were denied. Irrespective of newspaper reports to the contrary, he refused to bind himself to the future Democratic platform or nominees.[8]

The New York delegation had its second caucus the day after the publication of Chase's platform. Seymour, Barlow, and Belmont backed the chief justice but faced opposition from Tilden and Church. A poll of the New York delegation revealed an even split between Hendricks and Chase, with a small segment for Pendleton. Stymied by the division, the New Yorkers cast their first ballot for Church as a favorite-son candidate. Those leaning towards the chief justice claimed the decision was to Chase's advantage, and they planned to nominate him at a later date. Tilden, on the other hand, concluded that the selection of Chase was now out of the question. Editor Bennett of the *Herald* thought he detected a conspiracy: "a stroke of strategy in the nice little game concocted by the Albany Regency for Seymour's nomination."[9]

The convention began its formal business on Saturday, July 4. Belmont made the opening speech, presented Henry Palmer as temporary chairman, and after disposing of preliminary matters, they voted to adjoun until the following Monday. The second session was more eventful. The Committee on Organization named Seymour permanent chairman and recommended adoption of the rules governing the previous national convention. Because these rules included a requirement that the nominees receive a two-thirds vote, their endorsement hurt the Pendleton forces. The Ohio Democrat did not challenge the traditional two-thirds rule and called instead for the adoption of the platform prior to the nominations. Midwesterners were heartened by its passage. They believed the majority of the delegates were sympathetic to greenbackism and predicted that any candidate selected would have to run on a soft-money platform.[10]

The report of the platform commmittee on Tuesday, which endorsed the Ohio Plan, confirmed their expectations. If midwesterners could find fault in the financial plank, it lay in the omission of any reference to the national banking system which they largely opposed. The call for economy in government and reduction of the armed forces was an issue conservatives of all hues could readily support. The committee tried to reconcile conflicting interests over the tariff by proposing "a tariff for revenue" that would provide incidental protection for domestic manufacturers.[11]

If the platform favored the Midwest on economic issues, it was more balanced on reconstruction. Johnson's supporters welcomed the section that expressed gratitude for the president's resistance to congressional "usurpations," while his critics applauded the demand for an extension of amnesty to include all political offenses. Party doctrinaires welcomed the branding of the reconstruction acts as "unconstitutional, revolutionary, and void." Moderate Democrats and conservative Republicans feared the statement might be interpreted as a pledge by the Democratic administration to overthrow the new Southern governments, and they were pleased that the platform was more temperate on the suffrage issue. Setting aside the demands of those who declared the race issue to be the "Alpha and Omega of the Democratic faith," the platform committee pronounced suffrage a matter for state regulation.[12]

The Pendleton forces hailed the platform as a victory but soon discovered it did little to augment their strength. In the week of preballot maneuverings they had revised their estimates of support on the first roll call downward from 170 to 125 votes. The initial poll of the convention on Tuesday gave them only 105. Andrew Johnson received 65, and all but a few votes were from the South.The remainder were scattered among Hancock and favorite son candidates. The next four ballots disappointed the Pendleton supporters. They had hoped for sizable gains from the South, but Governor Parsons of Alabama and serveral other influential Southerners were allied against them. Johnson's strength steadily declined but Pendleton's gains were negligible. He managed to pick up some Southern support, but his total increase by the end of the session was merely seventeen votes. The Indiana delegation did not help when they retreated into conference, prompting rumors of an impending bolt.[13]

Pendleton supporters' apprehensions were realized on Wednesday morning. An Indiana delegate, speaking for a majority of his state's representatives, announced the delegation's switch to Thomas Hendricks before the resumption of balloting. Pendleton continued to gain on the next two ballots, largely because of further shifts among Southerners. But the defection of Indiana, signalling a fragmentation of his midwestern base, was the beginning of the end. By afternoon, West Virginia, Illinois, and Kansas withdrew their support. At the end of the day only Ohio and a few other hard-core delegations remained, leaving Pendleton with a total of 56 votes.

Winfield Hancock became the immediate beneficiary of the change. Hancock's initial support came from Mississippi, Louisiana, and Massachusetts, and other delegations, particularly from Southern and border states, moved into the Hancock column after the Pendleton boom peaked. The executive committee of the conservative veterans' convention, although not mandated to do so, announced their unanimous support for the general. By 3:00 P.M. the Pennsylvania delegates went over to Hancock, and it appeared a nomination was in the making. On the next three ballots his tally climbed to 144 votes, and with Hancock apparently on the verge of final victory, the convention adjourned for the day.[14]

That evening the Ohio delegation held a prolonged and stormy meeting. Washington McLean read Pendelton's letter of withdrawal and noted that he was obliged to present it to the convention in the morning. Then the Ohioans talked over their strategy. Some favored casting their lot with Hancock, virtually guaranteeing the general the nomination. Those suspicious of Hancock's military background were adamantly opposed. Nor was there a consensus in behalf of Hendricks, because many delegates believed that the senator had violated his earlier pledges to Pendleton. Reports of a movement for Chase concerned them. Most Ohio Democrats tried to block this movement by voting to oppose any endorsement of Chase. They disbanded without indicating whom they would support.[15]

The tactics of prominent New Yorkers helped Ohio keep the situation fluid. The New York delegation had been voting for Hendricks since early morning and watched his total steadily increase as Pendleton's fell. Rumors of Pendleton's withdrawal might dramatically increase the Indiana senator's tally. Although some New Yorkers favored Hendricks' nomination, others viewed their support as a stopgap measure. Concerned over the possibility of a Hancock or Hendricks bandwagon, Seymour spent the evening buttonholing New York delegates for Chase. Meanwhile Barlow, Tilden, and Benjamin Wood met with Thurman, McLean, and George Pugh to discuss a common strategy[16]

The following morning the Ohio delegation caucused once again and agreed to cast their next ballot for Asa Packer, in an obvious move to wean Pennsylvania away from Hancock by resubmitting the name of its favorite son. At the same time Seymour introduced a formal resolution to support Chase before the New York delegation. A poll of the members indicated the majority leaned towards the chief justice, but proponents of Hendricks' candidacy countered that it would be not be wise to drop the Indiana senator before his vote peaked. This argument was respected, and the New Yorkers agreed to switch to Chase only when Hendricks's tally began to decline.[17]

When the balloting resumed Hancock's strength had crested and a Hendricks boom was in the making. On the nineteenth roll call Henricks's vote rose from a previous high of 87 to 107, and three additional ballots brought it to 145. At this point Clement Vallandigham, appointed to fill a sudden vacancy in the Ohio delegation, approached Samuel Tilden. Vallandigham was one of the few Ohio Democrats known to be sympathetic to Chase, and he urged New York to switch to the chief justice. Tilden replied that the caucus agreement of his delegation prohibited such a move. Vallandigham then sought out Seymour and asked him to step aside as presiding officer while Ohio placed his name in nomination. Seymour responded as he had to similar offers earlier in the convention—he flatly refused.

Under the circumstances, Vallandigham concluded he had no other option but to ignore Seymour's reply. He returned to his delegation and conferred with George McCook, a close personal friend since childhood. McCook called the Ohio contingent into hurried consultation, gained the floor, and nominated Seymour. The New Yorker immediately objected but Vallandigham and Francis Kernan of New York reflected the mood of the assemblage when they requested that the delegates ignore his protest. Seymour was suddenly and forcibly removed from the hall by political associates, and the stage was set for his nomination. Wisconsin requested that its vote be switched to Seymour, and one by one the other delegations followed suit until the New Yorker had the nomination by acclamation.[18]

The choice of the vice-presidential candidate was anticlimatic. Because Seymour was an easterner and a civilian, ticket-balancing dictated that the second spot go to a military man and westerner. There were a number of possibilities, including Thomas Ewing of Kansas, Asa Dodge of Iowa, John McClernand of Illinois, and Frank Blair of Missouri. Blair's earlier strategy finally paid off. By his sharp condemnation of the reconstruction acts in his Broadhead letter and his ability to hold the Missouri delegation to Pendleton until Pendleton's formal withdrawal, Blair generated sympathy among doctrinaire party regulars and hard-core Pendleton supporters. He easily won the nomination of the first ballot despite the conservative veterans' preference for Ewing.[19]

The New York convention provided the country with a confusing and paradoxical profile of the Democractic party. An obvious discrepancy existed between the platform provision on national finances and the economic activities of the party leadership. Seymour did not hold government bonds, but his position had always been closer to the bondholders than the greenbackers, and few took his immediate affirmation of support for the platform seriously. The National Democratic Committee once again chose Belmont as chairman, selecting a symbol of New York banking to manage a campaign supposedly directed against eastern banking interests. The party's stance on reconstruction further complicated the situation. Democrats made much of their desire to attract conservative Republicans and independents to the ticket, but the reconstruction plank was not likely to enlist their enthusiastic support. Nor did the choice of candidates provide a counterweight; Blair, theoretically picked to win over conservative Unionists, was even more vehemently opposed to the reconstruction process than Seymour.

Critics of the Democratic ticket detected what they believed to be a backstage conspiracy for Seymour. Some detractors traced the conspiracy to Wall Street bondholders who wanted to protect their investments. Others believed Tammany Hall was the culprit, and they charged the political machine sabotaged the party nationally in order to carry New York state and local elections. In either case critics claimed that the New Yorkers successfully schemed to eliminate the leading contenders and entered into an agreement with Ohio delegates on Wednesday evening that led to Seymour's selection. Rumors that Seymour may have been a party to the plot created obvious difficulties for those who planned on making Grant's alleged deceit as acting secretary of war a major issue in the campaign.[20]

Andrew Johnson believed Seymour was not above reproach. Angered at the New Yorkers for their previous lukewarm attitude toward his administration, Johnson was in no mood to be favorably disposed toward the ticket. Reports from his convention managers aroused his ire. They charged the New York delegation had swayed the convention away from any endorsement of the administration as part of their overall plan to nominate Seymour. They claimed the governor had reneged on a promise, made the evening prior to the final ballot, to refuse the nomination and support Johnson. Johnson understandably viewed requests to support Seymour's campaign as an added insult.[21]

The party could not afford to ignore a president whose control over patronage and the army might be decisive in the fall elections; so Democrats in Washington suggested that the New York leaders visit the White House and placate Johnson. Tilden, Seymour, Barlow, and Belmont were unwilling to make the trip and sent John D. Van Buren instead. Their meeting was a fiasco. Van Buren described the President as "not only cross but implacable." Johnson criticized Seymour for his failure to help the administration and brought up a statement, attributed to the governor during the impeachment trial, that the president's conviction would aid the Democrats. Van Buren responded with inferences that Johnson himself had acted less than honorably and that Seymour could win the election without his support. After their quarrel, the Democratic Resident Committee cancelled plans to serenade the president that evening, and Democrats in the capitol advised Tilden and Seymour never to use Van Buren as an emissary in the future.[22]

Although Johnson's hostility toward Seymour stemmed largely from personal difficulties with New York Democrats, he reflected a general attitude among conservative Unionists. Many conservative Republicans and War Democrats were dissatisfied with the platform and the ticket and questioned whether they could support the party's nominees. In Seymour's own state, Weed and

Seward publicized their intentions of voting for Grant, a position endorsed by the *Times* and the *Herald*. The executive committee of the New York conservative veterans' organization, representing 2,300 members, openly condemned the party's presidential nominee. Surveying the local scene, Samuel Barlow lamented that the convention had created "almost universal execration and despair."[23]

While some discontented conservatives endorsed Grant, others explored alternatives. One possibility was the formation of a third party, and this was widely discussed immediately following the convention. This movement made little headway because of the short time remaining before the elections to make arrangements and the obvious damage it could inflict on the conservative cause. Another option would be to encourage Seymour, who had not yet responded to the draft, to decline the nomination. If he could be induced to withdraw, it was reasoned, the National Democratic Committee would have to provide a substitute ticket. It was hoped the new candidates would be an improvement.[24]

Meanwhile Chase positioned himself to take advantage of the discontent among disgruntled conservatives. Confidants discounted his pledge to support the results of the convention and asserted that although Chase considered himself a Democrat he was unhappy with the party's reconstruction plank. Nor could he endorse Seymour. The chief justice refrained from public criticism of Seymour, but Chase's personal secretary and Alexander Long worked together to encourage Seymour's withdrawal. Letters poured into Utica advising the Democratic nominee to place party needs above personal ambition. William Rosecrans, an influential figure among conservative veterans, visited Seymour and counseled withdrawal. After a lengthy discussion, Rosecrans left without any firm indication of Seymour's eventual decision.[25]

Endorsements of the ticket by important segments of the Democratic party offset the activities of Chief Justice Chase's adherents. George Pendleton immediately gave his support and authorized Washington McLean to publicize a preconvention letter from Pendleton describing Seymour as a man highly qualified for the White House. Hendricks fell into line, and editorials in the *Columbus Crisis* and the *Old Guard* stressed Copperhead acceptance of the ticket in spite of the activities of Alexander Long and his clique. There was evidence that inroads had been made among conservative Unionists; Senator Doolittle campaigned for Seymour, Charles Halpine offered to solicit the veterans' vote, and Hancock, who next to Johnson was the candidate most disturbed by outcome of the convention, was ready by the end of July to give his assent.[26]

Those who awaited some sign of public reaction watched the Kentucky elections in early August. Kentucky may not have been the best barometer of Northern opinion, but it was the only one immediately available, and political observers gave it more than the customary attention. The returns favored the Democrats, and conservative candidates maintained control of statewide offices by increased margins of victory. The Northern elections of the previous fall and Kentucky's election returns appeared to confirm a rising voter dissatisfaction with Radical reconstruction. The Kentucky vote also suggested the national Democratic ticket and platform had strong potential appeal. Even a political independent such as James Gorden Bennett, who had earlier proclaimed that the nomination of Seymour and Blair guaranteed the election of Grant, made a sudden turnabout and suggested that the outcome was an open question.[27]

Seymour made his final decision to accept the Democratic nomination on August 4, the same day as the Kentucky elections. He told Doolittle that his delay in announcing was due to a "vague idea that the political programme might be changed" but concluded that the "uprising of the people" and the "spontaneous, unanimous and enthusiastic" nature of Democratic rallies had convinced him to accept the honor tendered him by his party. The draft of his letter of acceptance was moderate in tone. Seymour attacked the congressional program but claimed a Democratic victory would not entail revolutionary changes. Whatever the outcome of the contest, the Senate would remain under Republican control, and a Democratic president and House of Representatives would merely provide a check on future Radical excesses.[28]

The nature of the developing Republican campaign determined Seymour's defensive position. After years of political crisis, civil war, and economic dislocation, the public wanted stability. Grant capitalized on this desire by a plea for peace in his letter of acceptance. He retired to his Galena home in apparent serenity, while Republican orators campaigned on the theme that peace could come only through support of the congressional program. Conversely, they charged that the Democrats had started the Civil War and threatened the present peace. They cited the Democratic plank declaring the reconstruction acts unconstitutional and Blair's Broadhead letter as evidence that the Democrats intended to overthrow the new Southern state governments. They also claimed the Democrats wanted to repudiate the war debt and disrupt the nation's economy.[29]

Republicans lowered the tone of the campaign by implying that the Democratic candidate was an unstable person. They charged Seymour's family was afflicted with a history of hereditary insanity; his father and uncle committed suicide during periods of mental illness, his mother spent three years in an insane asylum, and the governor's personal record indicated he was probably subject to the same weaknesses. His ambivalence toward the Union cause illustrated a basic weakness in character, and his handling of the New York draft riots suggested an inability to function in a crisis. If Seymour had hesitated to accept the presidential nomination, it was because he recognized his own incapacity. Since he would not be able to stand the strain of the presidency, the office would eventually go to his running mate, and the country could not expect much improvement because Blair was an intemperate alcoholic.[30]

Democrats denied these allegations and devised a counteroffensive. Seymour's father had not committed suicide because of insanity but rather to end the misery of a debilitating physical illness. Nor had the mother been confined to a mental institution. Far from exhibiting a tendency toward psychological disorder, the Seymour genealogy was resplendent with men of distinction in law and politics. Democrats extolled their candidate for his intellectual abilities and denounced Grant as a fool. The governor composed his speech before the draft riot and subsequent address to the rioters to reduce, rather than inflame, passions. If there were any questions about the wisdom of his actions, Seymour's supporters pointed to letters of commendation from Lincoln and other high-ranking Republicans. And Blair's supposed intemperance was nothing when compared to Grant's own record of drunkenness.[31]

The Democrats had a harder time handling the financial issue. Midwestern Republicans sought to offset the appeal of the Democratic greenback plank by the charge that eastern bondholders engineered Seymour's nomination and the governor was a captive of creditor interests. Midwestern Democrats denied this and pointed out that Belmont and other bondholders favored Chase rather than Seymour at the convention. Yet the Republican propaganda was bothersome, and Seymour was deluged with requests to set the matter right by a public declaration of his support of the platform's greenback provisions. Seymour refused and continued his overall campaign strategy of maintaining dignified silence at home in Utica. Eastern Democrats either opposed greenbackism or shifted the focus of the financial issue away from the taxation and payment of government bonds to the costliness of congressional reconstruction.[32]

Problems emerged in handling reconstruction issues. Chief among these was the meaning of Blair's Broadhead letter and the Democrats' intention in declaring the reconstruction acts null and void. Republicans charged the Democrats with revolutionary motives and presented their party as the champions of constitutionalism and civil law. Democrats were hard pressed to explain the apparent inconsistency; if the party pledged to use the army to overthrow the Southern Radical governments, it would be acting outside the framework of law. Charles Buckalew recognized this dilemma and spoke for many of his fellow conservatives when he advised "no such extreme action." Buckalew's disavowal of Blair's threatened use of force did not answer the question of what Democrats would do if they gained the White House. Conservatives who shared Buckalew's perspective met this problem by claiming that all the president had to do was remove the army and Southern Radical governments would topple of their own accord. However, there were drawbacks to this solution; it implied that Democrats would fail to execute federal laws and would countenance domestic disorders.[33]

News reports from the South were far from reassuring to the Democratic leadership. Republicans claimed that the New York platform and the Broadhead letter were responsible for speeches by Southern conservatives that excited political and racial passions and led to armed attacks by vigilante groups on carpetbaggers and blacks alike. Northern Democrats questioned the truth of these Republican assertions. They charged the opposition with attributing fabricated statements to the ex-Confederates and distorting isolated incidents of civil strife deliberately. The New Orleans riot two years earlier was recalled, and Democratic spokesmen made clear that the Radicals were the ones who had used violence. "The Radicals want an outrage," proclaimed Alfred Burr of the *Hartford Times*. "They are suffering for an outrage. They want a mob, dearly want a mob, and down South they are resolved to have one."[34]

William Rosecrans sought to produce tangible evidence of the peaceful intentions of Southern conservatives. In late August he journeyed to White Sulpher Springs and conferred with the revered Confederate general, Robert E. Lee. The meeting produced a letter signed by Lee and thirty-one other prominent ex-Confederates. Southerners reaffirmed their desire for peace, denied hostility toward freemen or the federal government, and explained their opposition to black political control on the grounds that blacks were not yet capable of exercising it wisely. Rosecrans forwarded the letter to the press and wrote Seymour that the National Democratic Executive Committee should encourage its ratification by the various state committees. He also suggested that Southern Unionists and moderate former secessionists speak in selected Northern locales.[35]

Lee's moderate position, in opposing black domination rather than black suffrage per se, reflected a renewed effort by some Southern conservatives to capture the black vote. To offset the Republican offensive, Southerners created Seymour and Blair organizations for blacks, fostered black glee clubs, and entertained freedmen at political rallies. During August and early September reports reached the North that large numbers of blacks were being recruited by the conservatives. Thus many Northern Democrats downplayed their opposition to black suffrage, assured the freedmen they had nothing to fear from conservatives, and predicted major Democratic gains in the Southern elections. Others, while willing to accept a division of the Southern black vote, used the specter of black suffrage to solicit support in their own localities.[36]

Improved relations between the party and the president boosted Democratic morale. Seymour asked Senator Doolittle to act as intermediary between the party and Johnson after the Van Buren fiasco, and Doolittle arranged a meeting between Seymour and John Coyle of the *National Inelligencer*. Coyle subsequently reported that Seymour denied any hostility toward Johnson, welcomed the president's advice, and would consider Johnson for an appointment in a future Democratic administration. Johnson's response was cordial and he gave assurances through his aides of his support for the Seymour-Blair ticket. In a widely publicized interview with a delegation of Tennessee conservatives at the end of August, Johnson reaffirmed his support. Democrats recognized the limitations placed on Johnson by the Tenure-of-Office Act and the Southern situation, but they expected his endorsement of their ticket would mean patronage aid and restrictions on military intervention.[37]

The optimism of late August, occasioned by the Kentucky victory, reports of black recruitment, and Johnson's endorsement, began to dissipate in September. On the first of the month, Vermont went Republican by an increased majority. A week later Democrats managed to retain control of the California governorship by a slim margin but lost one congressional seat. On the basis of these returns, conservatives revised their predictions on the Maine contest to be held on the fifteenth. Democrats had hoped for a marked increase in the percentage of the popular vote and launched a spirited campaign that included speaking engagements by Pendleton in Augusta, Bangor, and Portland. But returns from the early September elections had a chilling effect, and party spokesmen cautioned against overoptimism. On election day their fears were confirmed when the Republican gubernatorial candidate nearly doubled his previous victory margin.[38]

Some observers perceived political organization to be the Democratic campaign's major problem. The National Democratic Committee and its executive superstructure constituted the official body representing the party-at-large, but the committee, because of its composition, had difficulty meeting with any regularity. Midwestern antipathy toward eastern bankers, the financial plank, and Belmont's own unenthusiastic response to the platform and candidates indicated that the chairman should not play a major role. Consequently Tilden, Seymour's campaign manager, maintained a discreet distance from Belmont and the national organization. Because Belmont had solicited large sums of money from wealthy friends and associates for the campaign, the New York banker did not accept his downgraded position cheerfully and complained of conspiracies to deny him a foreign mission if Seymour were elected.[39]

Seymour tried to strengthen the party's organization by creating local clubs similar to the Jackson Clubs in Connecticut and New Jersey. Their goal was to enlist young men who were not attracted by existing organizations, and Seymour believed the best way to do this would be to make the new Order of Union Democrats a secret society. James Spencer of New York, who conceived the idea, launched the movement. The response was mixed. Clubs took root in some localities, and membership grew rapidly. Elsewhere, particularly in urban areas, they encountered difficulties. Old-line politicos regarded these organizations as competitive with existing clubs and as unnecessary duplication. Spencer also faced opposition to a secret society because many recalled the earlier party struggles against Know-Nothingism.[40]

General Rosecran's plan to present the Southern conservative leadership as moderate and concilatory over black voting rights was another strategy yet to be fully implemented. In mid-September Rosecrans conferred with the New York State central committee and urged ratification of Lee's position on reconstruction. He left the state convinced that the New Yorkers would be "timid in executing the plan." He asked Seymour to urge the committee "to act promptly and boldly" and suggested that Horace Day be the coordinator for the Southern states. Day worked hard and had some success; Democrats in Tennessee, Georgia, Louisiana, and South Carolina endorsed resolutions for the protection of blacks exercising their legal right of suffrage. Elsewhere he found substantial resistance and urged Seymour to use the national committee to encourage Southern compliance.[41]

The attempts by Day and Rosecrans to develop a coordinated campaign policy were the exception rather than the rule. One member of the national committee from Nevada complained that the Democrats worked well individually but lacked overall organization and leadership. Seymour himself conferred regularly with Tilden and was kept informed about the activities of Spencer and Day. Regular reports from N. E. Paine, Seymour's Midwest field agent, and random correspondence from other Democrats across the country helped fill in the picture. Yet Seymour complained of being "almost isolated," and this condition of affairs was troublesome. Late in the month he confided to Tilden that the Democrats had confused the public by their conflicting statements on the issues. What was needed, he suggested, was a clarification of the party's position and systematic direction of its activities. To achieve this unity he recommended the creation of an informal "Privy Council" of ten or twelve advisers.[42]

Seymour's suggestion stemmed in part from pressure exerted upon him by Democrats in Ohio, Indiana, and Pennsylvania. These three states, containing a sizable bloc of electoral votes, held their elections in mid-October, and it was generally conceded they would have a major influence on the November presidential contest. Democrats had been optimistic about carrying all three, but the outcome in Maine and the Northern reaction to reports of Southern violence added a new note of apprehension. When it appeared that the Republicans were making inroads, Democratic activists became increasingly fearful that more defeats would follow, and they urged action by Seymour in soliciting New York funds and in public appearances.[43]

Seymour was unwilling to campaign in person, but other prominent Democrats converged on the states to stump for the party. On September 23 Hoosier conservatives dramatized their campaign with an immense rally in Indianapolis. After a procession led by the White Boys in Blue veterans' organization, Pendleton, Hendricks, Blair, and other distinguished party spokesmen addressed the gathering. Five days later a similar demonstration was held in Cincinnati before a crowd estimated at nearly 25,000. In both instances Democratic orators focused on Republican monetary policies and the issue of black equality. These efforts did not obscure the obvious signs of difficulty. In Ohio, Vallandigham's congressional candidacy was an embarrassment to the national leadership, as were the continued attacks by Alexander Long and his cohorts. Hendricks, an early favorite to win the Indiana gubernatorial election, became alarmed over the decline in the number of his supporters and challenged his relatively obscure opponent to public debate.[44]

Additional problems arose in Pennsylvania. The Democrats had been gaining in Philadelphia, and, with local party regulars in control of Navy Yard patronage, they expected to carry the city. But Democrats needed to curtail Republican strength in the west to carry the state. William Wallace, state party chairman, decided to concentrate on the western districts where the greenback issue had its strongest appeal. Pendleton appeared at rallies in Greensburg, Pittsburg, and elsewhere, and other soft-money advocates stumped the area. But their efforts were checked by local concerns over tariff policy. Meanwhile party leaders in Philadelphia resented Wallace's failure to concentrate on their city and complained of his mismanagement of the campaign.[45]

In Philadelphia on October 2 Republicans staged a huge parade of veterans that included wagonloads of disabled soldiers and former Confederate prisoners. Democrats attempted to counteract this extravaganza by enlisting the aid of prominent conservative generals. Seymour and Tilden, prodded by William Bigler and other state leaders, asked William Franklin, Hancock, and McClellan to enter the campaign. Franklin agreed, but Hancock refused because it would be unprofessional for army officers to engage in politics. McClellan gave half-hearted support; he refused an invitation to attend a large rally in New York on October 5, but he did forward a letter indicating his support of the Democratic party. However, he failed to mention either Seymour or Blair, and his tribute to Grant's military record weakened the effect of his endorsement. Republicans saw an opportunity to exploit the occasion and claimed McClellan personally preferred the election of Grant.[46]

The returns on October 13 confirmed Democratic apprehensions. Although the party's total vote in Pennsylvania, Indiana, and Ohio was larger than that of the previous year, the Republican tally was even greater. Pennsylvania Democrats carried the Philadelphia mayoral contest but fared less well throughout the state; Republicans won the election for auditor general and nearly doubled their majority in the legislature. Similar results were soon forthcoming from the Midwest. Ohio Democrats lost their bid for secretary of state, the only statewide office in contention, and in Indiana Thomas Hendricks saw his commanding lead turned into a narrow defeat.[47]

The setback provided a welcome opportunity for some disaffected conservatives. A small group of Chase supporters, including Alexander Long, Henry Reed of the Cincinnati *West and South,* and Col. William Brown of Frankfort, Kentucky, had continued to criticize Seymour's candidacy and predicted defeat if the New Yorker remained on the ballot. They calculated that the early fall election returns would confirm their predictions of disaster and force Seymour's withdrawal. The chief justice took exception to their efforts but refused to endorse either presidential candidate or rule out his own entry if the Democrats decided to change their ticket.[48]

In early September other prominent Democrats began considering the possibility of a new slate of nominees. Long conferred with Vallandigham, who agreed to withdraw from his congressional race and endorse Chase if the Democrats lost in Maine. Vallandigham had second thoughts about withdrawing after the Maine election but indicated he was willing to support Chase if Republican victories continued in October. Long was given similar assurances by William Rosecrans, who visited him in Cincinnati. Samuel Barlow also sounded out confidants about replacing Seymour with Chase if the opposition carried Pennsylvania, Ohio, and Indiana.[49]

The discouraging October returns gave new strength to the movement to change the presidential nominee. Washington McLean suddenly shifted his support to Chase and, together with Long, Vallandigham, and Pendleton, met with Frank Blair in Cincinnati. The vice-presidential candidate agreed that prospects for victory were slim and that he would submit his resignation as a candidate if requested to do so by the national committee. Blair went directly to St. Louis and announced his decision at a scheduled rally. In the interim, Long sent his law partner, George Hoeffer, to Washington to confer with Chase. Hoeffer wired Long that the chief justice was amenable to a draft, and Long announced that he had received a telegram from Chase that indicated he was willing to accept the nomination.[50]

Additional pressure to change the ticket came from conservatives outside of Cincinnati. Manton Marble, in an editorial in the *World*, called for the Democratic leadership to exercise a "bold stroke of policy" and cast aside "any impediment to success which can yet be removed. . . ." Marble inferred that it was Blair rather than Seymour who was the impediment, but the editorial was the first public proposal of a change in the nominees and focused attention on the issue. Wilbur Storey, influenced by Marble's comments, notified Tilden that there was strong support for Chase in the Chicago area. Washington conservatives identified with the Johnson administration also sprang into action. Alexander Randall urged Tilden and the national committee to replace Seymour with either Chase or Johnson, and John Coyle gave his support to the movement in the columns of the *Intelligencer*. Meanwhile Seward visited Democratic leaders in New York City on a mission of personal diplomacy.[51]

The final decision remained with Tilden and Belmont, and they faced significant problems if they chose to revise the ticket. With only a few weeks remaining before the presidential election, it would be virtually impossible to reconvene the national convention. If the national committee made the change on its own, it risked the charge of violating established democratic procedures. And the likelihood remained that any change of nominees would further divide the party. Chase was most frequently mentioned as a substitute for Seymour, but it was not clear whether the chief justice would consent to run on the existing platform. Supporters of Hendricks, Hancock, Johnson, and McClellan viewed this as an opportunity for their own favorites. The response to Marble's editorial also indicated that a segment of the Democratic party firmly supported candidates Seymour and Blair.[52]

Belmont and Tilden were not troubled by their decision. On October 17 they conferred with Seymour. He reminded them he had been drafted against his wishes and that any alteration of the ticket would prompt his own withdrawal, but that he was willing to step down in the interest of the party. The two committee members assured Seymour they did not want a change and that such an attempt would be catastrophic. Their decision was passed on to other national party leaders. When queried by Jonah Hoover of the Washington Resident Committee, Belmont and Tilden, joined by Augustus Schell, responded that any proposal for a new slate of candidates was impractical and would be made without endorsement of the national organization. Two days later they drafted an even stronger statement in reply to a telegram from Wilbur Storey; they asserted the proposal to scrap the current nominees was not only "wholly unauthorized" but also "absurd." Similar communications, released to the Associated Press, quickly killed the movement for a new ticket. Although there was lingering discussion of the idea, political leaders suggested as replacements soon disassociated themselves from it.[53]

Once again united behind Seymour and Blair, Democratic spokesmen worked to arouse the party rank-and-file for the final contest in November. Belmont distributed a statement that emphasized the common interests binding conservatives together, denied Republican charges that the Democratic party intended revolution, and extolled Seymour's patriotic record. On the same day the Indiana State Democratic Central Committee released a circular in which it claimed there were grounds for optimism in the recent Hoosier returns. The committee asserted that conservatives could have carried the statewide contests were it not for Republican fraud and corruption and noted that Indiana Democrats had increased their representation in the House in spite of a gerrymandering of the legislative districts. Conservatives stressed the increase of Democrats in the Pennsylvania and Ohio congressional delegations and concluded that Democrats did better on national than local issues. This evidence confirmed their belief that they still might carry the presidential election.[54]

To win, the Democrats had to capture the public's attention. On October 20 Seymour announced he would make a series of public speeches in the North. Democrats remembered all too well Johnson's "Swing around the Circle" and feared this "hazardous experiment" might tarnish Seymour's image. However, the candidate avoided personal attacks and volatile rhetoric. If the electorate feared extremism, he asserted, it should be wary of the Republicans, for the Democrats intended no violation of law and order. He conceded to the Midwest that there was an unequal regional distribution of money and agreed that transportation costs deprived farmers of reasonable profits. But Seymour would not cater to the demands of the soft-money proponents and continued to claim that goverment retrenchment was the major solution for the nation's economic difficulties.[55]

Seymour's last minute effort had little impact on the election's final outcome. When the voters went to the polls on November 3 they simply confirmed the predictions of most political analysts. Grant won 52.75 percent of the popular vote and 214 of the 294 votes to be cast in the electoral college. Seymour's strongest support came from the mid-Atlantic region—he carried New York and New Jersey—and from the border states of Maryland, Delaware, and Kentucky. Outside these two areas he won only Oregon, Georgia, and Louisiana. Three additional states—Virginia, Mississippi, and Texas—might have voted for the Democratic nominee but could not participate, since they had not completed the reconstruction process. A comparison of the presidential returns with those cast in state and congressional elections underlined the significant role played by the national candidates. Democratic candidates for state offices, including those in New York, tended to poll a larger percentage of the vote than Seymour and Blair, and Democratic congressional nominees increased their strength in the House of Representatives. The probable coattail effect of the Republican national ticket, and the public's perception of the presidential candidates, obviously had a major influence on the election.[56]

It would be misleading to overemphasize the role of personalities. Seymour and Blair symbolized the Democrats, and their defeat was as much a rejection of the party as of the candidates themselves. Their failure arose from the legacy Democrats inherited from the war. Republicans repeatedly reminded voters that when the Union cause seemed darkest there were Democrats who called for peaceful separation of the states or criticized the Lincoln administration's conduct of the war. To dismiss this as mere rhetoric ignores the depth of emotions evoked by the Civil War. The war was still too close in time and too costly in human terms for Americans to react in a strictly pragmatic manner.

Democrats inadvertently rekindled wartime passions by their postwar strategy. They championed full restoration of political rights for prominent ex-Confederates and seized upon the Radical Republican movement for black civil and political equality as confirmation of their predictions about the consequences of emancipation. Their strategy stressed conservative domination of Southern state governments and vindication of previous Democratic policies. If Republicans had successfully manipulated the race issue to achieve power, Democrats resolved that it could be used equally well to bring about Republican defeat.

Northern attitudes on black suffrage constituted the crucial element in the strategy. Early postwar referendums indicated most Northern whites strongly opposed voting rights for blacks in their own states. Moreover, Northerners appeared reluctant to concede Radical Republican demands for an extension of the ballot to Southern freedmen. If voting rights for Northern and Southern blacks were interdependent and inseparable, Democrats could rightly conclude that they had the opposition cornered. If Republicans failed to press for black suffrage in the South, they faced the prospect of a revitalized Southern Democratic party. If they campaigned for votes for blacks, they could expect a widespread Northern backlash. Either way Democrats stood to gain both compensation for their wartime tribulations and a guarantee of their party's future success.

Their grand design governed their tactical relationship with the Johnson administration. Democrats courted the president when he entered the White House and championed him when he rejected the Radicals' demands. They assumed that Johnson and other like-minded Unionists would return to the Democratic party, augment its ranks, and share in its future victories. The president rejected Democratic overtures because he feared association with the party's wartime heritage of treason and defeatism. Instead he attempted to fashion a new organization in which conservative Unionists were dominant. Democrats regarded Johnson's plans for a new party as an attack on their legitimacy and a personal affront. They refused even symbolic admissions of their alleged treason and defeatism and clung to their partisan identification. Confident in their strategy on black suffrage, they were certain the president would eventually accede to their terms.

The Democratic position produced unexpected results. Angered by the Democratic rejection of the Fourteenth Amendment, congressional Republicans used their 1866 election triumphs as a mandate to impose black suffrage upon the South. Democrats waited in vain for the predicted Northern white backlash. Although the 1867 state elections indicated some initial disenchantment with Radical reconstruction, a transformation of Northern opinion was already underway. By the fall of 1868 the shift in public attitude became fully evident when two states—Iowa and Minnesota—passed referendums endorsing black enfrancisement. Democrats had correctly predicted a correlation between Northern and Southern Negro suffrage but not the form in which it finally arrived. The returns indicated that most Northerners preferred granting blacks the ballot to elevating ex-Confederates or suspected Copperheads to power. For Republicans, the presidential contest cleared the way for universal black male suffrage by constitutional amendment. For Democrats, it marked the bankruptcy of their strategy pursued since the end of the war.[57]

# NOTES

## CHAPTER 1

1. Allan Nevins and Milton Thomas, eds., *The Diary of George Templeton Strong,* 4 vols. (New York: Macmillan, 1952), 4:15.

2. An extensive treatment of the War Democrats may be found in Christopher Dell, *Lincoln and the War Democrats: The Grand Erosion of a Conservative Tradition* (Madison, N.J.: Farleigh Dickinson University Press, 1957). Dell's classification includes many party regulars as well as Democrats who supported coalition tickets.

3. Wood Gray, *The Hidden Civil War: The Story of the Copperheads* (New York: Viking Press, 1942), pp. 32, 61, 109, 152, 205; Erwin Stanley Bradley, *The Triumph of Militant Republicanism: A Study of Pennsylvania and Presidential Politics* (Philadelphia: Pennsylvania University Press, 1964), pp. 424–30; Charles Knapp, *New Jersey Politics during the Period of the Civil War and Reconstruction* (Geneva, N.Y.: Humphrey, 1924), pp. 13, 83; Stewart Mitchell, *Horatio Seymour of New York* (Cambridge, Mass.: Harvard University Press, 1938), pp. 256, 382.

4. Gray, *The Hidden Civil War,* pp. 21–26; Frank Klement, *The Copperheads in the Middle West* (Chicago: University of Chicago Press, 1960), pp. 13–14, 33–34; Paul Kleppner, *The Cross of Culture: A Social Analysis of Midwestern Politics, 1850–1890* (New York: Free Press, 1970), pp. 38–48.

5. Ibid., pp. 71–82.

6. Leonard Curry, *Blueprint for Modern America: Non-Military Legislation of the First Civil War Congress* (Nashville, Tenn.: Vanderbilt University Press, 1968), pp. 149–206; Klement, *Copperheads in the Middle West,* pp. 3–11, 83; Gray, *Hidden Civil War,* pp. 126–27; Arnold Shankman, "Conflict in the Old Keystone: Anti-war Sentiment in Pennsylvania" (Ph.D. diss., Emory University, 1972) pp. 133–34.

7. V. Jacque Voegeli, *Free But Not Equal: The Midwest and the Negro during the Civil War* (Chicago: University of Chicago Press, 1967), pp. 125–27; Roy Abrams, "Copperhead Newspapers and the Negro," *Journal Negro History* 20 (1935): 131–52; Forrest Wood, *Black Scare: The Racist Response to Emancipation and Reconstruction* (Berkeley: University of California Press, 1968), pp. 17–38; Frank Klement, "Midwestern Opposition to Lincoln's Emancipation Proclamation," *Journal of Negro History* 49 (1964): 169–83.

8. For an introduction to Copperheadism see William Carleton, "Civil War Dissidence in the North; The Perspective of a Century," *South Atlantic Quarterly* 65 (1966): 390–402; and Richard Curry, "The Union as it Was: A Critique of Recent Interpretations of the Copperheads," *Civil War History* 13 (1967): 25–39.

9. There is no general study of the moderates as a prototype, but Leonard Curry's "Congressional Democrats, 1861–1863," *Civil War History* 12 (1966): 213–29; Joel Silbey's *A Respectable Minority: The Democratic Party in the Civil War Era, 1860–1868* (New York: Norton, 1977), pp. 89–144; and Michael Les Benedict's *A Compromise of Principle: Congressional Republicans and Reconstruction* (New York: Norton, 1974), pp. 339–48 are instructive.

10. Coverage of Ohio politics can be found in George Porter, *Ohio Politics in the Civil War Period,* Columbia Studies in History, Economics, and Public Law, vol. 40 (New York: Longmans, Green, 1911).

11. Frank Klement, *The Limits of Dissent: Clement L. Vallandigham and The Civil War* (Lexington: University Press of Kentucky, 1970), pp. 123–25, 138–84.

12. Robert Rutland, "The Copperheads of Iowa: A Re-examination," *Iowa Journal of History* 52 (1954): 1–30; Hubert H. Wubben, "Dennis Mahoney and the *Dubuque Herald,* 1860–1863," *Iowa Journal of History* 56 (1958): 289–20; Olynthus Clark, *The Politics of Iowa during the Civil War and Reconstruction* (Iowa City: Clio Press, 1911), pp. 187–90.

13. Frank Klement, "Copperheads and Copperheadism in Wisconsin: Democratic Opposition to the Lincoln Administration," *Wisconsin Magazine of History* 42 (1959): 182–88; Frank Klement, "Brick Pomeroy: Copperhead and Curmudgeon," *Wisconsin Magazine of History* 35 (1951): 106–13, 156–57; Alfons Beitzinger, *Edward G. Ryan: Lion of the Law* (Madison: State Historical Society of Wisconsin, 1960), 67–81; Richard Current, *The History of Wisconsin,* vol. 2, *The Civil War Era, 1848–1973* (Madison: State Historical Society of Wisconsin, 1976), pp. 404–7.

14. Arthur Cole, *The Centennial History of Illinois,* vol. 3, *The Civil War Era, 1848–1870* (Springfield: Illinois Centennial Commission, 1919), pp. 298–300; Kenneth Stampp, *Indiana Politics during the Civil War,* Indiana Historical Collections, vol. 31 (Indianapolis: Indiana Historical Bureau, 1949), pp. 170–75.

15. Knapp, *New Jersey Politics,* pp. 79–91.

16. John Talmadge, "A Peace Movement In Civil War Connecticut," *New England Quarterly* 38 (1964): 306–20; John Niven, *Connecticut for the Union: The Role of the State in the Civil War* (New Haven: Yale University Press, 1965), pp. 306–8.

17. Arnold Shankman, "William B. Reed and the Civil War," *Pennsylvania Magazine of History and Biography* 53 (1964): 294–315; Irwin Greenberg, "Charles Ingersoll, The Aristocrat as Copperhead," *Pennsylvania Magazine of History and Biography* 93 (1969): 190–217; William Dusinberre, *Civil War Issues in Philadelphia, 1856–1865* (Philadelphia: University of Pennsylvania Press, 1965), pp. 153–54, 166; Shankman, "Conflict in the Old Keystone," pp. 159–61; Bradley, *The Triumph of Militant Republicanism,* p. 161; Alexander McClure, *Old Times Notes of Pennsylvania,* 2 vols. (Philadelphia: Winston, 1905), 2:44.

18. Coverage of New York politics may be found in Sidney Brummer, *Political History of New York State during the Period of the Civil War,* Columbia Studies in History, Economics, and Public Law, vol. 39 (New York: Longmans, Green, 1911); and Jerome Mushkat, *Tammany: The Evolution of a Political Machine, 1789–1865* (Syracuse: Syracuse University Press, 1971).

19. Brummer, *Political History of New York,* pp. 262–63, 341–42.

20. Ibid., pp. 371–72; Klement, *The Limits of Dissent,* 266–67; Samuel Pleasants, *Fernando Wood of New York* (New York: Columbia University Press, 1948), pp. 155–56.

21. Silbey, *A Respectable Minority,* pp. 115–24.

22. Charles Wilson, "McClellan's Changing Views on the Peace Platform of 1864," *American Historical Review* 38 (1933): 498–505.

23. Klement, *Limits of Dissent,* pp. 288-289; Pleasants, *Fernando Wood,* p. 160; Porter, *Ohio Politics,* pp. 197-98.

24. G. R. Tredway, *Democratic Opposition to the Lincoln Administration in Indiana* (Indianapolis: Indiana Historical Bureau, 1973), pp. 108–248.

## CHAPTER 2

1. Samuel S. Cox, *Union-Disunion-Reunion: Three Decades of Federal Legislation, 1855–1885* (Providence, R.I.: Reid, 1885), p. 310.

2. David Lindsay, *"Sunset" Cox: Irrepressible Democrat* (Detroit: Wayne State University Press, 1959), p. 93; Montgomery Blair to Barlow, n.d., S. L. M. Barlow Papers, Huntington Library, San Marino, Calif.

3. Barlow to Blair, Jan. 10, 16, 1865, Barlow Papers.

4. Diary of Charles Mason, Jan. 1, 29, 1865, Charles Mason Papers, Iowa State Department of History and Archives, Des Moines; George Pendleton to Barlow, Jan. 31, 1865, Barlow Papers; Fernando Wood to George O'Shea, Jan. 15, 1865, Fernando Wood Papers, New York Public Library; Samuel Cox, *Eight Years in Congress from 1857–1865* (New York: Appleton, 1865), pp. 397–98.

5. Bancroft to S. S. Cox, Jan. 28, 1865, in M. A. DeWolfe Howe, *Life and Letters of George Bancroft,* 2. vols. (New York: Scribners, 1908), 2: 156–58; *New York World,* May 18, 1865; *Milwaukee Daily News,* Apr. 15, 1865.

6. *Columbus Crisis,* Feb. 8, 1865; *Harrisburg Patriot and Union,* Feb. 25, 1865.

7. *American Annual Cyclopaedia and Register of Important Events for the Year 1865* (New York: Appleton, 1866), pp. 577, 823, 304; *Detroit Free Press,* Apr. 14, 1865; *Cincinnati Daily Enquirer,* Mar. 10, 1865.

8. Herman Belz, *Reconstructing the Union: Theory and Practice During the Civil War* (Ithaca, N.Y.: Cornell University Press, 1969), pp. 244–76; U.S., Congress, Senate, *Congressional Globe,* 38th Cong., 2d sess., Feb. 25, 1865, 2:1111.

9. *Detroit Free Press,* July 1, 1865; *Cincinnati Daily Enquirer,* June 2, 16, 1865.

10. *American Annual Cyclopaedia, 1865,* pp. 301, 577.

11. *Hartford Daily Times,* Apr. 17, 1865; *New York World,* Apr. 17, 1865; *Chicago Times,* Apr. 17, 1865; James A. Bayard to Barlow, Apr. 19, 1865, Barlow Papers; Buchanan to John Blake, Apr. 28, 1865, in John B. Moore, ed., *The Works of James Buchanan, Comprising his Speeches, State Papers, and Private Correspondence,* 12 vols. (Philadelphia: Lippincott, 1908–1910), 11: 385–86.

12. *Old Guard,* 3 (1865): 190; *New York World,* Mar. 7, 1865.

13. *New York World,* Apr. 19, 1865; J. Glancey Jones to Johnson, Apr. 18, 1865, Reverdy Johnson to Johnson, Apr. 24, 1865, Andrew Johnson Papers, Library of Congress, Washington, D.C.; *Hartford Daily Times,* Apr. 28, 1865.

14. Diary of Charles Mason, Apr. 19, 1865; *Chicago Times,* Apr. 21, 27, 1865; *New York World,* Apr. 25, May 4, 13, 1865; William A. Richardson to Morton, May 17, 1865, J. Sterling Morton Papers, Nebraska State Historical Society, Lincoln; *Detroit Free Press,* May 14, 1865; *Hartford Daily Times,* May 14, 15, 1865.

15. John and LaWanda Cox, *Politics, Principle, and Prejudice, 1865–1866: Dilemma of Reconstruction America* (New York: Free Press, 1963), pp. 50–67; Montgomery Blair to Barlow, May 13, 1865, Barlow Papers.

16. *New York World,* Apr. 26, 28, May 6, 14, 19, 1865.

17. Edward McPherson, ed., *The Political History of the United States during the Period of Reconstruction* (Washington, D.C.: Philp & Solomons, 1871), pp. 44–47; *Chicago Times,* Apr. 23, 1865; *Columbus Crisis,* Apr. 26, 1865; *Harrisburg Patriot and Union,* May 4, 1865; *Hartford Daily Times,* May 6, 15, 1865; Bigler to J. D. Stiles, May 14, 1865, Vallandigham to Bigler, May 20, 1865, William Bigler Papers, Historical Society of Pennsylvania, Philadelphia; *Albany Argus,* May 16, 1865; *Dubuque Weekly Herald,* May 24, 1865; Montgomery Blair to Barlow, May 25, 1865, Barlow Papers; *New York World,* May 26, 1865.

18. James Richardson, ed., *Compilation of the Messages and Papers of the Presidents, 1789–1897,* 10 vols. (Washington, D.C.: Bureau of National Literature and Art, 1896–1899), 6:310–14.

19. Diary of Charles Mason, May 20, 1865; *New York World,* May 30, 1865; *Hartford Daily Times,* May 31, 1865; *Chicago Times,* May 31, June 2, 1865; *Albany Argus,* May 31, 1865; *Chicago Times,* May 31, 1865; *Milwaukee Daily News,* June 1, 1865; *Cincinnati Daily Enquirer,* June 2, 1865; *Harrisburg Patriot and Union,* June 3, 1865; J. Glancy Jones to Buchanan, June 6, 1865, James Buchanan Papers, Historical Society of Pennsylvania, Philadelphia; *Illinois State Register,* June 7, 1865; *Dubuque Weekly Herald,* June 14, 1865.

20. *Albany Argus,* June 19, 1865; *Chicago Times,* June 6, 1865.

21. *Columbus Crisis,* June 7, 1865.

22. *New York World,* May 3, 1865; *Detroit Free Press,* May 31, 1865; *Albany Argus,* June 19, 1865; *Boston Post,* June 14, 1865.

23. *New York World,* June 3, 5, 1865; *Dubuque Weekly Herald,* June 7, 1865; *Hartford Daily Times,* June 15, 1865; M. Blair to Barlow, June 14, 1865, Barlow Papers; Barlow to M. Blair, June 15, 1865, Johnson Papers.

24. Solomon Parsons to Johnson, June 14, 1865, Barlow to M. Blair, June 15, 1865, M. Blair to Johnson, June 16, 1865, Johnson Papers; M. Blair to Barlow, June 15, 1865, Barlow Papers.

25. *American Annual Cyclopaedia, 1865,* p. 802; *New York World,* June 22, 26, 1865; *Columbus Crisis,* June 21, 1865; *Detroit Free Press,* June 22, 1865; *Albany Argus,* June 26, 1865; *Chicago Times,* June 27, 1865; *Milwaukee Daily News,* June 28, 1865.

26. Diary of Charles Mason, June 18, 1865; *Columbus Crisis,* July 19, 1865.

27. *Albany Argus,* July 3, 1865; *New York World,* July 7, 1865; *Milwaukee Daily News,* July 9, 1865; *Chicago Times,* July 17, 1865; *Columbus Crisis,* July 19, 1865; J. W. Bryce To Mason, July 7, 1865, Mason Papers; William Shipman to Barlow, July 12, 1865, Barlow Papers; J. S. Black to Blair, July 15, 1865, Barlow to M. Blair, July 19, 1865, Johnson Papers.

28. Mason to Black, July 8, 1865, Jeremiah Black Papers, Library of Congress, Washington, D.C.; George W. Jones to Buchanan, July 30, 1865, Buchanan Papers; Barlow to M. Blair, July 24, 1865, Johnson Papers.

29. Jewett to Long, Jan. 11, 20, 1865, Vallandigham to Long, June 11, 1865, Murrell to Long, June 17, 1865, Alexander Long Papers, Cincinnati Historical Society; *Old Guard* 3 (1865): 381.

30. E. Merton Coulter, *The Civil War and Readjustment in Kentucky* (Chapel Hill: University of North Carolina Press, 1926), pp. 281–83; Eric McKitrick, *Andrew Johnson and the Politics of Reconstruction* (Chicago: University of Chicago Press, 1960), p. 80; *New York World,* Aug. 1, 14, 28, 1865; *Hartford Daily Times,* Aug. 8, 1865; *Harrisburg Patriot and Union,* Aug. 16, 1865.

31. *Dubuque Weekly Herald,* Aug. 23, 1865; M. Blair to Barlow, Aug. 11, 1865, Barlow Papers.

32. *New York World,* Aug. 10, 1865; *Detroit Free Press,* Aug. 15, 1865; McPherson, *History of Reconstruction,* pp. 19–20.

33. Bigler to Stiles, May 14, 1865, Bigler Papers; Glossbrenner to Black, June 23, 1865, Black Papers; Black to M. Blair, July 15, 1865, Johnson Papers; Buchanan to John Blake, July 25, 1865, in Moore, *The Works of James Buchanan,* 11:394–95.

34. *Harrisburg Patriot and Union,* Aug. 25, 1865; *American Annual Cyclopaedia, 1865,* pp. 693–94; Alexander McClure, *Old Time Notes of Pennsylvania,* 2 vols. (Philadelphia: Winston, 1905), 2:186; Erwin Bradley, *The Triumph of Militant Republicanism: A Study of Pennsylvania and Presidential Politics* (Philadelphia: University of Pennsylvania Press, 1964), pp. 253–54; M. Blair to Black, Aug. 31, 1865, Black Papers; Horatio King to Buchanan, Sept. 26, 1865, Buchanan Papers; Buchanan to King, Oct. 5, 1865, in Moore, *The Works of James Buchanan,* 11:400–401.

35. *Cincinnati Daily Enquirer,* Aug. 26, 1865; *American Annual Cyclopaedia, 1865,* p. 685; George Porter, *Ohio Politics in the Civil War Period,* Columbia Studies in History, Economics, and Public Law, vol. 40 (New York: Longmans, Green, 1911), pp. 214–15.

36. *Davenport Daily Democrat,* Aug. 26, 1865; *American Annual Cyclopaedia, 1865,* p. 441.

37. *Dubuque Weekly Herald,* Sept. 6, 1865; Mahoney to Mason, Sept. 16, 1865, Byington to Mason, Sept. 16, 1865, Mason Papers; W. A. Murrell to Long, June 17, 1865, Long Papers; Porter, *Ohio Politics,* p. 214.

38. Pratt to Barlow, Aug. 18, 22, 1865, Barlow to Pratt, Sept. 11, 1865, Barlow Papers; Barlow to Pratt, Aug, 21, 1865, Johnson Papers; Barlow to Tilden, Aug. 31, 1865, Samuel J. Tilden Papers, New York Public Library.

39. *New York World,* Aug. 25, 28, 31, 1865.

40. Pratt to Barlow, Aug. 18, 1865, Barlow Papers; Barlow to Pratt, Aug. 21, 1865, Johnson Papers.

41. Barlow to Tilden, Aug. 31, 1865, Tilden to T. N. Parmley, Aug. 31, 1865, Tilden Papers; Barlow to M. Blair, Sept. 11, 1865, Barlow Papers; *American Annual Cyclopaedia, 1865,* p. 614; *Albany Argus,* Sept. 8, 1865.

42. Homer Stebbins, *A Political History of the State of New York, 1865–1869,* Columbia Studies in History, Economics and Public Law, vol. 60 (New York: Columbia University Press, 1913), pp. 48–49; *New York World,* Sept. 9, 1865.

43. *American Annual Cyclopaedia, 1865,* pp. 577, 824; *St. Paul Pioneer,* Sept. 8, 1865; R. C. Olin to Sibley, Oct. 5, 1865, Henry Sibley Papers, Minnesota State Historical Society, St. Paul; Moses Bates to Johnson, Oct. 3, 1865, Johnson Papers; Arthur Cole, *The Centennial History of Illinois,* vol. 3, *The Civil War Era, 1848–1870* (Springfield: Illinois Centennial Commission, 1919), p. 393.

44. *American Annual Cyclopaedia, 1865,* p. 614; Stebbins, *Political History of New York,* pp. 37–64.

45. G. Galen Berrier, "The Negro Suffrage Issue in Iowa, 1865–1868, *Annuals of Iowa* 39 (1968): 248–54; Richard Current, *The History of Wisconsin,* vol. 2, *The Civil War Era, 1848–1873* (Madison: State Historical Society of Wisconsin, 1976), p. 568; Porter, *Ohio Politics,* pp. 207–11.

46. *Davenport Daily Democrat,* Sept. 8, 1865; *Harrisburg Patriot and Union,* Sept. 12, 1865; *Milwaukee Daily News,* Sept. 17, 1865; *Hartford Daily Times,* Sept. 27, 1865; *Detroit Free Press,* Sept. 26, 1865; *Columbus Crisis,* Oct. 4, 1865.

47. *Milwaukee Daily News,* Sept. 17, 1865; *New York World,* Sept. 13, 16, 18, 28, 1865; *St. Paul Pioneer,* Sept. 16, 20, 1865; *Hartford Daily Times,* Sept. 13, 20, 1865; *Columbus Crisis,* Sept. 20, 1865.

48. *American Annual Cyclopaedia, 1865,* pp. 304, 441; McClure, *Old Time Notes,* 2:189; Porter, *Ohio Politics,* p. 219.

49. McPherson, *History of Reconstruction,* pp. 48–49; *New York World,* Oct. 24, 1865; *Harrisburg Patriot and Union,* Oct. 25, 1865; *Chicago Times,* Oct. 26, 1865.

50. *New York World,* Oct. 7, 1865; Barlow to Shipman, Oct. 25, 1865, Barlow to Taylor, Oct. 21, 1865, Barlow Papers.

## CHAPTER 3

1. *Hartford Daily Times,* Aug. 16, 23, 1865; *New York World,* Aug. 19, 22, 1865; *St. Paul Pioneer,* Sept. 22, 1865.

2. *Cincinnati Daily Enquirer,* Nov. 22, 1865; *New York World,* Sept. 21, 1865.

3. *New York World,* Sept. 21, Oct. 12, 14, 1865; *Hartford Daily Times,* Nov. 24, 28, 1865; *St. Paul Pioneer,* Nov. 21, 1865.

4. Edward McPherson, ed., *The Political History of the United States of America during the Period of Reconstruction* (Washington: Philp & Solomons, 1871), pp. 18–28.

5. *Hartford Daily Times*, Nov. 11, 20, 1865; *New York World*, Nov. 14, 1865; *Harrisburg Patriot and Union*, Dec. 5, 1865; *Dubuque Weekly Herald*, Dec. 6, 1865; Barlow to M. Blair, Nov. 13, S. L. M. Barlow Papers, Huntington Library, San Marino, Calif.; Diary of Charles Mason, Nov. 19, 1865, Charles Mason Papers, Iowa State Department of History and Archives, Des Moines.

6. Seventeen percent of the Democrats had served more than one term compared to 24 percent of the Republicans and Unionists.

7. Biographical information on Democratic congressmen can be found in Allen Johnson and Dumas Malone, eds., *Dictionary of American Biography*, 20 vols. (New York: Scribners, 1928–1940); and Clifford Reynolds, ed., *Biographical Directory of the American Congress, 1774–1961* (Washington, D.C.: USGPO, 1961).

8. M. Blair to Barlow, Nov. 12, 1865, Barlow Papers; *New York World*, Nov. 14, 1865; Diary of Charles Mason, Nov. 19, 1865; *Cincinnati Daily Enquirer*, Nov. 25, 30, 1865.

9. U.S. Congress, House, *Congressional Globe*, 39th Cong., 1st sess., Dec. 4, 1865, 1:3–4; *New York Times*, Dec. 5, 1865.

10. James Richardson, ed., *A Compilation of the Messages and Papers of the Presidents, 1789–1897*, 10 vols. (Washington, D.C.: Bureau of National Literature and Art, 1896–1899), 6:333–71; *Detroit Free Press*, Dec. 2, 6, 1865; *New York World*, Dec. 5, 6, 1865; *Harrisburg Patriot and Union*, Dec. 5, 1865; *Albany Argus*, Dec. 6, 1865; *Cincinnati Daily Enquirer*, Dec. 7, 1865; Irish to Mason, Dec. 11, 1865, Dunlovy to Mason, Dec. 11, 1865, Mason Papers; *Dubuque Weekly Herald*, Dec. 13, 1865.

11. *Columbus Crisis*, Dec. 6, 1865.

12. Blair to Barlow, Dec. 7, 1865, Barlow to Richard Taylor, Dec. 9, 1865, Barlow Papers; U.S., Congress, Senate, *Congressional Globe*, 39th Cong., 1st sess., Dec. 12, 1865, 1:29–30; *New York World*, Dec. 19, 1865.

13. Diary of Charles Mason, Dec. 31, 1865; J. Glancy Jones to Buchanan, Dec. 29, 1865, James Buchanan Papers, Historical Society of Pennsylvania, Philadelphia; *Albany Argus*, Dec. 30, 1865; *Chicago Times*, Jan. 24, 1866.

14. House, *Congressional Globe*, 39th cong., 1st sess., Dec. 5, 1865; 1:10, Dec. 11, 1865, 1:20, Dec. 19, 1865, 1:87.

15. Francis Brown, *Raymond of the "Times"* (New York: Norton, 1951), p. 286; Senate, *Congressional Globe*, 39th Cong., 1st sess., Dec. 20, 1865, 1:96–97; House, *Congressional Globe*, 39th Cong., 1st sess., Dec. 21, 1865, 1:115; Balcolm to Johnson, Jan. 2, 1866, Andrew Johnson Papers, Library of Congress, Washington, D.C.

16. *New York World*, Dec. 22, 1865; House, *Congressional Globe*, 39th Cong., 1st sess., Jan 26, 1866, 1:454.

17. *Illinois State Register*, Jan. 19, 1866; *Detroit Free Press*, Jan. 20, 1866; *Chicago Times*, Jan. 20, 1866.

18. Senate, *Congressional Globe*, 39th Cong., 1st sess., Jan 16, 1866, 1:246.

19. House, *Congressional Globe*, 39th Cong., 1st sess., Jan 10, 1866, 1:175–78, Jan. 11, 1866, 1:196–206.

20. Richard Current, *Old Thad Stevens: A Story of Ambition* (Madison: University of Wisconsin Press, 1942), p. 231; House, *Congressional Globe*, 39th Cong., 1st sess., Jan 18, 1866, 1:310–11.

21. *New York Times*, Jan. 22, 1866; Benjamin Rush to Johnson, Jan. 20, 1866, W. Patton to Johnson, Jan. 30, 1966, Johnson Papers; *New York World*, Jan. 20, Feb. 1, 1866; Diary of Charles Mason, Jan. 21, 28, 1866; *Columbus Crisis*, Jan. 24, 1866; *Chicago Times*, Jan. 26, 1866; Senate, *Congressional Globe*, 39th Cong., 1st sess., Jan 19, 1866, 1:520.

22. McPherson, *History of Reconstruction*, pp. 51–52; James Dixon to Winthrop, Feb. 1, 1866, Robert Winthrop Papers, Massachusetts Historical Society, Boston.

23. Joseph James, *The Framing of the Fourteenth Amendment*, Illinois Studies in the Social Sciences, vol. 37 (Urbana: University of Illinois Press, 1956), pp. 55–60.

24. House, *Congressional Globe*, 39th Cong., 1st sess., Dec. 17, 1865, 1:258, Jan. 22, 1866, 1:354, Jan. 31, 1866, 1:538; Benjamin Kendrick, *Journal of the Joint Committee of Fifteen on Reconstruction, 1865–1867*, Columbia Studies in History, Economics, and Public Law, vol. 62 (New York: Columbia University Press, 1914), pp. 43–46.

25. *Hartford Daily Times*, Jan. 30, Feb. 3, 1866; *New York World*, Jan. 30, Feb. 6, 1866; James Guthrie to Pierce, Feb. 4, 1866, Franklin Pierce Papers, Library of Congress, Washington, D.C.; W. W. White to Mason, Feb. 5, 1866, Mason Papers; *Columbus Crisis*, Feb. 7, 1866.

26. Senate, *Congressional Globe,* 39th Cong., 1st sess., Jan 19, 1866, 1:315–19, Feb. 5, 1866, 1:575; House, *Congressional Globe,* 39th Cong., 1st sess., Feb. 3, 1866, 1:628, 639.

27. McPherson, *History of Reconstruction,* pp. 53–55; *Cincinnati Daily Enquirer,* Feb. 9, 15, 1866; *New York World,* Feb. 9, 1866; *Chicago Times,* Feb. 9, 1866; *Detroit Free Press,* Feb. 12, 1866; Phillip Ripley to Marble, Feb. 8, 1866, Manton Marble Papers, Library of Congress, Washington, D.C.

28. Richardson, *Messages and Papers of the Presidents,* 6:398–405.

29. Benjamin Kendrick, *The Journal of the Joint Committee of Fifteen on Reconstruction,* pp. 239–41; *Hartford Daily Times,* Feb. 21, 1866; House, *Congressional Globe,* 39th Cong., 1st sess., Feb. 21, 1866, 1:950.

30. Senate, *Congressional Globe,* 39th Cong., 1st sess., Feb. 21, 1866, 1:957; *New York Tribune,* Feb. 22, 1866.

31. Diary of Charles Mason, Feb. 8, 1866; *National Intelligencer,* Feb. 23, 1866; McPherson, *History of Reconstruction,* pp. 58–63.

32. *Hartford Daily Times,* Feb. 20, 1866; *Illinois State Register,* Feb. 20, 1866; *Milwaukee Daily News,* Feb. 21, 1866; S. S. Cox to Marble, Feb. 20, 1866, Marble Papers; J. S. Black to Johnson, Feb. 20, 1866, A. B. Butler to Johnson, Feb. 20, 1866, Fernando Wood to Johnson, Feb. 24, 1866, John Dix to Johnson, Mar. 2, 1866, Johnson Papers; Henry Watterson, *History of the Manhattan Club* (New York: privately printed, 1915), p. xxviii; Barlow to Richard Taylor, Mar. 7, 1866 Barlow Papers; *New York World,* Feb. 23, 1866; *Cincinnati Daily Enquirer,* Feb. 20, 23, 1866.

33. Senate, *Congressional Globe,* 39th Cong., 1st sess., Mar. 8, 1866, 2:1284, 1288–89.

34. *American Annual Cyclopaedia and Register of Important Events for the Year 1866* (New York: Appleton, 1867), p. 536; Howard K. Beale, ed., *The Diary of Gideon Welles,* 3 vols. (New York: Norton, 1960), 2:443; Diary of Charles Mason, Mar. 18, 1866.

35. Edmund Burke to Johnson, Mar. 12, 1866, Johnson Papers; *Hartford Daily Times,* Mar. 8, 1866; *American Annual Cyclopaedia, 1866,* p. 537.

36. *Hartford Daily Times,* Feb. 6, 7, 1866; *American Annual Cyclopaedia, 1866,* p. 252.

37. *National Intelligencer,* Mar. 20, 1866; *New York World,* Mar. 13, 1866; Barlow to Thomas Pratt, Mar. 16, 1866, Barlow Papers; A. E. Burr to Welles, Mar. 12, 1866, Gideon Welles Papers, Library of Congress, Washington, D.C.

38. Beale, *Welles Diary,* 2:454, 457–58.

39. *Hartford Daily Times,* Mar. 24, 26, 27, 1866; *New York World,* Mar. 24, 1866; Beale, *Welles Diary,* 2:461–62.

40. Edmund Burke to Johnson, Mar. 12, 1866, John Haskins to Johnson, Mar. 21, 1866, Johnson Papers; Barlow to Thomas Pratt, Mar. 16, 1866, James A. Bayard to Barlow, Apr. 17, 1866, Barlow Papers.

41. Eric McKitrick, *Andrew Johnson and Reconstruction* (Chicago: University of Chicago Press, 1960), pp. 298–306; McPherson, *History of Reconstruction,* pp. 78–80.

42. Senate, *Congressional Globe,* 39th Cong., 1st sess., Jan. 30, 1866, 1:504–6, Jan. 31, 1866, 1:530, Feb. 2, 1866, 1:606; House, *Congressional Globe,* 39th Cong., 1st sess., Mar. 1, 1866, 2:1121–22, Mar. 2, 1866, 2:1156–57.

43. *Cincinnati Daily Enquirer,* Mar. 17, 1866; *New York World,* Mar. 17, 1866; *Columbus Crisis,* Mar. 21, 1866; F. P. Blair to Johnson, Mar. 18, 1866, George Morgan to Johnson, Mar. 19, 1866, Cowan to Johnson, Mar. 13, 1866, Johnson Papers; Richardson, *Messages and Papers of the Presidents,* 6:398–413, 429–32.

44. P. A. Ogden to Blair, Mar. 28, 1866, Johnson Papers.

45. Senate, *Congressional Globe,* 39th Cong., 1st sess., Mar. 12, 1866, 2:1327–31, Mar. 13, 2:1352–65.

46. Charles Knapp, *New Jersey Politics during the Period of Civil War and Reconstruction* (Geneva, N.Y.: Humphrey, 1924), pp. 142–48.

47. Senate, *Congressional Globe,* 39th Cong., 1st sess., Mar. 22, 1866, 2:1564–73, 1589–1602, Mar. 26, 1866, 2:1635–48, Mar. 27, 1866, 2:1666–79; Stockton to Marble, Apr. 31, 1866, Marble Papers.

48. *Hartford Daily Times,* Apr. 3, 1866; Shipman to Barlow, Apr. 8, 1866, Barlow Papers; Senate, *Congressional Globe,* 39th Cong., 1st sess., Apr. 6, 1866, 2:1809; House, *Congressional Globe,* 39th Cong., 1st sess., Apr. 9, 1866, 2:1861.

49. James English to Cox, n.d., Samuel S. Cox Papers, Brown University Library, Providence, R.I.; *New York World,* Apr. 3, 1866; *Hartford Daily Times,* Apr. 11, 1866; House, *Congressional Globe,* 39th Cong., 1st sess., Apr. 7, 1866, 2:1822.

## CHAPTER 4

1. *National Intelligencer,* Apr. 2, 11, 1866; Diary of Charles Mason, Apr. 1, 8, 1866, Charles Mason Papers, Iowa State Department of History and Archives, Des Moines; Montgomery Blair to Barlow, Apr. 7, 1866, S. L. M. Barlow Papers, Huntington Library, San Marino, Calif.

2. *New York Herald,* Apr. 10, 26, 1866; C. H. Ray to M. Blair, Apr. 10, 1866, Andrew Johnson Papers, Library of Congress, Washington, D.C.; *Detroit Free Press,* Apr. 18, 1866; *Dubuque Weekly Herald,* Apr. 25, 1866; *Illinois State Register,* May 12, 1866; Buchanan to Horatio King, Apr. 21, 1866, in John B. Moore, ed., *The Works of James Buchanan, Comprising His Speeches, State Papers, and Private Correspondence,* 12 vols. (Philadelphia: Lippincott, 1910), 11:415–17.

3. *New York Herald,* Apr. 23, 1866; *National Intelligencer,* Apr. 25, 1866.

4. John and LaWanda Cox, *Politics, Principle, and Prejudice, 1865–1866: Dilemma of Reconstruction America* (New York: Free Press, 1963), pp. 107–28.

5. *Hartford Daily Times,* Apr. 30, May 10, 1866; Alexander McClure, *Old Time Notes of Pennsylvania,* 2 vols. (Philadelphia: Winston, 1905), 2:193–96; Edward McPherson, ed., *The Political History of the United States during the Period of Reconstruction* (Washington, D.C.: Philp & Solomons, 1871), p. 123.

6. Eric McKitrick, *Andrew Johnson and Reconstruction* (Chicago: University of Chicago Press, 1960), pp. 384–87; U.S., Congress, House, *Congressional Globe,* 39th Cong., 1st sess., May 5, 1866, 3:2401, 2408, 2409, 2411; U.S. Congress, Senate, *Congressional Globe,* May 5, 1866, 3:2428, 2857.

7. McPherson, *History of Reconstruction,* p. 17; *New York World,* Apr. 19, May 30, 1866; *Illinois State Register,* May 14, 16, 1866.

8. Mabel Walker, *The Fenian Movement* (Colorado Springs: Myles, 1969), pp. 94–101; *New York World,* June 8, 1866; *St. Paul Pioneer,* June 9, 1866; *Milwaukee Daily News,* June 14, 1866; J. W. Bryce to Mason, June 21, 1866, Mason Papers; Diary of Charles Mason, June 24, 1866.

9. Joseph James, *The Framing of the Fourteenth Amendment,* Illinois Studies in the Social Sciences, vol. 37 (Urbana: University of Illinois Press, 1956), pp. 91–116.

10. *New York Tribune,* Mar. 21, 1866; House, *Congressional Globe,* 39th Cong., 1st sess., Mar. 8, 1866, 2:1158, Mar. 24, 1866, 2:1632, May 8, 1866, 3:2467.

11. *Illinois State Register,* May 2, 1866; House, *Congressional Globe,* 39th Cong., 1st sess., May 8, 1866, 3:2461, 2465, 2467, May 10, 1866, 3:2530.

12. Ibid., May 8, 1866, 3:2462, 2467, May 10, 1866, 3:2538.

13. Ibid., May 8, 1866, 3:2465–66, May 10, 1866, 3:2530–31; *New York World,* Apr. 30, 1866.

14. House, *Congressional Globe,* 39th Cong., 1st sess., May 10, 1866, 3:2545; *New York Times,* May 11, 1866.

15. James, *The Framing of the Fourteenth Amendment,* pp. 132–152.

16. *New York Times,* May 12, 14, 1866; *Detroit Free Press,* June 5, 1866; *St. Paul Pioneer,* June 22, 1866.

17. McPherson, *History of Reconstruction,* pp. 83, 93–101; *Hartford Daily Times,* June 23, 1866; *New York World,* June 23, 1866; *Illinois State Register,* June 23, 1866; *Cincinnati Daily Enquirer,* June 25, 1866.

18. James G. Randall and Theodore Pease, eds., *The Diary of Orville Hickman Browning,* 2 vols. (Springfield: Illinois State Historical Library, 1933), 2:79.

19. Henry W. Raymond, "Extracts from the Journal of Henry J. Raymond," *Scribner's Monthly* 20 (1880):276.

20. Howard K. Beale, ed., *The Diary of Gideon Welles,* 3 vols. (New York: Norton, 1960), 2:527–29.

21. Raymond, "Extracts From the Journal of Henry J. Raymond," p. 276; Beale, *Welles Diary,* 2:529–31.

22. Randall, *Browning Diary,* 2:81, Beale, *Welles Diary,* 2:540.

23. McPherson, *History of Reconstruction,* p. 119; J. W. Bryce to Mason, June 27, 1866, A. G. Gillet to Mason, June 29, 1866, Mason Papers; *Milwaukee Daily News,* June 30, July 1, 1866; *Illinois State Register,* June 30, July 5, 1866; *St. Paul Pioneer,* July 1, 1866; *Columbus Crisis,* July 11, 1866.

24. *New York Herald,* July 6, 1866; J. Reinhart to Mason, July 7, 1866, Mason Papers.

25. *Cincinnati Daily Enquirer,* July 27, 1866; George Porter, *Ohio Politics in the Civil War Period,* Columbia Studies in History, Economics, and Public Law, vol. 40 (New York: Longmans, Green, 1911), pp. 231–32; George W. Morgan to Johnson, July 13, 1866, Johnson Papers.

26. August Belmont to Barlow, June 26, 1866, Barlow Papers; *New York World,* June 27, 1866.

27. S. S. Marshall to Morrison, July 2, 1866, William Ralls Morrison Papers, Chicago Historical Society; M. Blair to Barlow, July 5, 1866, Barlow Papers.

28. Randall, *Browning Diary,* 2:83; *New York Herald,* July 11, 1866; *American Annual Cyclopaedia and Register of Important Events for the Year 1866* (New York: Appleton, 1867), pp. 754–55.

29. Thomas Wagstaff, "Andrew Johnson and the National Union Movement, 1865–1866" (Ph.D. diss., University of Wisconsin, 1967), pp. 287–89; *New York World,* July 7, 1866.

30. *American Annual Cyclopaedia, 1866,* pp. 755–56.

31. *American Annual Cyclopaedia, 1866,* pp. 478, 755–56; *St. Paul Pioneer,* July 14, 31, Aug. 1, 1866; Porter, *Ohio Politics,* pp. 228–29; George W. Morgan to Johnson, July 14, 1866, Johnson Papers.

32. William E. Smith, *The Francis Preston Blair Family in Politics,* 2 vols. (New York: Macmillan, 1933), 2:366; F. Wood to Johnson, Aug. 1, 1866, Johnson Papers; *Dubuque Weekly Herald,* July 23, 1866; R. M. D. France to Bigler, July 21, Aug. 6, 1866; William Bigler Papers, Historical Society of Pennsylvania, Philadelphia; F. M. Irish to Mason, Aug. 1, 1866, Mason Papers; H. H. Mitchell to Allen, July 26, 1866, William Allen Papers, Library of Congress, Washington, D.C.

33. *New York Herald,* July 13, 1866; *Cincinnati Daily Enquirer,* July 20, 1866; James T. Pratt to Welles, July 19, 1866, Gideon Welles Papers, Library of Congress, Washington, D.C.

34. Raymond, "Extracts From the Journal of Henry J. Raymond," p. 276; Raymond to Ransom Balcolm, July 17, 1866 in August Maverick, *Henry J. Raymond and the New York Times for Thirty Years* (Hartford, Conn.: Hale, 1870), pp. 173–74; *New York Times,* July 17, 19, 23, 25, 1866.

35. McKitrick, *Andrew Johnson and Reconstruction,* pp. 422–27; *New York World,* Aug. 1–6, 1866.

36. *New York Herald,* Aug. 3, 1866; *Milwaukee Daily Times,* Aug. 4, 1866; *Hartford Daily Times,* Aug. 2, 1866; James Babcock to Welles, Aug. 5, 1866, Welles Papers; Robert Winthrop to R. S. Spofford, Aug. 9, 1866, Robert B. Winthrop Papers, Massachusetts Historical Society, Boston; R. B. Carnahan to Johnson, Aug. 7, 1866, Johnson Papers.

37. John Dix to Doolittle, July 23, 1866, James Doolittle Papers, Wisconsin State Historical Society, Madison; *New York World,* July 28, 1866; Fernando Wood to Johnson, Aug. 1, 1866, Johnson Papers; Homer Stebbins, *A Political History of the State of New York, 1865–1869,* Columbia Studies in History, Economics, and Public Law, vol. 55 (New York: Columbia University Press, 1913), p. 90.

38. J. H. Geiger to Johnson, Aug. 2, 1866, Randall to Johnson, Aug. 12, 1866, Johnson Papers; Raymond, "Extracts From the Journal of Henry J. Raymond," p. 278; Mason to Vallandigham, Aug. 5, 1866, Mason Papers; Samuel Pleasants, *Fernando Wood of New York* (New York: Columbia University Press, 1948), p. 167; *Milwaukee Daily News,* Aug. 15, 1866.

39. Diary of Charles Mason, Aug. 19, 1866; *New York World,* Aug. 16, 1866.

40. Thomas Wagstaff, "The Arm-and-Arm Convention," *Civil War History* 14 (1968):101–19.

41. Raymond, "Extracts From the Journal of Henry J. Raymond," pp. 278–81.

42. *Columbus Crisis,* Aug. 22, 1866; *New York Daily News* in *Illinois State Register,* Aug. 27, 1866; Diary of George B. Smith, Aug. 17, 1866, George B. Smith Papers, Wisconsin State Historical Society, Madison; W. W. White to Mason, Aug. 18, Mason Papers; Washington Bigler to Bigler, Aug. 20, Bigler Papers; *New York World,* Aug. 17, 1866; *Chicago Times,* Aug. 17, 1866; *Hartford Daily Times,* Aug. 21, 1866.

43. *New York World,* Sept. 25, 1866.

44. Leslie Fischel, "Wisconsin and Negro Suffrage," *Wisconsin Magazine of History* 46 (1963): 180–96; *Detroit Free Press,* Sept. 25–26, 1866.

45. McKitrick, *Andrew Johnson and Reconstruction,* pp. 428–38.

46. *New York World,* Sept. 6, 1866; *Davenport Daily Democrat,* Sept. 16, 1866; *Cincinnati Daily Enquirer,* Sept. 25, 1866; Diary of Charles Mason, Sept. 9, 1866; Buchanan to Nahum Capen, Oct. 2, 1866, in Moore, *The Works of James Buchanan,* 11:428.

47. Richard Curran to Lasselle, Aug. 24, 1866, Charles Lasselle Papers, Indiana State Library, Indianapolis; William Wallace to Bigler, Aug. 28, Oct. 3, 1866, H. Clymer to Bigler, Sept. 6, 20, 1866, Edward Clymer to Bigler, Sept. 20, Bigler Papers; J. Glancy Jones to Johnson, Sept. 22, 1866, Bigler to Johnson, Oct. 18, 1866, Johnson Papers.

48. *American Annual Cyclopaedia, 1866,* pp. 478, 508.

49. Stebbins, *Political History of New York,* 92–94; Barlow to Smythe, Aug. 25, 1866, Johnson Papers; Marble to Joseph Warren, n.d., Manton Marble Papers, Library of Congress, Washington, D.C.; J. D. VanBuren to Tilden, Aug. 31, Sept. 3, 1866, Samuel J. Tilden Papers, New York Public Library.

50. Stebbins, *Political History of New York,* pp. 91–106.

51. *New York Herald,* Sept. 14, 1866; *New York Times,* Sept. 17, 1866; S. S. Cox to Marble, Sept. 21, 1866, Marble Papers; William Bigler to Johnson, Oct. 1, 1866, Johnson Papers; *New York World,* Sept. 24, 1866.

52. J. Mullaly to Mason, Oct. 7, 1866, Mason Papers; Diary of Charles Mason, Oct. 12, 1866; *Davenport Daily Democrat,* Oct. 8, 1866; S. S. Cox to Marble, Oct. 9, 1866, Marble Papers; *Chicago Times,* Oct. 15, 1866; Hiram Ketchum to Johnson, Oct. 17, 1866, Johnson Papers; Barlow to Reverdy Johnson, Oct. 24, 1866, Barlow Papers; Randall, *Browning Diary,* 2:101; *New York Times,* Oct. 24, 1866.

53. *Chicago Times,* Oct. 11, 1866; T. Dwight to Morton, Oct. 14, 1866, J. Sterling Morton Papers, Nebraska State Historical Society, Lincoln; *New York World,* Oct. 18, 1866; Diary of Charles Mason, Oct. 21, 28, 1866; Hugh McCulloch to Tilden, Oct. 22, 1866, Tilden Papers.

54. Walker, *The Fenian Movement,* pp. 111–19; David Montgomery, *Beyond Equality: Labor and the Radical Republicans* (New York: Knopf, 1967), pp. 132–33; J. W. Bryce to Mason, Aug. 20, 25, 1866, Mason Papers; Tilden to Johnson, Sept. 20, 1866, Johnson Papers; *Milwaukee Daily News,* Oct. 30, 1866; *Detroit Free Press,* Nov. 1, 1866; *New York World,* Nov. 3, 1866.

## CHAPTER 5

1. John A. Dix to Johnson, Nov. 7, 1866, Samuel Smith to Johnson, Nov. 10, 1866, Andrew Johnson Papers, Library of Congress, Washington, D.C.; Howard K. Beale, ed., *The Diary of Gideon Walles,* 3 vols. (New York: Norton, 1960), 2:817; *Old Guard* 4 (1866):767; Oscar Stephenson to Mason, Dec. 10, 1866, Charles Mason Papers, Iowa State Department of History and Archives, Des Moines; *Hartford Daily Times,* Dec. 14, 1866; Buchanan to G. G. Leiper, Nov. 30, 1866, in John B. Moore, ed., *The Works of James Buchanan, Comprising His Speeches, State Papers, and Private Correspondence,* 12 vols. (Philadelphia: Lippincott, 1908–1910), 11:428–29.

2. Irving Katz, *August Belmont: A Political Biography* (New York: Columbia University Press, 1968), pp. 157–58; *Cincinnati Daily Enquirer,* Jan. 7, 1867; George Porter, *Ohio Politics in the Civil War Period,* Columbia Studies in History, Economics, and Public Law, vol. 40 (New York: Longmans, Green, 1911), p. 239; *Hartford Daily Times,* Jan. 9, 1867.

3. *Columbus Crisis,* Jan. 2, Feb. 13, 1867; Edward McPherson, ed., *The Political History of the United States of America during the Period of Reconstruction* (Washington, D.C.: Philp & Solomons, 1871), pp. 245, 248; Diary of Charles Mason, Jan. 13, 23, 1867, Henry Clay Dean to Mason, Feb. 12, 1867, Mason Papers; *Milwaukee Daily News,* Jan. 26, 1867.

4. *Milwaukee Daily News,* Nov. 11, 1866; *Detroit Free Press,* Nov. 17, 1866; Henry Clay Dean to Mason, Nov. 9, 1866, G. W. Jones to Mason, Nov. 25, 1866, M. S. Bonnifield to Mason, Dec. 22, 1866, Mason Papers; *Chicago Times,* Nov. 12, 1866.

5. *Cincinnati Daily Enquirer,* Nov. 14, 1866; *Milwaukee Daily News,* Nov. 14, 1866.

6. P. W. Bartley to Johnson, Nov. 9, 1866, Samuel Smith to Johnson, Nov. 10, 1866, James Taylor to Johnson, Nov. 16, 1866, Johnson Papers; *Chicago Times,* Nov. 8, 1866; *New York World,* Nov. 16, 1866; for Southern attitudes see Michael Perman, *Reunion Without Compromise: The South and Reconstruction, 1865–1868* (London: Cambridge University Press, 1973), pp. 229–65.

7. *New York World,* Nov. 8, 9, 14, 1866.

8. *Detroit Free Press,* Nov. 10, 1866; *Milwaukee Daily News,* Nov. 16, 1866; T. F. Bayard to J. A. Bayard, Thomas Bayard Papers, Library of Congress, Washington, D.C.; *Albany Argus* in *Milwaukee Daily News,* Nov. 16, 1866; William Cassidy to Johnson, Nov. 16, 1866, Johnson Papers.

9. *Chicago Times,* Nov. 12, 14, 15, 1866.

10. *Illinois State Register,* Nov. 13, 1866; *Cincinnati Daily Enquirer,* Nov. 14, 1866; *Milwaukee Daily News,* Nov. 14, 1866; *Davenport Daily Democrat,* Nov. 17, 1866; *Hartford Daily Times,* Nov. 19, 1866; *Boston Post,* Nov. 19, 1866.

11. Diary of Charles Mason, Nov. 11, 18, 1866; *New York Herald,* Nov. 15, 1866; *Detroit Free Press,* Nov. 20, 1866.

12. *Milwaukee Daily News,* Nov. 19, 1866; *Chicago Times,* Nov. 19, 20, 1866; *Hartford*

*Daily Times,* Nov. 27, 30, 1866; *New York Herald,* Nov. 30, 1866; Manton Marble to Burke, Edmund Burke Papers, Library of Congress, Washington, D.C.; I. C. to Marble, Dec. 2, 1866, Manton Marble Papers, Library of Congress, Washington, D.C.

13. James Richardson, ed., *A Compilation of the Messages and Papers of the Presidents, 1789–1987,* 10 vols. (Washington, D.C.: Bureau of National Literature and Art, 1896–1899), 6:445–59; *Chicago Times,* Dec. 4, 1866; *Hartford Daily Times,* Dec. 4, 1866; *New York World,* Dec. 4, 1866; *Milwaukee Daily News,* Dec. 5, 1866; *Columbus Crisis,* Dec. 5, 1866; *Dubuque Weekly Herald,* Dec. 12, 1866.

14. *New York Times,* Dec. 6, 1866.

15. U.S., Congress, House, *Congressional Globe,* 39th Cong., 2d sess., Dec. 3, 1866, 1:4, Dec. 6, 1866, 1:33, Dec. 10, 1866, 1:39.

16. U.S. Congress, Senate, *Congressional Globe,* 39th Cong., 2d sess., Dec. 12, 1866, 1:84–85, Dec. 13, 1866, 1:97–100, 107, 109.

17. Ibid., Dec. 14, 1866, 1:130, Dec. 17, 1866, 1:145, Dec. 19, 1866, 1:188–90.

18. McPherson, *History of Reconstruction,* pp. 209–20; *Milwaukee Daily News,* Dec. 19, 1866; *Hartford Daily Times,* Dec. 22, 26, Jan. 5, 1867; *New York World,* Jan. 1, 15, 1867; *Boston Post,* Jan. 3, 1867.

19. James G. Randall and Theodore Pease, eds., *The Diary of Orville Hickman Browning,* 2 vols. (Springfield: Illinois State Historical Library, 1933), 2:122; Richardson, *Messages and Papers of the Presidents,* 6:472–73.

20. House, *Congressional Globe,* 39th cong., 2d sess., Jan. 8, 1867, 1:344; Senate, *Congressional Globe,* 39th Cong., 2d sess., Jan. 7, 1867, 1:303–13.

21. Ibid., Jan. 10, 1867, 1:381, Jan. 11, 1867, 1:404–406; House, *Congressional Globe,* 39th Cong., 2d sess., Jan. 7, 1867, 1:319–21.

22. Ibid., Jan 15, 1867, 1:481–82; Senate, *Congressional Globe,* 39th Cong., 2d sess., Jan. 9, 1867, 1:359–62, Jan. 10, 1867, 1:382, 399.

23. *New York World,* Jan. 9, 14, 1867; *Hartford Daily Times,* Jan. 10, 1867; Diary of Charles Mason, Jan. 13, 1867.

24. House, *Congressional Globe,* 39th Cong., 2d sess., Jan. 16, 1867, 1:500–505.

25. Perman, *Reunion Without Compromise,* pp. 256–59; *Illinois State Register,* Jan. 19, 1867.

26. George Sioussant, ed., "Notes of Colonel W. G. Moore, Private Secretary to President Johnson, 1865–1868," *American Historical Review* 14 (1913):104; Beale, *Welles Diary,* 3:32; McPherson, *History of Reconstruction,* pp. 258–59; *Chicago Times,* Feb. 4, 5, 1867.

27. *Chicago Times,* Feb. 5, 1867; *Boston Post,* Feb. 8, 1867; *Albany Argus* in the *Chicago Times,* Feb. 14, 1867; *Milwaukee Daily News,* Feb. 5, 1867; *Hartford Daily Times,* Feb. 6, 1867; A. E. Burr to Welles, Feb. 11, 1867, Gideon Welles Papers, Library of Congress, Washington, D.C.; Senate, *Congressional Globe,* 39th Cong., 2d sess., Feb. 6, 1867, 2:1045–47.

28. House, *Congressional Globe,* 39th Cong., 2d sess., Feb. 1, 1867, 2:944, Feb. 2, 1867, 2:969–70, Feb. 6, 1867, 2:1036–37.

29. Ibid., Feb. 8, 1867, 2:1103–4, Feb. 12, 1867, 2:1182.

30. *Detroit Free Press,* Feb. 13, 1867; *Cincinnati Daily Enquirer,* Feb. 16, 1867; *Chicago Times,* Feb. 17, 1867; *Columbus Crisis,* Feb. 20, 1867; John Nugent to Barlow, Feb. 17, 1867, S. L. M. Barlow Papers, Huntington Library, San Marino, Calif.; *New York World,* Feb. 14, 1867.

31. House, *Congressional Globe,* 39th Cong., 2d sess., Dec. 20, 1866, 1:212–215; *New York Times,* Feb. 14, 1867.

32. Senate, *Congressional Globe,* 39th Cong., 2d sess., Feb. 15, 1867, 2:1361, 1374–75.

33. Ibid., Feb. 3, 1867, 2:1459–67.

34. House, *Congressional Globe,* 39th Cong., 2d sess., Feb. 18, 1867, 2:1315–1340; *New York World,* Feb. 18, 1867.

35. House, *Congressional Globe,* 39th Cong., 2d sess., Feb. 19, 1867, 2:1352–1400; Senate, *Congressional Globe,* 39th Cong., 2d sess., Feb. 19, 1867, 3:1570.

36. Ibid., Feb. 20, 1867, 3:1627; Beale, *Welles Diary,* 3:55–56, 59.

37. Wood to Johnson, Feb. 21, 1867, Johnson Papers; *New York World,* Feb. 21, 1867; *Detroit Free Press,* Feb. 22, 1867.

38. Richardson, *Messages and Papers of the Presidents,* 6:492–511; John Nugent to Barlow, Feb. 28, 1867, Barlow Papers; House, *Congressional Globe*, 39th Cong., 2d sess., Mar. 2, 1867, 3:1732–33, Senate, *Congressional Globe,* Mar. 2, 1867, 3:1973–96.

39. *The Nation,* 4 (1867):141.

## CHAPTER 6

1. *Chicago Times,* Mar. 18, 1867; *National Intelligencer,* Mar. 11, 13, 1867; Edward McPherson, *A Political History of the United States of America during the Period of Reconstruction* (Washington, D.C.: Philp & Solomons, 1871), pp. 141–43.

2. Charles Halpine to Johnson, Mar. 13, 25, 1867, Andrew Johnson Papers, Library of Congress, Washington, D.C.

3. *New York World,* Feb. 27, Mar. 4, May 11, 1867; Manton Marble to Buchanan, Feb. 25, 1867, in John B. Moore, ed., *The Works of James Buchanan, Comprising His Speeches, State Papers, and Private Correspondence,* 12 vols. (Philadelphia: Lippincott, 1908–1910), 11:434–35.

4. *New York World,* Feb. 23, 26, Mar. 6, 1867.

5. Irving Katz, *August Belmont: A Political Biography* (New York: Columbia University Press, 1968), p. 159; *National Intelligencer,* Mar. 15, 1867; *New York World,* March 16, 19, Apr. 16, 1867.

6. U.S., Congress, House, *Congressional Globe,* 40th Cong., 1st sess., Mar. 11, 1867, 1:65, Mar. 19, 1867, 1:215; U.S. Congress, Senate, *Congressional Globe,* 40th Cong., 1st sess., Mar. 11, 1867, 1:157; *U.S. Statutes at Large,* vol. 15, pp. 2–4; Diary of Charles Mason, Mar. 24, 1867, Charles Mason Papers, Iowa State Department of History and Archives, Des Moines.

7. *New York World,* Mar. 25, 1867.

8. Hampton to John Mullaly, Mar. 31, 1867, in Charles Cauthen, ed., *Family Letters of the Three Wade Hamptons* (Columbia: University of South Carolina Press, 1953), p. 42; Francis Simkins and Robert Woody, *South Carolina during Reconstruction* (Chapel Hill: University of North Carolina Press, 1932), pp. 83–86.

9. Walter Fleming, *Civil War and Reconstruction in Alabama* (New York: Columbia University Press, 1905), pp. 503–5; J. G. de Roulhac Hamilton, *Reconstruction in North Carolina* (New York: Columbia University Press, 1914), pp. 243–44; Alan Conway, *The Reconstruction of Georgia* (Minneapolis: University of Minnesota Press, 1966), pp. 139–41; John Ficklin, *History of Reconstruction in Louisiana,* John Hopkins Studies in Historical and Political Science, ser. 27 (Baltimore: John Hopkins Press, 1910), 185; *Chicago Times,* Mar. 9, 1867; *Boston Post,* Apr. 27, 1867; William Harris, *Presidential Reconstruction in Mississippi* (Baton Rouge: Louisiana State University Press, 1967), pp. 241–42; James Patton, *Unionism and Reconstruction in Tennessee, 1860–1869* (Chapel Hill: University of North Carolina Press, 1934), pp. 134–36; *New York World,* Mar. 9, 1867.

10. *Chicago Times,* Mar. 10, 13, 20, 31, Apr. 20, 26, 1867; *Boston Post,* Mar. 21, 26, 28, 1867; *Davenport Daily Democrat,* Apr. 1, 1867; *Detroit Free Press,* Apr. 25, 1867.

11. *Old Guard,* 5 (1867):318–19, 526–32, 558–59; *Philadelphia Age,* Mar. 6, 1867; *Columbus Crisis,* May 1, 1867; *Cincinnati Daily Enquirer,* Mar. 6, 21, Apr. 16, May 14, 1867.

12. Buchanan to Marble, Mar. 4, 1867, in Moore, *The Works of James Buchanan,* 11:437–38; *Philadelphia Age,* Mar. 8, 13, 28, 1867; *Milwaukee Daily News,* Mar. 22, May 4, 1867; *Cincinnati Daily Enquirer,* Mar. 12, 20, May 3, 1867; *Columbus Crisis,* Mar. 6, Apr. 9, 1867.

13. *Cincinnati Daily Enquirer,* Apr. 4, 9, 1867; *Philadelphia Age,* Mar. 5, 7, 13, Apr. 4, 1867.

14. *Old Guard,* 5 (1867):81–89, 230–32, 280–86; James Wall to Buchanan, Mar. 27, 1867, James Buchanan Papers, Historical Society of Pennsylvania, Philadelphia; Henry Clay Dean to Mason, Mar. 5, 1867, Mason Papers.

15. *Boston Post,* Jan. 16, Feb. 8, 9, 18, 1867; *American Annual Cyclopaedia and Register of Important Events for the Year 1867* (New York: Appleton, 1868), pp. 535–37; *Hartford Daily Times,* Feb. 6, 1867; *New Haven Register* in *National Intelligencer,* Apr. 2, 1867.

16. *Boston Post,* Mar. 27, 1867; *Hartford Daily Times,* Mar. 26, 29, 30, 1867.

17. *National Intelligencer,* Mar. 15, Apr. 3, 9, 1867; *Chicago Times,* Apr. 4, 1867; *Philadelphia Age,* Apr. 3, 1867.

18. *Dubuque Weekly Herald,* Apr. 10, 1867; *Columbus Crisis,* Apr. 10, 1867; *Cincinnati Daily Enquirer,* Apr. 12, May 29, 1867; Joseph Buchanan to Mason, Apr. 22, 1867, Mason Papers; unsigned to Long, Apr. 13, 1867, Alexander Long Papers, Cincinnati Historical Society; *Boston Post,* Apr. 20, July 13, 1867.

19. Stanley Kutler, *Judicial Power and Reconstruction Politics* (Chicago: University of Chicago Press, 1968), pp. 96–99; *Cincinnati Daily Enquirer,* Apr. 15, 1867.

20. William Russ, Jr., "Registration and Disfranchisement under Radical Reconstruction," *Mississippi Valley Historical Review* 21 (1934): 163–80; Jonathan Dorris, *Pardon and Amnesty under Lincoln and Johnson* (Chapel Hill: University of North Carolina Press, 1953), pp. 333–34.

21. James Sefton, *The United States Army and Reconstruction, 1865–1877* (Baton Rouge: Louisiana State University Press, 1967), pp. 130–41.

22. *Hartford Daily Times,* June 3, 1867; Tilden to Marble, Apr. 23, 1867, Manton Marble Papers, Library of Congress, Washington, D.C.

23. *Chicago Times,* May 4, 28, 29, 1867; *Detroit Free Press,* May 38, 1867; *Boston Post,* June 1, 1867.

24. Ibid., June 28, 1867; *Cincinnati Daily Enquirer,* June 28, 1867.

25. *New York World,* June 29, Aug. 3, 1867; Senate, *Congressional Globe,* 40th Cong., 1st sess., July 11, 1867, 1:573–77; *Boston Post,* July 23, Aug. 6, 1867; *Chicago Times,* July 20, 1867; *Detroit Free Press,* Aug. 18, 1867.

26. U.S., *Statutes at Large,* vol. 15, pp. 14–16; *Chicago Times,* July 15, 1867.

27. *New York World,* Mar. 18, 19, 1867; *Davenport Daily Democrat,* May 7, July 16, 1867.

28. Senate, *Congressional Globe,* 29th Cong., 1st sess., Feb. 5, 1866, 1:667, 2d sess., Feb. 25, 1867, 3:1837, 40th Cong., 1st sess., July 21, 1867, 1:797; *Cincinnati Daily Enquirer,* Mar. 4, 1867; *New York World,* June 28, 1867; *Philadelphia Age,* June 12, 1867.

29. David Montgomery, *Beyond Equality: Labor and the Radical Republicans* (New York: Knopf, 1967), pp. 234, 242–43, 298–303; *Cincinnati Daily Enquirer,* Apr. 19, 1867.

30. *New York World,* Feb. 8, 16, June 15, 1867; *Chicago Times,* May 8, 1867.

31. *New York World,* Feb. 11, 1867; House, *Congressional Globe,* 39th Cong., 2d sess., Jan. 18, 1867, 1:554, Feb. 18, 1867, 2:1314–15; *New York Herald,* Feb. 1, 3, 1867; Buchanan to Blake, Jan. 19, 1867, Buchanan Papers.

32. *New York Herald,* Feb. 5, 1867; House, *Congressional Globe,* 29th Cong., 2d sess., Feb. 20, 1867, 2:1417–24, Feb. 28, 1867, 3:1663–68; Mar. 2, 1867, 3:1734–35.

33. *New York World,* Mar. 13, 1867.

34. Irwin Unger, *The Greenback Era: A Social and Political History of American Finance, 1865–1879* (Princeton: Princeton University Press, 1964), pp. 72–79; *Cincinnati Daily Enquirer,* Apr. 19, 1867.

35. Chester Destler, "The Origin and Character of the Pendleton Plan," *Mississippi Valley Historical Review* 24 (1837):171–84; McLean to Barlow, Feb. 4, 1867, S. L. M. Barlow Papers, Huntington Library, San Marino, Calif.

36. Unger, *The Greenback Era,* pp. 80–82.

37. *Cincinnati Daily Enquirer,* Aug. 1, 1867; *Boston Post,* 1867, Aug. 23, 1867; *New York World,* Sept. 6, 1867.

38. *Chicago Times,* June 15, 20, 1867; *Boston Post,* 1867, Aug. 23, 1867; *Cincinnati Daily Enquirer,* June 27, 1867; *Hartford Daily Times,* Aug. 6, 1867; *Illinois State Register,* Aug. 6, 1867; *Detroit Free Press,* July 28, 1867.

39. *National Intelligencer,* July 20, Aug. 1, 1867; *Cincinnati Daily Enquirer,* July 13, 1867.

40. *Hartford Daily Times,* July 29, Aug. 17, 1867; Patton, *Union and Reconstruction in Tennessee,* pp. 139–40; Simkins and Woody, *South Carolina during Reconstruction,* p. 86; *New York World,* Aug. 6, 12, 1867; *Cincinnati Daily Enquirer,* Aug. 7, 1867; *Boston Post,* Aug. 8, 1867.

41. William B. Hesseltine, *Ulysses S Grant: Politician* (New York: Dodd, Mead, 1935), pp. 87–88; Benjamin Thomas and Harold Hyman, *Stanton: The Life and Times of Lincoln's Secretary of War* (New York: Knopf, 1962), pp. 547–51.

42. *Detroit Free Press,* Aug. 15, 1867; *New York World,* Aug. 26, 1867; *Chicago Times,* Aug. 30, Sept. 5, 11, 1867; *Hartford Daily Times,* Sept. 6, 9, 1867; James Richardson, ed., *A Compilation of the Messages and Papers of the Presidents, 1789–1897,* 10 vols. (Washington, D.C.: Bureau of National Literature and Art, 1896–1899), 6:547–49; *Boston Post,* Sept. 10, 1867; *Cincinnati Daily Enquirer,* Sept. 10, 1867; *Illinois State Register,* Sept. 10, 1867.

43. George Fort Milton, *The Age of Hate: Andrew Johnson and the Radicals* (New York: Coward-McMann, 1930), pp. 195–96; S. M. Ribbin to Bigler, Aug. 25, 1867, William Bigler Papers, Historical Society of Pennsylvania, Philadelphia; M. Blair to Johnson, Aug. 26, 1867, J. B. Stoll to Johnson, Aug. 29, 1867, Cassidy to Blair, Sept. 1, 1867, B. Boyer to Johnson, Sept. 4, 1867, Alexander to Johnson, Sept. 8, 1867, Hendricks to Voorhees, Oct. 23, 1867, Johnson Papers; *New York World,* Aug. 14, 1867; Howard Beale, ed., *The Diary of Gideon Welles,* 3 vols. (New York: Norton, 1960), 3:195–96; F. Blair to Tilden, Sept. 6, 1867, Samuel J. Tilden Papers, New York Public Library; M. Blair to Barlow, Sept. 9, 1867, Barlow Papers.

44. *Cincinnati Daily Enquirer,* Sept. 7, 11, 1867; *Hartford Daily Times,* Sept. 10, 1867.

45. *New York World,* Sept. 12, 1867; Beale, *Welles Diary,* 3:199–200; Welles to Tilden, Sept. 14, 1867, Tilden Papers; *Boston Post,* Nov. 9, 1867.

46. Beale, *Welles Diary,* 3:203–4; Blair to Barlow, Sept. 20, 1867, Barlow Papers; Philo Durfee to Seymour, Oct. 5, 1867, Horatio Seymour Papers, New York State Library, Albany; *New York World,* Sept. 25, 18, 1867.

47. *American Annual Cyclopaedia, 1867,* p. 620; Samuel Randall to Johnson, Aug. 15, 1867, Johnson Papers; *New York Herald,* Aug. 22, 1867; *Boston Post,* Sept. 14, 1867; Beale, *Welles Diary,* 3:205; *Philadelphia Age,* Aug. 14, 17, 24, 26, Sept. 3, 11, 13, 14, Oct. 9, 14, 1867.

48. George Porter, *Ohio Politics in the Civil War Period,* Columbia Studies in History, Economics, and Public Law, vol. 15 (New York: Longmans, Green, 1911), pp. 239, 244–46; *Cincinnati Daily Enquirer,* Sept. 5, Oct. 1, 1867; *Columbus Crisis,* Sept. 18, 1867.

49. Robert Sharkey, *Money, Class and Party: An Economic Study of Civil War and Reconstruction,* John Hopkins Studies in Historical and Political Science, ser. 77 (Baltimore: John Hopkins Press, 1959), pp. 92–96; Unger, *The Greenback Era,* pp. 83–84; *Cincinnati Daily Enquirer,* Apr. 24, June 21, July 6, Aug. 16, 1867.

50. Washington McLean to Barlow, Oct. 10, 1867, Barlow Papers; *Cincinnati Daily Enquirer,* Oct. 12, 17, 1867; Porter, *Ohio Politics in the Civil War Period,* p. 248; *Detroit Free Press,* Oct. 10, 1867; *Chicago Times,* Oct. 11, 1867; *New York World,* Oct. 12, 1867; *Illinois State Register,* Oct. 15, 1867; *Columbus Crisis,* Oct 23, 1867.

51. *American Annual Cyclopaedia, 1867,* pp. 544–45; *Boston Post,* Oct. 4, 1867.

52. Beale, *Welles Diary,* 3:223; *Boston Post,* Oct. 12, 1867; Barlow to Tilden [Oct. 1867], in John Bigelow, ed., *Letters and Literary Memorials of Samuel J. Tilden,* 2 vols. (New York: Harper, 1908), 1:149; *Cincinnati Daily Enquirer,* Oct. 11, 1867; *Chicago Times,* Oct. 15, 1867; *St. Paul Pioneer,* Oct. 17, 1867.

53. Sanford Church to Tilden, Oct. 12, 1867, Tilden Papers; *New York World,* Oct. 12, 15, 21, 1867; *New York Times,* Oct. 19, 1867; Georges Clemenceau, *American Reconstruction, 1865–1870* (New York, MacVeagh, 1928), pp. 130–31.

54. *Milwaukee Daily News,* Oct. 5, 1867; *Detroit Free Press,* Aug. 21, 1867; *St. Paul Pioneer,* Oct. 15, 1867.

55. *American Annual Cyclopaedia, 1867,* pp. 513, 544–45; Clemenceau, *American Reconstruction,* p. 134.

## CHAPTER 7

1. William Shipman to Barlow, Oct. 15, 1867, McClellan to Barlow, n.d., S. L. M. Barlow Papers, Huntington Library, San Marino, Calif.; S. S. Nichols to Seymour, Oct. 19, 1867, Horatio Seymour Papers, New York Historical Society, New York; William Bell to Bigler, Nov. 7, 1867, William Bigler Papers, Historical Society of Pennsylvania, Philadelphia; *St. Paul Pioneer,* Nov. 10, 1867; *Hartford Daily Times,* Nov. 12, 1867.

2. Michael Perman, *Reunion Without Compromise: The South and Reconstruction, 1865–1868* (London: Cambridge University Press, 1973), p. 304–36.

3. *New York World,* Nov. 7, 13, 21, 22, 1867.

4. W. N. Halderman to Marble, Nov. 13, 1867, George S. Curtis to Marble, Nov. 7, 1867, Manton Marble Papers, Library of Congress, Washington, D.C.; *Cincinnati Daily Enquirer,* Nov. 21, 1867; *Chicago Times,* Nov. 1, 1867; *Old Guard* 5 (1867):881–86; *New York World,* Dec. 7, 1867.

5. *Boston Post,* Nov. 20, 1867.

6. *Old Guard,* 5 (1867):886.

7. James Sefton, *The United States Army and Reconstruction* (Baton Rouge: Louisiana State University Press), pp. 175–77; Jeremiah Black to Hancock, Nov. 30, 1867, in Almira Hancock, *Reminiscences of Winfield Scott Hancock* (New York: Webster, 1887), pp. 225–26; *Boston Post,* Dec. 7, 12, 1867; *Cincinnati Daily Enquirer,* Dec. 21, 1867; *Philadelphia Age,* Jan. 3, 1867.

8. *Cincinnati Daily Enquirer,* Aug. 23, 1867; *Old Guard* 5 (1867):801–10; Howard K. Beale, ed., *The Diary of Gideon Welles,* 3 vols. (New York: Norton, 1960), 3:184; William Shipman to Barlow, Sept. 16, 1867, Barlow Papers; *Hartford Daily Times,* Nov. 11, 1867.

9. Ibid., Nov. 27, 1867; *Cincinnati Daily Enquirer,* Nov. 27, 1867; *St. Paul Pioneer,* Dec. 11, 1867; Sylvester Mowry to Doolittle, Dec. 12, 1867, James Doolittle Papers, Wisconsin State Historical Society, Madison; *Illinois State Register,* Dec. 13, 1867.

10. David DeWitt, *The Impeachment and Trial of Andrew Johnson* (New York: Macmillan, 1903), pp. 200–94; *St. Paul Pioneer,* Nov. 26, 1867.

11. *Cincinnati Daily Enquirer,* Nov. 29, 1867; Black to Johnson, Nov, 16, 25, Andrew Johnson Papers, library of Congress, Washington D.C.

12. *National Intelligencer,* Nov. 14, 16, 27, 1867; George Fort Milton, *The Age of Hate: Andrew Johnson and the Radicals* (New York: Coward-McCann, 1930), pp. 474–75.

13. U.S., Congress, House, *Congressional Globe,* 40th Cong., 2d sess., Dec. 3, 1867, 1:11–12; Senate, *Congressional Globe,* 40th Cong., 2d sess., Dec. 4, 1867, 1:20–22, Dec. 10, 1867, 1:100–101; *Boston Post,* Dec. 4, 1867; *Hartford Daily Times,* Dec. 4, 1867; *St. Paul Pioneer,* Dec. 4, 1867; *Cincinnati Daily Enquirer,* Dec. 4, 1867; *Columbus Crisis,* Dec. 11, 1867.

14. *Detroit Free Press,* Dec. 1, 1867; *Cincinnati Daily Enquirer,* Dec. 3, 1867; House, *Congressional Globe,* 40th Cong., 2d sess., Dec. 6, 1867, 1:64–68; *St. Paul Pioneer,* Dec. 10, 1867; D. A. Ogden to Johnson, Dec. 11, 1867, Johnson Papers.

15. James Richardson, ed., *A Compilation of the Messages and Papers of the Presidents, 1789–1897,* 10 vols. (Washington: Bureau of National Literature and Art, 1896–99), 6:583–94.

16. Martin Mantell, *Johnson, Grant, and the Politics of Reconstruction* (New York: Columbia University Press, 1973), pp. 74–75.

17. *St. Paul Pioneer,* Dec. 10, 1867; House, *Congressional Globe,* 40th Cong., 2d sess., Dec. 13, 1867, 1:177–78; *Cincinnati Daily Enquirer,* Dec. 23, 1867.

18. House, *Congressional Globe,* 40th Cong., 2d sess., Dec. 17, 1867, 1:240–41.

19. Blair to Barlow, Dec. 23, 1867, Barlow Papers; *St. Paul Pioneer,* Dec. 19, 1867; *Cincinnati Daily Enquirer,* Dec. 19, 1867; Marble to Doolittle, Dec. 29, 1867, Doolittle Papers; Doolittle to Marble, Jan. 2, 1868, Marble Papers.

20. Sever Eubank, "The McCardle Case: A Challenge to Radical Reconstruction," *Journal of Mississippi History* 18 (1965):111–27; *Boston Post,* Jan. 11, 1868; *Cincinnati Daily Enquirer,* Jan. 11, 1868.

21. House, *Congressional Globe,* 40th Cong., 2d sess., Jan. 13, 1868, 1:477–89; *Detroit Free Press,* Jan. 14, 1868; *Philadelphia Age,* Jan. 14, 1868; *Boston Post,* Jan. 16, 1868; *Illinois State Register,* Jan. 17, 1868.

22. House, *Congressional Globe,* 40th Cong., 2d sess., Jan. 13, 1868, 1:476, Jan. 14, 1868, Jan. 21, 1868, 1:664.

23. William B. Hesseltine, *Ulysses S. Grant: Politician* (New York: Knopf, 1935), pp. 103–5.

24. J. Glancey Jones to Johnson, Jan. 14, 1868, John A. McClernand to Johnson, Jan. 14, 1868, Johnson Papers; *Illinois State Register,* Jan. 14, 1868; *Boston Post,* Jan. 14, 1868; *Philadelphia Age,* Jan. 16, 1868; *National Intelligencer,* Jan. 15, 1868; *New York World,* Jan. 15, 20, 23, 27, 1868; *Cincinnati Daily Enquirer,* Jan. 16, 1868; *Hartford Daily Times,* Jan. 23, 1868; Georges Clemenceau, *American Reconstruction, 1865–1870* (New York: MacVeagh, 1926), p. 144.

25. House, *Congressional Globe,* 40th Cong., 2d sess., Feb. 4, 1868, 1:977, Feb. 10, 1868, 2:1087; *New York World,* Feb. 5, 7, 10–12, 1868; *Cincinnati Daily Enquirer,* Feb. 5, 6, 1868; Horatio King to Buchanan, Feb. 5, 1868, James Buchanan Papers, Historical Society of Pennsylvania, Philadelphia; Jerome Stillson to Barlow, Feb. 12, 1868, Barlow Papers; *Boston Post,* Feb. 12, 1868; *Illinois State Register,* Feb. 12, 1868; *St. Paul Pioneer,* Feb. 12, 1868.

26. Edward McPherson, ed., *The Political History of the United States of America during the Period of Reconstruction* (Washington: Philp & Solomons, 1871), p. 353.

27. Senate, *Congressional Globe,* 40th Cong., 2d sess., Feb. 13, 1868, 2:1144–56, Feb. 14, 1868, 2:1166–77, Feb. 19, 1868, 2:1271.

28. Milton, *Age of Hate,* pp. 496–501.

29. Henry Smythe to W. G. Moore, Feb. 27, 1868, Johnson Papers.

30. Jerome Stillson to Barlow, Feb. 27, 1868, Barlow Papers; *Cincinnati Daily Enquirer,* Feb. 25, 1868; *Illinois State Register,* Feb. 25, 27, 1868; Clemenceau, *American Reconstruction,* p. 158; *St. Paul Pioneer,* Mar. 3, 4, 1868; *Columbus Crisis,* Mar. 4, 1858; T. F. Bayard to J. A. Bayard, Feb. 23, 1868, Thomas F. Bayard Papers, Library of Congress, Washington, D.C.

31. Sam Ward to Barlow, Feb. 25, 1868, Barlow Papers; *Hartford Daily Times,* Feb. 28, 1868.

32. *Hartford Daily Times,* Feb. 27, 1868; *New York Herald,* Mar. 1, 1868; U.S. Congress, House, *Congressional Globe,* 40th Cong., 2d sess., Feb. 22, 1868, 2:1337; *Cincinnati Daily Enquirer,* Feb. 26, 1868.

33. House, *Congressional Globe,* 40th Cong., 2d sess., Feb. 22, 1868. 2:1336–38, 1342, 1349, 1359; Michael Les Benedict, *The Impeachment and Trial of Andrew Johnson* (New York: Norton, 1973), pp. 105–6.

34. *Cincinnati Daily Enquirer,* Mar. 27, 29, 1868; *New York Herald,* Mar. 1, 1868, *New York World,* Mar. 2, 1868; *Hartford Daily Times,* Mar. 6, 1868.

35. Senate, *Congressional Globe,* 40th Cong., 2d sess., Feb. 29, 1868, 2:1521–22, Mar. 2, 1868, 2:1602–1603.

36. Ibid., Mar. 2, 1868, 2:1595–1601.

37. Ibid., Feb. 29, 1868, 2:1520–22.
38. DeWitt, *Impeachment and Trial of Andrew Johnson*, pp. 388–89.
39. *Hartford Daily Times*, Mar. 6, 1868; Senate, *Congressional Globe*, 40th Cong., 2d sess., Mar. 5, 1868, 2:1671–80.
40. Ibid., Mar. 6, 1868, 2:1696–1700.
41. Ibid., Mar. 9, 1868, 2:1742–44.
42. *Illinois State Register*, Mar. 11, 1868; *New York Herald*, Mar. 12, 1868; House, *Congressional Globe*, 40th Cong., 2d sess., Mar. 12, 1868, 2:1859–60, Mar. 21, 1868, 3:2060.
43. Thomas Ewing to Johnson, Mar. 1, 1868, Johnson Papers; Beale, *Welles Diary*, 3:305; C. Wendell to Tilden, Samuel J. Tilden Papers, New York Public Library.
44. Black to Johnson, Mar. 18, 1868, Johnson Papers; William Brigance, "Jeremiah Black and Andrew Johnson," *Mississippi Valley Historical Review* 19 (1932):205–18.
45. *Hartford Daily Times*, Mar. 21, 24, 1868; *Chicago Times*, Mar. 24, Apr. 1, 1868; House, *Congressional Globe*, 40th Cong., 2d sess., Mar. 26, 1868, 3:2137–39, Mar. 28, 1868, 3:2193–94, 2216.
46. *Chicago Times*, Mar. 30, Apr. 2, 1868; *Cincinnati Daily Enquirer*, Mar. 31, 1868.
47. *Illinois State Register*, Apr. 1, 1868; *Cincinnati Daily Enquirer*, Apr. 1, 3, 1868.
48. Senate, *Congressional Globe*, 40th Cong., 2d sess., *Supplement Containing the Proceedings of the Senate Sitting for the Trial of Andrew Johnson*, Mar. 31, 1868, pp. 59–63; *Philadelphia Age*, Apr. 1, 1868; *Boston Post*, Apr. 1, 1868; *Chicago Times*, Apr. 2, 1868; *St. Paul Pioneer*, Apr. 4, 1868; *Cincinnati Daily Enquirer*, Apr. 4, 1868.
49. *Chicago Times*, Apr. 6, 13, 1868; *St. Paul Pioneer*, Apr. 10, 12, 1868.
50. *Hartford Daily Times*, Apr. 7, 1868; *Boston Post*, Apr. 9, 1868; *Cincinnati Daily Enquirer*, Apr. 7, 9, 13, 15, 1868.
51. *National Intelligencer*, Apr. 8, 20, 1868; *Chicago Times*, Apr. 20, 1868; *Hartford Daily Times*, Apr. 24, 1868.
52. John D. Van Buren to Seymour, Apr. 21, 1868, Seymour Papers; *Cincinnati Daily Enquirer*, Apr. 22, May 1, 1868; *Hartford Daily Times*, Apr. 23, 1868; Jerome Mushkat, "The Trial of Andrew Johnson: A Contemporary View," *New York History* 48 (1967):280.
53. *Cincinnati Daily Enquirer*, Apr. 29, 1868; *Chicago Times*, May 2, 1868; Senate, *Congressional Globe*, 40th Cong., 2d sess., *Supplement*, Apr. 24, 1868, p. 295; House, *Congressional Globe*, 40th Cong., 2d sess., Apr. 29, 1868, 3:2333–34; Mushkat, "The Trial of Andrew Johnson," p. 280; *National Intelligencer*, May 4, 1868; *New York Herald*, May 4, 1868; *Hartford Daily Times*, May 5, 1868.
54. Ibid., Apr. 25, 27, 1868.
55. Samuel S. Cox, *Union-Disunion-Reunion: Three Decades of Federal Legislation, 1865–1885* (Providence, R.I.: Reid, 1885), pp. 592–94.
56. House, *Congressional Globe*, 40th Cong., 2d sess., May 8, 1868, 3:2390–99, May 11, 1868, 3:2412.
57. *Illinois State Register*, May 12, 1868.
58. Senate, *Congressional Globe*, 40th Cong., 2d sess., *Supplement*, May 16, 1868, pp. 410–12.
59. *New York Herald*, May 19, 23, 1868.
60. Clemenceau, *American Reconstruction*, p. 186.
61. John D. Van Vuren to Seymour, May 20, 1868, Seymour Papers; *Cincinnati Daily Enquirer*, May 27, June 3, 1868; *Hartford Daily Times*, June 3, 1868.

## CHAPTER 8

1. Charles Coleman, *The Election of 1868: The Democratic Effort to Regain Control*, Columbia Studies in History, Economics, and Public Law, vol. 302 (New York: Columbia University Press, 1933), pp. 60–61; *New York Herald*, Jan. 10, 1868; *Cincinnati Daily Enquirer*, Feb. 28, 1868; *Illinois State Register*, Jan. 9, 11, 1868; *Chicago Times*, Jan. 21, 1868.
2. *New York World*, Nov. 19, 29, Dec. 4, 1867, Jan. 29, 1868; *New York Herald*, Nov. 15, 30, Dec. 4, 1867; *Cincinnati Daily Enquirer*, Mar. 13, 1868; *American Annual Cyclopaedia and Register of Important Events for the Year 1868* (New York: Appleton, 1869), p. 203.
3. *New York Herald*, Dec. 4, 1867; *New York Times*, Dec. 4, 1867; Robert Sharkey, *Money, Class and Party: An Economic Study of Civil War and Reconstruction*, John Hopkins Studies in Historical and Political Science, ser. 77 (Baltimore: John Hopkins Press, 1959), pp. 106–10.

4. Coleman, *The Election of 1868*, p. 37; *New York Herald*, Feb. 9, 1868; George Cass to Tilden, Feb. 24, 1868, Samuel J. Tilden Papers, New York Public Library.

5. *New York World*, Jan. 30, Feb. 1, 1868; George McJimsey, *Genteel Partisan: Manton Marble, 1834–1917* (Ames: Iowa State University Press, 1971), p. 122.

6. Sharkey, *Money, Class, and Party*, pp. 110–17.

7. Bigler to Tilden, Feb. 3, 1868, in John Bigelow, ed., *Letters and Literary Memorials of Samuel J. Tilden*, 2 vols. (New York: Harper, 1908), p. 217; Tilden to Bigler, Feb. 28, 1868, William Bigler Papers, Historical Society of Pennsylvania, Philadelphia; Mason to Byington, Feb. 13, 1868, LeGrand Byington Papers, State Historical Society of Iowa, Iowa City.

8. *Boston Post*, Dec. 14, 1867; *Cincinnati Daily Enquirer*, Jan. 25, 1868; *National Intelligencer*, Dec. 23, 1867; *Philadelphia Age*, Jan. 22, 1868; *St. Paul Pioneer*, Feb. 18, 21, 1868.

9. *Old Guard* 6 (1868):160; *Columbus Crisis*, Feb. 5, 1868; Belmont to Tilden, Feb. 19, Tilden Papers; Irving Katz, *August Belmont: A Political Biography* (New York: Columbia University Press, 1968), p. 160.

10. Coleman, *The Election of 1868*, p. 61; *Chicago Times*, May 4, Apr. 22, 1868; Homer Stebbins, *Political History of New York, 1865–1869*, Columbia Studies in History, Economics, and Public Law, vol. 55 (New York: Columbia University Press, 1913), pp. 321–24; James Burr to Bigler, Jan. 7, 1868, Bigler Papers; Bigler to Tilden, Mar. 4, 1868, Tilden Papers; Erwin Bradley, *The Triumph of Militant Republicanism: A Study of Pennsylvania and Presidential Politics* (Philadelphia: Pennsylvania University Press, 1964), p. 293.

11. James Noble to Marble, Feb. 4, 1868, Manton Marble Papers, Library of Congress, Washington, D.C.

12. Corse to Sibley, Jan. 18, Feb. 26, 1868, Henry Sibley Papers, Minnesota State Historical Society, St. Paul; *National Intelligencer*, May 19, 1868; Mary Dearing, *Veterans in Politics: The Story of the G.A.R.* (Baton Rouge: Louisiana State University Press, 1952), pp. 153, 167–68.

13. Corse to Sibley, Jan. 17, 1868, Sibley Papers; *New York Herald*, Jan. 12, Mar. 30, 1868; *New York World*, Nov. 7, 1867.

14. Charles Mason to Morton, Jan. 20, 1868, J. Sterling Morton Papers, Nebraska State Historical Society, Lincoln; Coleman, *The Election of 1868*, pp. 55–56; *National Intelligencer*, Mar. 20, 1868; Katz, *Belmont*, pp. 162, 166.

15. Frank Klement, *The Limits of Dissent: Clement L. Vallandigham and the Civil War* (Lexington: University of Kentucky Press, 1970), pp. 305–6; George Porter, *Ohio Politics in the Civil War Period*, Columbia Studies in History, Economics, and Public Law, vol. 40 (New York: Longmans, Green, 1911), p. 253.

16. *New York Herald*, Feb. 1, Mar. 12, 1868; *Boston Post*, Mar. 2, 1868; *Hartford Daily Times*, Mar. 11, 1868.

17. *Hartford Daily Times*, Feb. 13, Apr. 7, 1868; Howard K. Beale, *The Diary of Gideon Welles*, 3 vols. (New York: Norton, 1960), 2:527–29.

18. William Smith, *The Francis Preston Blair Family in Politics*, 2 vols. (New York: Macmillan, 1933), 2:391–400; Montgomery Blair to Barlow, Jan. 29, 1868, S. L. M. Barlow Papers, Huntington Library, San Marino, Calif.

19. Martin Mantell, *Johnson, Grant, and The Politics of Reconstruction* (New York: Columbia University Press, 1973), pp. 74–75, 89–90.

20. *Columbus Crisis*, Jan. 1, 1868; *Cincinnati Daily Enquirer*, Dec. 20, 1867; M. Blair to Barlow, Apr. 15, 1868, S. M. Marshall to Barlow, May 5, 1868, Barlow Papers; Joseph Warren to Marble, Jan. 28, 1868, Marble Papers.

21. Richard Taylor to Barlow, Jan. 16, 1868, John B. Gordon to Barlow, Apr. 6, 1868, Barlow Papers; John D. Van Buren to Seymour, Apr. 21, May 1, 1868, Horatio Seymour Papers, New York Historical Society, New York; *Boston Post*, Apr. 17, 1868; Seymour to Tilden, May 9, 1868, Tilden Papers; Dearing, *Veterans in Politics*, pp. 154–55.

22. Jerome Stillson to Barlow, Feb. 7, 1868, McClellan to Barlow, Mar. 13, 1868, Barlow Papers; Smythe to Moore, Feb. 27, 1868, Andrew Johnson Papers, Library of Congress, Washington, D.C.; William Myers, *General George Brinton McClellan: A Study in Personality* (New York: Appleton, 1934), pp. 482–83.

23. *New York Herald*, Feb. 15, 1868; James Buchanan to Bigler, Feb. 15, 1868, Bigler Papers; Bigler to Buchanan, Feb. 21, Mar. 5, 10, 1868, James Buchanan Papers, Historical Society of Pennsylvania, Philadelphia.

24. Bigler to Buchanan, Mar. 10, 1868, Buchanan Papers; Buchanan to Bigler, Mar. 13, 1868, Bigler Papers; *New York Herald*, Mar. 13, Apr. 24, 1868.

25. *Columbus Crisis*, Jan. 1, 1868; *Old Guard* 6 (1868):158; Pomeroy to Marble, Jan. 3, 1868, Marble Papers.

26. Harlow Orton to Smith, Jan. 17, 1868, George B. Smith Papers, Wisconsin State Historical Library, Madison; *Chicago Times,* Apr. 28, 1868.

27. Stewart Mitchell, *Horatio Seymour of New York* (Cambridge, Mass.: Harvard University Press, 1938), p. 396; *Cincinnati Daily Enquirer,* Dec. 3, 1867.

28. Seymour to Tilden, Nov. 29, 1867, Tilden Papers; Church to Seymour, Dec. 27, 1868, G. L. Miller to Seymour, Jan. 4, 1868, Cassidy to Seymour, Jan. 15, 1868, Horatio Seymour Papers, New York State Library, Albany; Mitchell, *Seymour,* p. 397.

29. Seymour to Tilden, Jan. 20, 1868, Francis Kernan to Tilden, Mar. 7, 1868, Tilden Papers; *New York Herald,* Mar. 12, 1868.

30. *Illinois State Register,* Mar. 14, 1868; *St. Paul Pioneer,* Mar. 22, 23, 1868; Tilden to Bigler, Apr. 6, 1868, Bigler Papers; N. E. Paine to Tilden, June 26, 1868, Tilden Papers.

31. *Cincinnati Daily Enquirer,* Jan. 9, Mar. 7, 1868; Seymour to Tilden, Mar. 4, 1868, Tilden Papers; U.S., Congress, Senate, *Congressional Globe,* 40th Cong., 2d sess., Feb. 25, 1868, 1:1416, June 10, 1868, 3:2999–3008.

32. William Browne to Barlow, Jan. 26, 1868, Reverdy Johnson to Barlow, Apr. 25, 1868, Barlow Papers; *Boston Post,* Feb. 25, 1868; *Old Guard* 6 (1868):89–90; *Columbus Crisis,* May 20, 1868.

33. William Browne to Barlow, Apr. 9, 22, May 15, 1868, R. Ould to Barlow, Apr. 18, 27, May 6, 1868, John Gordon to Barlow, Apr. 23, May 19, 1868, Reverdy Johnson to Barlow, May 16, 1868, D. L. Yulee to Barlow, June 22, 1868, Barlow Papers; *Old Guard* 6 (1868):317; Van Evrie to Seymour, [June 1968], Seymour Papers, New York State Library.

34. Coleman, *The Election of 1868,* p. 22.

35. *Chicago Times,* Apr. 15, 1868; *American Annual Cyclopaedia, 1868,* p. 203; *Hartford Daily Times,* Feb. 10, Mar. 12, 1868; *Philadelphia Age,* May 13, 1868; Harriet Dilla, *The Politics of Michigan, 1865–1868,* Columbia Studies in History, Economics and Public Law, vol. 47 (New York: Columbia University Press, 1912), pp. 91–92; *Detroit Free Press,* Apr. 8, 1868.

36. Coleman, *The Election of 1868,* pp. 103–4; *New York World,* Mar. 26, 1868; *New York Herald,* Mar. 6, 1868; *Cincinnati Daily Enquirer,* May 19, 1868.

37. Edward Perzel, "Alexander Long, Salmon P. Chase, and the Election of 1868," *Bulletin of the Cincinnati Historical Society* 23 (1865):3:18.

38. Chase to Long, Apr. 8, 1868, J. W. Schuckers to Long, Apr. 29, 30, 1868, Alexander Long Papers, Cincinnati Historical Society; Chase to Long, Apr. 19, 1868, in Jacob W. Schuckers, *The Life and Public Services of Salmon Portland Chase* (New York: Appleton, 1874), pp. 578–79.

39. *Cincinnati Daily Enquirer,* Mar. 25, 1868; *Chicago Times,* Mar. 27, 1868; *New York World,* Mar. 31, 1868.

40. Mantell, *Johnson, Grant, and the Politics of Reconstruction,* pp. 97–99.

41. Pendleton to Morton, Apr. 26, May 9, 23, 1868, Emma Morton to Morton, May 29, 1868, Morton Papers; *New York Herald,* May 27, 1868; Smith, *Blair Family,* 2:397; Frank Blair to Tilden, May 30, 1868, Tilden Papers.

42. Van Buren to Seymour, May 20, 1868, Seymour Papers, New York Historical Society; *New York Herald,* May 31, 1868; James Bayard to Barlow, May 21, 31, June 3, 1868, Barlow Papers; Barlow to Tilden, June 31, 1868, in John Bigelow, ed., *Letters and Literary Memorials of Samuel J. Tilden,* 2 vols. (New York: Harper, 1908), pp. 231–32; *New York Herald,* June 2, 1868; William Hanchett, *Irish: Charles G. Halpine in Civil War America* (Syracuse: Syracuse University Press, 1970), p. 172.

43. Chase to Belmont, May 30, 1868, in Schuckers, *Chase,* pp. 584–86; *New York World,* June 2, 8, 1868.

44. *Cincinnati Daily Enquirer,* June 10, 13, 1868; Church to Tilden, June 10, 1868, in Bigelow, *Letters of Samuel J. Tilden,* 1:229; *Illinois State Register,* June 13, 1868; *Hartford Daily Times,* June 15, 1868; Charles Brown to Allen, June 10, 1868, William Allen Papers, Library of Congress, Washington, D.C.; Bayard to Barlow, June 10, 1868, M. Blair to Barlow, June 10, 1868, Barlow Papers; *Columbus Crisis,* June 10, 1868; *New York Herald,* June 21, 1868.

45. *New York World,* June 17, 1868.

46. Chase to Van Buren, June 17, 1868, Salmon P. Chase Papers, Library of Congress, Washington, D.C.; James Kennedy to William Cassidy, June 18, 1868, Seymour Papers, New York State Library; Chase to William C. Bryant, June 19, in Schuckers, *Chase,* pp. 588–89; *New York Herald,* June 19, 1868.

47. F. A. Aiken to Cox, June 22, Samuel Cox Papers, Brown University Library, Providence, R.I.; Cassidy to Seymour, June 20, 1868, Seymour Papers, New York State Library; *New*

*York World,* June 19, 22, 1868; *Chicago Times,* June 10, 1868; Kate Sprague to Barlow, June 23, 1868, Samuel Ward to Barlow, June 24, 1868, Barlow Papers; Barlow to Tilden, June 24, 1868, Tilden Papers; *New York Herald,* June 26, 1868.

48. *New York Herald,* May 16, 1868; William Hawley to Tilden, May 23, 1868, Tilden Papers.

49. Beale, *The Diary of Gideon Welles,* 2:381; *National Intelligencer,* June 12, 1868; *New York World,* June 16, 1868.

50. Philo Durfee to Seymour, June 10, 16, 22, 26, 1868, Seymour Papers, New York State Library; R. W. Latham to Johnson, June 29, 1868, Johnson Papers.

## CHAPTER 9

1. W. Warden to Johnson, July 1, 1868, Andrew Johnson Papers, Library of Congress, Washington, D.C.

2. *Cincinnati Daily Enquirer,* July 1, 2, 1868; *St. Paul Pioneer,* July 2, 3, 1868; *Hartford Daily Times,* July 2, 1868.

3. *Cincinnati Daily Enquirer,* July 5, 1868; Harriet Dilla, *The Politics of Michigan, 1865–1878,* Columbia Studies in History, Economics, and Public Law, vol. 47 (New York: Columbia University Press, 1912), p. 96.

4. William Smith, *The Francis Preston Blair Family in Politics,* 2 vols (New York: Macmillan, 1933), 2:402–6.

5. *Boston Post,* June 30, 1868; W. Warden to Johnson, July 1, 1868, Johnson Papers; *Hartford Daily Times,* July 7, 1868.

6. *Philadelphia Age,* July 6, 1868; Warden to Johnson, July 3, 5, 1868, Johnson Papers.

7. *St. Paul Pioneer,* July 1, 1868; *Hartford Daily Times,* July 2, 1868; *New York Herald,* July 2, 1868; Kate Sprague to Chase, July 2, 1868, Salmon Chase Papers, Historical Society of Pennsylvania, Philadelphia.

8. Jacob W. Schuckers, *The Life and Public Services of Salmon Portland Chase* (New York: Appleton, 1874), pp. 589–90, 750–51; McCormick to Van Buren, July 2, 1868, McCormick to Chase, July 2, 1868, Cyrus Hall McCormick Papers, Wisconsin State Historical Society, Madison; Chase to Long, July 4, 1868, Alexander Long Papers, Cincinnati Historical Society.

9. *Cincinnati Daily Enquirer,* July 2, 1868; *Hartford Daily Times,* July 6, 1868; *Boston Post,* July 6, 1868; *New York Herald,* July 5, 1868.

10. *New York Herald,* July 4, 6, 7, 1868.

11. *Philadelphia Age,* July 8, 9, 1868.

12. *Cincinnati Daily Enquirer,* July 6, 1868; *New York World,* July 8, 1868; Chase to Van Buren, July 8, 1868 in Schuckers, *Chase,* p. 590.

13. *Cincinnati Daily Enquirer,* July 8, 1868.

14. Ibid., July 9, 1868.

15. Charles Coleman, *The Election of 1868: The Democratic Effort to Regain Control,* Columbia Studies in History, Economics, and Public Law, vol. 392 (New York: Columbia University Press, 1933), pp. 228, 235.

16. Van Buren, to Chase, July 24, 1868, Salmon Chase Papers, Library of Congress, Washington, D.C.; *New York Herald,* Sept. 6, 1868.

17. *St. Paul Pioneer,* July 29, 1868; *New York Herald,* July 10, 1868.

18. *Cincinnati Daily Enquirer,* July 10, 1868; *St. Paul Pioneer,* July 29, 1868; Coleman, *The Election of 1868,* p. 227.

19. Mary Dearing, *Veterans in Politics: The Story of the G.A.R.* (Baton Rouge: Louisiana State University Press, 1952), p. 158; *Cincinnati Daily Enquirer,* July 10, 1868.

20. *New York Herald,* July 10, Sept. 5, 1868; Samuel Ward to Barlow, July 16, 1868, S. L. M. Barlow Papers, Huntington Library, San Marino, Calif.; R. B. Harley to Seymour, July 23, Horatio Seymour Papers, New York State Library, Albany.

21. Howard K. Beale, ed., *The Diary of Gideon Welles,* 3 vols. (New York: Norton, 1960), 3:403; Hiram Ketchum to Johnson, July 9, 1868, Philo Durfee to Johnson, July 9, 13, 1868, J. D. Perryman to Johnson, July 10, 1868, Johnson Papers.

22. R. W. Latham to Tilden, July 14, 1868, Fernando Wood to Tilden, July 21, 1868, Samuel Tilden Papers, New York Public Library; J. D. Hoover to Seymour, July 15, 1868, R. W. Latham to F. Wood, July 20, 1868, John D. Van Buren to Seymour, July 20, 1868, Seymour Papers, New York State Library.

23. Dearing, *Veterans in Politics,* p. 161; Anonymous to Seymour, July 10, 1868, Seymour

Papers, New York State Library; *New York Herald,* July 10, 1868; *New York Times,* July 10, 1868; Barlow to Tilden, July 10, 1868, Tilden Papers.

24. *New York Herald,* July 10, 1868; "Any Democrat" to Seymour, July 17, 1868, W. E. W. to Seymour, July 24, 1868, Seymour Papers, New York State Library.

25. *Hartford Daily Times,* July 15, 1868; J. W. Schukers to Long, July 13, 14, 17, 27, 1868, John Cahill to Long, July 23, 24, 25, 27, 30, 31, 1868, W. Rosecrans to Long, Aug. 5, 1868, Long Papers.

26. *Cincinnati Daily Enquirer,* July 10, 1868; Samuel Ryan to Seymour, July 14, 1868, Horatio Seymour Papers, New York Historical Society, New York; *Columbus Crisis,* July 15, 1868; *Old Guard* 6 (1868):628–31; Halpine to Anne Halpine, July 27, 1868, Charles Halpine Papers, Huntington Library, San Marino, Calif.

27. *Cincinnati Daily Enquirer,* Aug. 4, 1868; *Hartford Daily Times,* Aug. 5, 1868; *New York Herald,* Aug. 8, 1868.

28. Seymour to Doolittle, Aug. 4, 1868, in "Selections From the Correspondence of the Late Senator James R. Doolittle: Post Bellum Days," *Magazine of History* 7 (1913):58–59; *New York World,* Aug. 5, 1868.

29. *New York Herald,* July 11, 1868; *New York Tribune,* Aug. 5, 1868.

30. *New York Herald,* July 11, 1868; *New York Tribune,* July 16, 25, 1868.

31. *St. Paul Pioneer,* July 11, Aug. 8, 1868; *Cincinnati Daily Enquirer,* July 14, 17, 21, 1868; *New York World,* July 16, 1868; *Hartford Daily Times,* July 18, Aug. 25, 1868; *Illinois State Register,* Sept. 24, 25, 1868; *Milwaukee Daily News,* Aug. 31, 1868.

32. J. S. Bridgeman to Seymour, July 20, 1868, R. B. Harley to Seymour, July 23, 1868, John Chisholm to Seymour, July 31, 1868, N. D. Martin to Seymour, Sept. 7, 1868, Seymour Papers, New York State Library; Horace Day to Seymour, Sept. 7, 1868, Seymour Papers, New York Historical Society; *Cincinnati Daily Enquirer,* Aug. 4, 1868; *Hartford Daily Times,* July 15, 1868; *Philadelphia Age,* Aug. 25, 26, 1868.

33. U.S., Congress, Senate, *Congressional Globe,* 40th Cong., 2d sess., July 9, 1868, 4:3878; *New York World,* Aug. 5, 1868; *St. Paul Pioneer,* Sept. 8, 1868; John D. Van Buren to Seymour, Aug. 23, 1868, Seymour Papers, New York Historical Society.

34. *New York Herald,* July 22, Aug. 4, Sept. 1, 1868; *Milwaukee Daily News,* Aug. 22, 1868; *St. Paul Pioneer,* Sept. 11, 1868; *Hartford Daily Times,* Aug. 25, 29, 1868.

35. Rosecrans to Seymour, Aug. 6, Sept. 6, 1868, Seymour Papers, New York Historical Society; *Philadelphia Age,* Aug. 31, 1868, *Cincinnati Daily Enquirer,* Sept. 5, 1868.

36. *Milwaukee Daily News,* Aug. 13, 1868; *Hartford Daily Times,* Aug. 15, 1868; *New York Herald,* Aug. 24, Sept. 9, 1868; *St. Paul Pioneer,* Aug. 28, 1868; *New York World,* Sept. 3, 1868; *Chicago Times,* Sept. 12, 1868; Eugene Tisdale to Seymour, Sept. 4, 1868, S. A. Benjamin to Seymour, Sept. 7, 1868, Seymour Papers, New York State Library.

37. Seymour to Doolittle, Aug. 4, 1868, in "Selections From the Correspondence of the Late Senator James Doolittle," pp. 57–58; Coyle to Johnson, Aug. 28, 1868, Johnson Papers; Philo Durfee to Seymour, Aug. 25, 1868, Seymour Papers, New York Historical Society; *Philadelphia Age,* Aug. 31, 1868.

38. *Hartford Daily Times,* Aug. 21, 22, 24, Sept. 12, 1868; George Miller to Seymour, Sept. 4, 1868, N. E. Paine to Seymour, Sept. 8, 11, 1868, Morris Miller to Seymour, Sept. 10, 1868, Seymour Papers, New York State Library; *New York Herald,* Sept. 15, 1868; *American Annual Cyclopaedia and Register of Important Events for the Year 1868* (New York: Appleton, 1869), pp. 448–49.

39. Samuel Ward to Marble, Aug. 1, 1868, Belmont to Marble, Aug. 17, 1868, Manton Marble Papers, Library of Congress, Washington, D.C.; J. L. Douglas to Seymour, Sept. 5, 1868, J. W. McCerkle to Seymour, Sept. 16, 1868, Seymour Papers, New York State Library; Irving Katz, *August Belmont: A Political Biography* (New York: Columbia University Press, 1968), p. 179.

40. Seymour to Tilden, July 20, 21, 1868, Tilden Papers; D. Paine to Spencer, Aug. 10, 1868, Shakelford to Spencer, Aug. 12, 1868, Charles Mott to Seymour, Sept. 28, 1868, Seymour Papers, New York State Library.

41. Rosecrans to Seymour, Sept. 15, 1868, Seymour Papers, New York Historical Society; Day to Seymour, Sept. 16, 24, 29, 1868, Seymour Papers, New York State Library.

42. J. W. McCerkle to Seymour, Sept. 16, 1868, Paine to Seymour, Aug. 17, Sept, 8, 11, 12, 1868, Seymour Papers, New York State Library; Paine to Tilden, Aug. 12, 1868, Seymour to Tilden, Aug. 12, 20, Sept. 26, 1868, Tilden Papers.

43. Aquila Jones to N. E. Paine, Sept. 8, 1868, J. N. Way to Seymour Sept. 14, 1868, E. E. Davis to Seymour, Sept. 18, 1868, B. T. Cooper to Seymour, Sept. 23, 1868, W. A. Wallace

to Seymour, Sept. 24, 1868, William Cassidy to Seymour, Sept. 25, 1868, Seymour Papers, New York State Library; T. C. Fields to Seymour, Sept. 26, 1868, Seymour Papers, New York Historical Society.

44. *Cincinnati Daily Enquirer,* Sept. 24, 29, 1868.

45. George Magee to Seymour, Sept. 8, 1868, D. S. Rook to Seymour, Sept. 13, 1868, S. S. Remah to Seymour, Sept. 17, 22, 1868, J. C. Jones to Seymour, Sept. 18, 1868, Robert Polithorp to Seymour, Sept. 19, 1868, J. McKibben to Seymour, Sept. 23, 1868 Gideon Tucker to Seymour, Oct. 1, 1868, Seymour Papers, New York State Library; Samuel Randall to William Moore, Oct. 1, 1868, Gideon Welles Papers, Huntington Library.

46. John Abbott to Seymour, Sept. 24, 1868, Seymour Papers, New York State Library; William Bigler to Tilden, Sept. 25, 1868, Seymour to Tilden, Oct. 1, 2, 1868, Hancock to Tilden, Oct. 10, 1868, Tilden Papers; *New York Herald,* Oct. 6, 7, 1868; Georges Clemenceau, *American Reconstruction, 1865–1870* (New York: MacVeagh, 1926), pp. 248–50; William Myers, *General George Brinton McClellan: A Study in Personality* (New York: Appleton, 1934), pp. 486–87; Dearing, *Veterans in Politics,* pp. 168–73.

47. *Cincinnati Daily Enquirer,* Oct. 15, 1868; *Philadelphia Age,* Oct. 15, 1868; *American Annual Cyclopaedia, 1868,* pp. 377–78, 603–604; Erwin Bradley, *The Triumph of Militant Republicanism: A Study of Pennsylvania and Presidential Politics* (Philadelphia: University of Pennsylvania Press, 1964), p. 298.

48. Chase to William Brown, Sept. 2, 1868, Salmon Chase Papers, Library of Congress, Washington, D.C.; Seymour to Van Buren, Sept. 8, 1868, Hiram Barney to Seymour, Sept. 10, 1868, Van Buren to Seymour, Sept. 24, 1868, Seymour Papers, New York Historical Society; Brown to Long, Aug. 27, Sept. 14, 1868, Long Papers; *Hartford Daily Times,* Oct. 12, 1868.

49. Long to Chase, Sept. 10, 30, Oct 3, 1868, Long Papers; Thomas Pratt to Barlow, Sept. 4, 1868, Barlow Papers.

50. Washington McLean to Barlow, Oct. 14, 15, 16, 1868, Barlow Papers; Vallandigham to Tilden, Oct. 17, F. P. Blair to Tilden, Oct. 19, 1868, Tilden Papers; Long to Chase, Oct. 15, 1868, George Hoeffer to Long, Oct. 17, 1868, Long Papers; *Illinois State Register,* Oct. 17, 1868; *National Intelligencer,* Oct. 27, 1868; Smith, *Blair Family,* 2:423.

51. *New York World,* Oct. 15, 1868; *National Intelligencer,* Oct. 16, 1868; Randall to Tilden, Oct. 15, 1868, Storey to Tilden, Oct. 16, 1868, Tilden Papers; Clemenceau, *American Reconstruction,* p. 255.

52. George Henry to Bigler, Oct. 14, 1868, William Bigler Papers, Historical Society of Pennsylvania, Philadelphia; James Noble to McLean [Oct. 1868], Barlow Papers; J. Antheum et. al to Tilden, Oct. 16, 1868, Tilden Papers; William Cassidy to Marble, Oct. 16, 1868, Seymour Papers, New York Historical Society; *St. Paul Pioneer,* Oct. 17, 1868; *Hartford Daily Times,* Oct. 17, 1868; *Milwaukee Daily News,* Oct. 17, 1868.

53. *New York Herald,* Oct. 17, 19, 1868; Katz, *Belmont,* p. 181; Tilden, Belmont and Schell to Storey, Oct. 17, 1868, Tilden Papers; *Illinois State Register,* Oct. 19, 1868; Chase to Long, Oct. 27, 1868, Long Papers.

54. August Belmont, *Letters, Speeches, and Addresses* (New York, 1890), pp. 188–190; "To the Voters of Indiana," in the Charles Lasselle Papers, Indiana State Library, Indianapolis; *Hartford Daily Times,* Oct. 19, 20, 1868.

55. *New York World,* Oct. 21, 23, 1868; *St. Paul Pioneer,* Oct. 24, 1868; Stewart Mitchell, *Horatio Seymour of New York* (Cambridge, Mass.: Harvard University Press, 1938), p. 473.

56. Coleman, *The Election of 1868,* pp. 362–67; Martin Mantell, *Johnson, Grant, and the Politics of Reconstruction* (New York: Columbia University Press, 1973) pp. 143–49.

57. *American Annual Cyclopaedia, 1868,* pp. 504–404; Robert Dykstra and Harlan Hahn, "Northern Voters and Negro Suffrage: The Case of Iowa, 1865–1868," *Public Opinion Quarterly* 32 (1968):202–15; Lawrence Grossman, *The Democratic Party and the Negro: Northern and National Politics* (Urbana: University of Illinois Press, 1976).

# BIBLIOGRAPHIC ESSAY

MANUSCRIPT MATERIAL on the early postwar era is uneven, often fragmentary, and more extensive for Republicans than for Democrats. The Andrew Johnson Papers, Library of Congress, provide the most comprehensive collection for the period 1865–1868 and are indispensable for understanding the interplay of conservative Unionist and Democratic forces. Other collections illuminating the role of conservative Unionists are the James Doolittle Papers, Wisconsin State Historical Society; Charles Halpine Papers, Henry E. Huntington Library; Henry Sibley Papers, Minnesota State Historical Society; Gideon Welles Papers, Henry E. Huntington Library and Library of Congress; and Robert Winthrop Papers, Massachusetts Historical Society.

New York Democrats occupied a crucial position in national party councils and have left a number of major collections. The voluminous Samuel L. M. Barlow Papers, Henry E. Huntington Library, are rich source material on Northern Democrats and Southern conservatives, and other aspects of Northern Democratic policy. The Manton Marble Papers, Library of Congress, include extensive correspondence from a wide assortment of Democrats. Horatio Seymour's collections, at the New York State Library and New York Historical Society, are primarily valuable for the presidential contest of 1868. The Samuel J. Tilden Papers, New York Public Library, contain important additional information. Unfortunately, the Samuel S. Cox Papers, Brown University Library, are quite limited for the early postwar era.

The Charles Mason Papers, Iowa State Department of History and Archives, have significant material on national politics for the period 1865–1866. The Diary of Charles Mason reveals his role as chairman of the Washington Resident Committee, and his correspondence includes letters from influential Copperheads. Manuscript sources of Democratic hard-liners are meager. The most useful are the Thomas F. Bayard Papers, Library of Congress, and the Alexander Long Papers, Cincinnati Historical Society. The LeGrand Byington Papers, State Historical Society of Iowa, and the Fernando Wood Papers, New York Public Library, have a few items of importance.

Further collections included in this study are the William Allen Papers, Library of Congress; the William Bigler Papers, Historical Society of Pennsylvania, illuminate Pennsylvania politics; the Jeremiah Black Papers, Library of Congress, reflect Black's close relationship with the Johnson administration; the James Buchanan Papers, Historical Society of Pennsylvania; the Edmund Burke Papers, Library of Congress, reveal aspects of New Hampshire politics; the Salmon P. Chase Papers, Library of Congress and Historical Society of Pennsylvania, cover the Democratic courtship of Chase in 1868; the Charles Lasselle Papers, Indiana State Library; the Cyrus Hall McCormick Papers, Wisconsin State Historical Society; the William Ralls Morrison Papers, Chicago Historical Society; the J. Sterling Morton Papers,

Nebraska State Historical Society; the Franklin Pierce Papers, Library of Congress; and the George B. Smith Papers, Wisconsin State Historical Society.

Published speeches, letters, autobiographies, reminiscences, and other contemporary accounts supplement the manuscript collections. Howard K. Beale, ed. *The Diary of Gideon Welles,* 3 vols. (New York, 1960), and James G. Randall and Theodore C. Pease eds., *The Diary of Orville Hickman Browning,* 2 vols. (Springfield, Ill., 1933) provide information on the inner workings of the Johnson Administration. Georges Clemenceau, *American Reconstruction, 1865–1870* (New York, 1926), and Allan Nevins and Milton Thomas, eds., *The Diary of George Templeton Strong,* 4 vols. (New York, 1952) are two sources highly critical of the Democrats. Henry W. Raymond, "Extracts from the Journal of Henry J. Raymond," *Scribner's Monthly* 20 (1880) gives important information on the National Union Convention.

Democratic material is provided by August Belmont, *Letters, Speeches, and Addresses* (New York, 1890); John Bigelow, ed., *Letters and Literary Memorials of Samuel J. Tilden,* 2 vols. (New York, 1908); Samuel S. Cox, *Eight Years in Congress* (New York, 1865) and *Union-Disunion-Reaction: Three Decades of Federal Legislation, 1865–1885* (Providence, 1885); Almira Hancock, *Reminiscences of Winfield Scott Hancock* (New York, 1887); John B. Moore, ed., *The Works of James Buchanan, Comprising his Speeches, State Papers, and Private Correspondence,* 12 vols. (Philadelphia, 1908-1910); Jerome Mushkat, "The Impeachment of Andrew Johnson: A Contemporary View," *New York History* 48 (1967): 276–86; and Charles Remey, "Life and Letters of Charles Mason: Chief Justice of Iowa," 16 vols. (unpublished manuscript, Washington, D.C., 1939).

Additional references are Charles Cauthen, *Family Letters of the Three Wade Hamptons, 1782–1901* (Columbia, S. C., 1953); M. A. DeWolfe Howe, *The Life and Letters of George Bancroft,* 2 vols. (New York, 1908); Duane Mowry, ed., "Selections from the Correspondence of the Late Senator James R. Doolittle: Post Bellum Days," *Wisconsin Magazine of History* 17 (1913): 56–64; Jacob Shuckers, *The Life and Public Services of Salmon Portland Chase* (New York, 1874); and St. George Souissant, "Notes of Colonel W. G. Moore, Private Secretary to President Johnson, 1866–1868," *American Historical Review* 14 (1913): 98–132.

Collections of government documents and other sources that include formal partisan or government actions are the *American Annual Cyclopaedia and Register of Important Events for the year 1865 [through 1868],* (New York, 1866–1869); *Congressional Globe,* 38th through 40th Congresses; Edward McPherson, ed., *The Political History of the United States of America during the Period of Reconstruction* (Washington, D.C., 1871); James Richardson, ed., *A Compilation of the Messages of the Presidents, 1789–1897,* 10 vols. (Washington, D.C., 1896–1899); and *United States Statutes at Large.*

Contemporary newspapers and periodicals reflect partisan opinions, intraparty maneuvers, and actions. The *Columbus Crisis, Dubuque Weekly*

*Herald,* and the monthly *Old Guard* were consistent representatives of Democratic hard-liners. The *Albany Argus, Boston Post, Chicago Times, Davenport Daily Democrat,* and the *New York World* were the more progressive of the Democratic papers. Other Democratic papers consulted were the *Cincinnati Daily Enquirer, Detroit Free Press, Harrisburg Patriot and Union, Hartford Daily Times, Milwaukee Daily News, Philadelphia Age, St. Paul Pioneer,* and the Springfield *Illinois State Register.*

The *New York Herald* carried extensive reports on political events around the country and adopted a conservative but independent outlook. The *New York Times* is excellent for political coverage and for delineating the differences between conservative Republicans and the Democrats. The *New York Tribune* and the *Nation* were Republican in sentiment, and the Washington *National Intelligencer* closely identified with the Johnson administration.

Secondary works on reconstruction politics by Howard K. Beale, *The Critical Year: A Study of Andrew Johnson and Reconstruction* (New York, 1930) and George Fort Milton, *The Age of Hate: Andrew Johnson and the Radicals* (New York, 1930) trace Radical reconstruction from opposing anti-Radical perspectives. Eric McKitrick's more recent study, *Andrew Johnson and Reconstruction* (Chicago, 1960) suggests that the Democrats helped pave the way for congressional reconstruction. Martin Mantell, *Johnson, Grant, and the Politics of Reconstruction* (New York, 1973) emphasizes the often neglected period of 1867 to 1868 and gives considerable attention to the Democrats.

Relevant topical studies on reconstruction politics and policies on the national level are Herman Belz, *Reconstructing the Union: Theory and Practice during the Civil War* (Ithaca, N.Y., 1969); Michael Les Benedict, *A Compromise of Principle: Congressional Republicans and Reconstruction, 1863–1869* (New York, 1974) and *The Impeachment and Trial of Andrew Johnson* (New York, 1973); Mary R. Dearing, *Veterans in Politics: The Story of the G.A.R.* (Baton Rouge, La., 1952); David De Witt, *The Impeachment and Trial of Andrew Johnson, Seventeenth President of the United States: A History* (New York, 1903); Harriet Doris, *Pardon and Amnesty under Lincoln and Johnson: The Restoration of the Confederates to their Rights and Privileges* (Chapel Hill, N.C., 1953); Sever Eubank, "The McCardle Case: A Challenge to Radical Reconstruction," *Journal of Mississippi History* 18 (1956): 111–27; Joseph James, *The Framing of the Fourteenth Amendment* (Urbana, Ill., 1956); Harold Hyman, *Era of the Oath: Northern Loyalty Tests during the Civil War and Reconstruction* (Philadelphia, 1954); Benjamin Kendrick, *The Journal of the Joint Committee of Fifteen on Reconstruction, 39th Congress, 1865–1867,* Columbia Studies in History, Economics, and Public Law, vol. 42 (New York, 1914); Stanley Kutler, *Judicial Power and Reconstruction Politics* (Chicago, 1968); and James E. Sefton, *The United States Army and Reconstruction* (Baton Rouge, La., 1967).

Northern attitudes toward blacks during the Civil War and early reconstruction period are examined in Roy Abrams, "Copperhead Newspapers and the Negro," *Journal of Negro History* 20 (1935): 131–52; G. Galen Berrier, "The Negro Suffrage Issue in Iowa, 1865–1868," *Annals of Iowa* 39 (1968): 241–61; Robert Dykstra and Harlan Hahn, "Northern Voters and Negro Suffrage: The Case of Iowa, 1865–1868," *Public Opinion Quarterly* 32 (1968): 202–15; Leslie Fischel, "Northern Prejudice and Negro Suffrage, 1865–1870," *Journal of Negro History* 24 (1954): 8–26, and "Wisconsin and Negro Suffrage," *Wisconsin Magazine of History* 46 (1963): 180–86; Lawrence Grossman, *The Democratic Party and the Negro: Northern and National Politics, 1868–1892* (Urbana, Ill., 1976); Frank Klement, "Midwestern Opposition to Lincoln's Emancipation Proclamation," *Journal of Negro History* 46 (1963): 180–96; Jacque Voegli, *Free but Not Equal: The Midwest and the Negro during the Civil War* (Chicago, 1967); and Forrest Wood, *Black Scare: The Racist Response to Emancipation and Reconstruction* (Berkeley, 1968).

Economic issues are covered by Stanley Coben, "Northeastern Business and Radical Reconstruction: A Re-examination," *Mississippi Valley Historical Review* 46 (1959): 67–90; Chester Destler, "The Origin and Character of the Pendleton Plan," *Mississippi Valley Historical Review* 24 (1937): 171–84; David Montgomery, *Beyond Equality: Labor and the Radical Republicans* (New York, 1967); Robert Sharkey, *Money, Class, and Party: An Economic Study of Civil War and Reconstruction,* John Hopkins Studies in Historical and Political Science, ser. 77 (Baltimore, 1959); and Irwin Unger, *The Greenback Era: A Social and Political History of American Finance, 1865–1879* (Princeton, N.J., 1964).

Michael Perman, *Reunion Without Compromise: The South and Reconstruction* (London, 1973) discusses the debate among Southern conservatives over reconstruction policy, that frequently paralleled the divisions among Northern Democrats. Studies of the Southern states during reconstruction include Alan Conway, *The Reconstruction of Georgia* (Minneapolis, 1966); John Ficklin, *History of Reconstruction in Louisiana,* John Hopkins Studies in Historical and Political Science, ser. 27 (Baltimore, 1910); Walter Fleming, *Civil War and Reconstruction in Alabama* (New York, 1905); Joseph G. de Roulhac Hamilton, *Reconstruction in North Carolina* (New York, 1914); William Harris, *Presidential Reconstruction in Mississippi* (Baton Rouge, La., 1967); James Patton, *Unionism and Reconstruction in Tennessee* (Chapel Hill, N.C., 1934); and Francis Simkins and Robert Woody, *South Carolina during Reconstruction* (Chapel Hill, N.C., 1932); E. Merton Coulter, *The Civil War and Readjustment in Kentucky* (Chapel Hill, N.C., 1926), covers a border state that occasionally influenced Northern politics.

Numerous studies analyze the crisis faced by the Democratic party in the Civil War. Roy Nichols, the *Disruption of American Democracy* (New York, 1948) and Robert Johannsen, "The Douglas Democracy and the Crisis of Disunion," *Civil War History* 9 (1963): 229–47 examine the party on the eve of the war. Joel Silbey, *A Respectable Minority: The Democratic Party in the Civil War era, 1860–1868* (New York, 1977) provides a sympathetic treatment of the Democrats, with the main emphasis on the war years. Van M.

Davis, "Individualism on Trial: The Ideology of the Northern Democracy during the Civil War" (Ph.D. diss., University of Virginia, 1972) covers the ideals governing Democrats. Paul Kleppner, *The Cross of Culture: A Social Analysis of Midwestern Politics, 1850–1890* (New York, 1970) analyzes the party's constituencies. Congressional Democrats are studied in Leonard Curry, "Congressional Democrats, 1861–1863," *Civil War History,* 12 (1966): 213–29 and in his *Blueprint for Modern America Non-military legislation of the First Civil War Congress* (Nashville, Tenn., 1968).

John and LaWanda Cox, in *Politics, Principle, and Prejudice, 1865–1868: Dilemma of Reconstruction America* (New York, 1963) examine the relations between conservative Unionists and Democrats and emphasize New York politics. Thomas Wagstaff, "Andrew Johnson and the National Union Movement, 1865–1866" (Ph.D. diss., Emory University, 1972) and "The Arm-and-Arm Convention," *Civil War History* 14 (1968): 101–19 looks at the background and deliberations of the Philadelphia Convention. Albert V. House Jr., "Northern Congressional Democrats as Defenders of the South during Reconstruction," *Journal of Southern History* 6 (1940): 46–71 provides a general treatment of this subject. William A. Russ Jr., "Was there Danger of a Second Civil War during Reconstruction?" *Mississippi Valley Historical Review,* 25 (1938): 49–55 looks at the Democratic reaction to the impeachment threat. William Brigance, "Jeremiah Black and Andrew Johnson," *Mississippi Valley Historical Review* 19 (1932): 205–18 analyzes relations between the president and an important Pennsylvania Democrat. Charles Coleman, *The Election of 1868: The Democratic Effort to Regain Control* (1933) has a wealth of information on the Democratic nominations and campaign. Horace Samuel Merrill, *Bourbon Democracy in the Middle West* (Baton Rouge, La., 1953) covers business-oriented midwestern Democrats.

Two major studies on the Copperheads are Wood Gray's, *The Hidden Civil War: The Story of the Copperheads* (New York, 1942) and Frank Klement's, *The Copperheads in the Middle West* (Chicago, 1960). Copperheads are scrutinized in a number of studies: William G. Carleton, "Civil War Dissidence in the North: The Perspective of a Century," *South Atlantic Quarterly* 45 (1966): 390–402; Richard O. Curry, "Copperheadism and Ideological Continuity: Anatomy of a Stereotype," *Journal of Negro History* 57 (1972): 29–36 and "The Union as it Was: A Critique of Recent Interpretations of the Copperheads," *Civil War History* 18 (1967): 25–39; Henry C. Hubbart, "Pro-southern Influences in the Free West, 1840–1865," *Mississippi Valley Historical Review* 20 (1933): 45–62; Frank Klement, "Copperheads and Copperheadism in Wisconsin: Democratic Opposition to the Lincoln Administration," *Wisconsin Magazine of History* 42 (1959): 182–88; Robert Rutland, "The Copperheads of Iowa: A Re-examination," *Iowa Journal of History* 52 (1954): 1–30; Arnold Shankman, "Conflict in the Old Keystone: Anti-war Sentiment in Pennsylvania" (Ph.D. diss., University of Wisconsin, 1967); John Talmadge, "A Peace Movement in Civil War Connecticut," *New England Quarterly,* 38 (1964): 306–20; G. R. Tredway, *Democratic Opposi-*

*tion to the Lincoln Administration in Indiana* (Indianapolis, 1973); and Nicholas B. Wainwright, "The Loyal Opposition in Civil War Philadelphia," *Pennsylvania Magazine of History and Biography* 80 (1964): 294–315.

Christopher Dell, *Lincoln and the War Democrats: The Grand Erosion of Conservative Tradition* (Madison, N. J., 1975) is the only significant work on the War Democrats. Dell's definition is a broad one and includes all Democrats who joined in the war effort. However, there is no study that deals with moderate Democratic regulars.

State, local, and institutional histories constitute a crucial source of information on the Democrats. De Alva Alexander, *A Political History of the State of New York,* 4 vols. (New York, 1906–1923); Sidney Brummer, *Political History of New York State during the Period of the Civil War* (New York, 1911); and Homer Stebbins, *Political History of New York, 1865–1869,* in Columbia Studies in History, Economics, and Public Law, vol. 55 (New York, 1913) are the major studies on New York politics. Also useful are Alexander Callow Jr., *The Tweed Ring* (New York, 1966); Seymour Mandlebaum, *Boss Tweed's New York* (New York, 1965); Jerome Mushkat, *Tammany: The Evolution of a Political Machine, 1789–1865* (Syracuse, 1971); and Henry Watterson, *History of the Manhattan Club: A Narrative of the Activities of Half a Century* (New York, 1915).

The politics of other mid-Atlantic states are analyzed by Erwin Bradley, *The Triumph of Militant Republicanism: A Study of Pennsylvania and Presidential Politics* (Philadelphia, 1964); Stanton Davis, *Pennsylvania Politics, 1860–1863* (Cleveland, 1935); William Dusinberre, *Civil War Issues in Philadelphia, 1856–1865* (Philadelphia, 1965); Charles Knapp, *New Jersey Politics during the Period of the Civil War and Reconstruction* (Geneva, N.Y. 1924); and Alexander McClure, *Old Time Notes of Pennsylvania,* 2 vols. (Philadelphia, 1905).

Several New England states lack scholarly treatment for the Civil War era. The best works are John Niven, *Connecticut for the Union: The Role of the State in the Civil War* (New Haven, 1965); and Edith Ware, *Political Opinion in Massachusetts during the Civil War and Reconstruction,* in Columbia Studies in History, Economics, and Public Law, vol. 84 (New York, 1916).

For coverage of midwestern states see Felice Bonadio, *North of Reconstruction: Ohio Politics, 1865–1870* (New York, 1970); Olynthus Clark, *Politics of Iowa during the Civil War and Reconstruction* (Iowa City, 1911); Authur Cole, *The Centennial History of Illinois,* vol. 3, *The Era of the Civil War, 1848–1870* (Springfield, Ill., 1919); Richard Current, *The History of Wisconsin,* vol. 2, *The Civil War Era, 1848–1873* (Madison, 1976); Harriet Dilla, *The Politics of Michigan, 1865–1878,* Columbia Studies in History, Economics, and Public Law, vol. 47 (New York, 1912); George Porter, *Ohio Politics in the Civil War Period,* in Columbia Studies in History, Economics, and Public Law, vol. 40 (New York, 1911); and Kenneth Stampp, *Indiana Politics during the Civil War* (Indianapolis, 1949).

Numerous and significant biographical studies are available. Probably the best study on Andrew Johnson is still Robert Winston *Andrew Johnson: Plebian and Patriot* (New York, 1928), and should be supplemented by Albert Castle's, "Andrew Johnson: His Historiographic Rise and Fall," *Mid-America* 45 (1963): 175–84. Influential conservative Unionists turned Democrat are covered by James Sellers, "James R. Doolittle," *Wisconsin Magazine of History* 17 (1933–1934): 168–78, 277–306, 393–401, 18 (1934–1935): 20–41, 178–87; William Ernest Smith, *The Francis Preston Blair Family in Politics,* 2 vols. (New York, 1933); and William Hanchett, *Irish: Charles G. Halpine in Civil War America* (Syracuse, 1970).

Thomas and Martha Belden, *So Fell the Angels* (Boston, 1956) touches on Salmon Chase's flirtation with the Democrats but should be supplemented with Edward Perzel, "Alexander Long, Salmon P. Chase, and the Election of 1868," *Bulletin of the Cincinnati Historical Society* 23 (1965): 3–18. Biographies of conservatives whom the Democrats tried to win over are Francis Brown's, *Raymond of the "Times"* (New York, 1951); Oliver Carlson's, *The Man Who Made the News: James Gordon Bennett* (New York, 1942); William Hesseltine's, *Ulysses S. Grant: Politician* (New York, 1935); Martin Lichterman's, "John Adams Dix, 1789–1897" (Ph.D., diss., Columbia University, 1952); and Glyndon Van Deusen's, *Thurlow Weed: Wizard of the Lobby* (Boston, 1947) and *William Henry Seward* (Oxford, 1967). There are a number of biographies on Democratic regulars from New York. George McJimsey, *Genteel Partisan: Manton Marble, 1834–1917* (Ames, Iowa, 1971) is a superior study of the *New York World* editor. Irving Katz, *August Belmont: A Political Biography,* makes effective use of the private Belmont collection. Alexander Flick and G. S. Labrano, *Samuel Jones Tilden, A Study in Political Sagacity* (New York, 1939); David Lindsey, *"Sunset" Cox, Irrepressible Democrat* (Detroit, 1959); and Stewart Mitchell, *Horatio Seymour of New York* (Cambridge, Mass., 1938) are excellent accounts of three major figures in New York politics. Jack Kofoed, *Brandy for Heroes: A Biography of the Honorable John Morrissey* (New York, 1938); Samuel Pleasants, *Fernando Wood of New York* (New York, 1948); and Joseph George Jr., "Abraham Africanus I: President Lincoln through the Eyes of a Copperhead Editor," *Civil War History* 14 (1968): 226–39 are significant and George's article provides some background on C. Chauncey Burr.

Among the studies on Pennsylvania Democrats are William Brigance, *Jeremiah Sullivan Black: A Defender of the Constitution and Ten Commandments* (Philadelphia, 1934); Irwin Greenberg "Charles Ingersoll: The Aristocrat as Copperhead," *Pennsylvania Magazine of History and Biography* 90 (1969): 190–217; Albert House, "The Political Career of Samuel Jackson Randall" (Ph.D. diss., University of Wisconsin, 1934); William Hummell, "Charles R. Buckalew: Democratic Statesman in a Republican Era" (Ph.D. diss., University of Pittsburgh, 1963); Charles Jones, *Life and Public Services of J. Glancy Jones,* 2 vols. (Philadelphia, 1910); Philip Klein, *President James Buchanan: A Biography* (University Park, Penn., 1962); Arnold

Shankman, "William B. Reed and the Civil War," *Pennsylvania History* 39 (1972): 455–68; and Milton Stuart, *Asa Packer* (Princeton, 1938).

Other useful biographies are Alfons Beitzinger, *Edward G. Ryan: Lion of the Law* (Madison, 1960); Earl D. Robbins Jr., "The Congressional Career of William Ralls Morrison" (Ph.D. diss., University of Illinois, 1963); John Hare, "Allen G. Thurman: A Political Study" (Ph.D. diss., Ohio State University, 1933); William Hutchinson, *Cyrus Hall McCormick,* 2 vols. (New York, 1930–1935); Leonard Kenworthy, *The Tall Syracuse of the Wabash: Danial Voorhees* (Boston, 1936); Frank Klement, "Brick Pomeroy: Copperhead and Curmudgeon," *Wisconsin Magazine of History* 35 (1951): 106–13, 156–57 and *The Limits of Dissent: Clement L. Vallandigham and the Civil War* (Lexington, Ky.); Reginald McGrane, *William Allen: A Study in Western Democracy* (Columbus, 1925); William Myers, *General George Brinton McClellan: A Study in Personality* (New York, 1934); Roy Nichols, *Franklin Pierce: Young Hickory from the Granite Hills;* James C. Olson, *J. Sterling Morton* (Lincoln, Nebr., 1942); and Bernard Steiner, *Life of Reverdy Johnson* (Baltimore, 1914).

# INDEX